Is man still relevant? A provocation

Technological evolution and human existence

Is man still relevant? A provocation

Technological evolution and human existence

Table of contents

Political Perspectives

Communal Perspectives

Preface

The question of whether humans are still relevant to the times may seem provocative. It touches on our self-image as a species, our relationship to progress, technology and the challenges that a rapidly changing world brings with it. But especially in the present, when technological evolution is advancing at an exponential rate, it is worth reflecting fundamentally: Do the biological, psychological and social characteristics of humans still fit the world they have created? Or is man, as we know him, a relic from another era that is finding it difficult to find his place in a reality dominated by algorithms, automation and artificial intelligence?

This book is not intended to be a simple treatise or a resigned cultural critique, but rather an analytical examination of the status quo of human existence. Popular scientific explanations are combined with factual presentations to offer readers a well-founded yet exciting approach to one of the most pressing questions of our time.

The technological developments of the last few decades have fundamentally changed our understanding of ourselves. We live in a world in which artificial intelligence already works faster, more efficiently and sometimes more accurately than we do in many areas. Even cognitive processes that were long considered the domain of the human mind - creativity, emotions, decision-making - are increasingly being simulated by machines. What does this mean for our self-image? Are humans losing relevance or are they being transformed into a new form of existence?

At the same time, advances in biotechnology and neuroscience are raising questions that go far beyond technological feasibility. Transhumanist concepts advocate an optimization of humans, a fusion with technology to compensate for their supposed weaknesses. But who decides what needs to be improved? Is the natural human an intermediate stage on the way to a new type of being? And can we do justice to the ethical implications of these developments?

There are no easy answers to these questions, and yet it is essential to address them. This book is aimed at all those who are not just witnesses but active participants in this change - people who think about the future, who question things critically, who are prepared to deal with the possibilities and risks. The following pages offer no dystopian doomsday scenarios or blind enthusiasm for technology, but a reflective and multidimensional analysis that puts people at the center: their strengths, their limitations and their future.

People are creatures of change. Since the beginning, they have shaped their environment, adapted and developed further. But perhaps we are now at a point where people are no longer shaping the world, but the world they have created is redefining them. So are people still relevant? The answer lies not only in science, but also in our willingness to question ourselves and our role in the future.

The real provocation lies in naming things ruthlessly. But it is necessary. Because only those who have the courage to ask uncomfortable and future-oriented questions can find answers that will decide tomorrow.

The question of whether humans are still contemporary is intentional and urgent. It arises not only in view of the rapidly advancing technological development, but also in the context of the fundamental changes that are permeating our social, cultural and ecological lives. It is not just about humans' ability to adapt to these changes, but also about their role as beings who both develop the tools that shape their environment and have the ability to think and reflect on their own existence. The tension between technological evolution and human existence could hardly be more topical.

Over the last few centuries, humans have undergone unprecedented development. What was considered science fiction just a few generations ago is now reality: artificial intelligence, genome research, autonomous driving, digital networking and many other innovations shape our everyday lives. But in the midst of this rapid development, the central question arises: are humans still able to keep up with this technology? Or is it on a path where it is increasingly being overtaken by its own creations?

It is easy to see technology as progress, as a constant improvement in human life. But the downside of this progress is often overlooked: The ethical, social and environmental consequences associated with the spread of new technologies. Technological change is occurring at a pace that is overwhelming humans in many ways – not only on a practical level, but also on an existential level. How do we react when machines begin to independently take on tasks that previously could only be performed by humans? What happens when machines surpass us not only in the production of goods, but also in the creation of art, in research and even in decision-making?

Technology is not just a tool that we hold in our hands – it has become an active agent in the design of our world. This fact leads to a fundamental reassessment of what it means to be human. Are we still the primary actors in the world, or are we increasingly becoming witnesses and perhaps even objects of a technological process that no longer fully belongs to us?

This analysis examines how humans can deal with the challenges of technological evolution in the 21st century. The line between what we consider human and what is considered technologically advanced is becoming increasingly permeable. Humans as biological beings have evolved over millions of years

- a process characterized by slow and steady adaptation to environmental conditions. But today, in a world where technology determines the speed of change, we must ask ourselves whether this biological evolution can still keep pace with technological development.

This book combines popular scientific observations with a factual presentation of technological advances to shed light on the question of human relevance in an increasingly digital world. It is a mix of facts and stories that not only aims to inform the reader, but above all to encourage them to think about the fundamental questions that are coming our way in the midst of the technological revolution: What does it mean to be human when machines begin to not only replace us, but also surpass us in areas that were once considered purely human? How can we as a society deal with the unstoppable changes triggered by technology? And what remains of humanity when our creations overtake us in more and more areas?

This is not intended to be a book that provides ready-made answers that are easy to consume. Rather, it is an invitation to lose yourself in the complexity of the topics in order to gain new perspectives through thought and reflection. In a world in which technological change seems to affect every facet of our lives, it is essential that we as humans not only recognize the advantages of new technologies, but also deal with the challenges and questions associated with their introduction.

This text is a deliberate provocation. It calls on us not only to accept the advances and challenges of technological evolution, but to actively enter into the discourse about the future of humanity. Because the question of whether humans are still contemporary does not only concern technology - it particularly concerns us humans, our interactions and our future. It challenges us to redefine ourselves and recognize our responsibility as designers of our coexistence.

Technological progress is unstoppable - but it is up to us how we shape it and deal with it. Will we see ourselves as mere spectators of our own development or as active players who help shape it and act responsibly? This question will accompany us not only in the coming years, but in the coming decades. And only if we consciously face this challenge can we shape the future in a way that both promotes progress and preserves the value and meaning of being human.

So embark on a journey through the world of technological and human development, where you will not only learn about the fascinating advances of recent years, but also take a look at the questions that affect us all. Because in the end, it is not just about whether people can keep up with technology - but about whether we as a society are prepared to face the responsibility that comes with this development.

I invite you to think further with me.

Hermann Selchow

Social Perspectives

Digital Loneliness and Interpersonal Relationships

Social life used to be a stage of physical presence. People met in cafes, went to events, made phone calls, talked face to face and maintained their relationships through the touch of hands, the smile in the corner of the eye and the exchange of glances. In today's world, where almost every moment of our lives is accompanied by digital devices, the way we connect with each other has changed dramatically. Communication and relationships have shifted from traditional physical encounters to a new world of digital interactions. This development has the potential to fundamentally change both the quality and the depth of interpersonal bonds.

Digitalization, driven by the Internet and social networks, has made the world of direct communication easier for us. A call, a message, a comment or a like - all of this is just a click away. And yet a central question arises: have these new forms of communication improved our relationships or have they devalued them? A paradox becomes apparent: despite the apparent closeness that digital platforms create, more and more people feel lonely, even in the midst of a virtual hustle and bustle.

The Rise of Digital Connections and the Paradox of Lone-liness

It is undeniable that social media platforms such as Facebook, Instagram, Twitter and TikTok offer us an unprecedented way to stay in touch. We are now able to communicate, share information and maintain relationships with people all over the world in real time, no matter how far away they are. These networks allow us to receive updates on other people's lives in seconds and share our own lives with others.

But at the same time, these digital connections represent a new kind of loneliness that many people increasingly find distressing. At first glance, it may seem that the world of social media is full of life, joy and sociable activity. We see pictures of friends travelling, sharing experiences and depicting moments of joy in public posts. But the more we delve into these surface relationships, the clearer it becomes that these connections are often just a fragmented and superficial form of communication.

Psychological studies have shown that digital platforms, although they increase the number of social interactions, often do not meet the same emotional needs as face-to-face, face-to-face encounters. In a world where we are constantly inundated with information and impressions, we find it increasingly difficult to create deeper, more meaningful connections. The constant distraction of notifications and the need to always be up to date can mean that real, authentic conversations and emotional intimacy are increasingly falling by the wayside.

Digital loneliness is not only reflected in the number of "real" friends we have on social media, but also in the quality of those relationships. A 2018 study by the Pew Research Center found that nearly 40 percent of adults in the United States say they regularly feel lonely despite being active on social media. This number continues to grow, and social networks are increasingly perceived as a source of loneliness.

It seems like a contradiction in terms: we are constantly connected, constantly reachable, and yet many people feel increasingly lonely. There is a growing gap between the apparent closeness that digital platforms promise us and the actual depth of these connections. To understand this contradiction, one must look at the mechanisms behind the way we connect with each other today.

First of all, the speed and scope of digital connections is remarkable. It is now possible to communicate with almost anyone in the world at any time and anywhere. We can send messages in seconds, share photos and even send videos of ourselves to friends and family in real time. Social networks give us access to a wealth of information and social circles that go far beyond what was available to us in the analog world. We can connect with people we have never met in person and still feel like we are part of a network. These networks are so ubiquitous that we hardly question them anymore - they are an integral part of our everyday lives.

Despite this apparent abundance of connections, the question arises: Why do so many people still feel lonely? Why is the number of people who say they feel isolated despite constant digital connectivity increasing? A crucial aspect of this phenomenon lies in the way social media is designed. Platforms such as Facebook, Instagram, X and TikTok are based on a reward system that is built on quick, superficial interactions. A "like" or a comment may represent a form of recognition, but it is not a real, deep interaction. The depth of a conversation, receiving and giving emotions, sharing experiences and showing understanding are difficult to achieve in this context.

The constant availability of information and the flood of messages that reach us from all sides create a constant state of distraction. Instead of being truly present, we are trapped in a world of permanent interruption. It is a paradoxical phenomenon: despite the multitude of connections we have in the digital world, we often no longer manage to really engage with the people around us. The focus is not on the quality of the connection, but on the quantity of interactions. We collect friends, followers and connections, but many of these relationships are fleeting and superficial. Constantly sharing pictures and posts gives the impression of closeness, but at the core, many of these connections remain empty.

Another factor contributing to the paradox of loneliness is social comparison, which plays a central role in social media. We constantly see what other people are doing, and the selection of content that is shared often only shows the best sides of life. Vacation pictures, successful careers, happy relationships - all of this is presented in an idealized form.

This constant comparison can lead us to feel inferior to ourselves or believe that our own lives do not meet popular expectations. The more we compare ourselves to the seemingly perfect lives of others, the more we distance ourselves from our own lives and the real relationships we could cultivate. A gap develops between the world that digital platforms show us and the reality we experience ourselves.

In addition, the increase in digital connections often leads to alienation from ourselves. As we increasingly define our identity through the lens of social media, we lose access to the deeper, authentic aspects of ourselves. We portray ourselves and our lives as we believe others should perceive them. This constant construction and self-dramatization leads us to distance ourselves from our true essence and only show the surface. Instead of seeking real, profound connections with other people, we seek validation in the form of likes, comments and follower numbers.

Another challenge in digital communication is the loss of non-verbal communication. In a face-to-face conversation, we can respond to body language, facial expressions and tone of voice - elements that often reveal more about the other person's feelings and intentions than words alone. This dimension is largely lost in digital communication. Emojis and short text messages can convey emotions, but they are often insufficient to fully express the complexity of human feelings. The lack of real closeness leads to the emotional depth of conversations decreasing. Relationships based only on text messages and pictures remain superficial without the personal context because they do not generate the same emotional resonance as real, face-to-face encounters.

The constant availability of social media also leads to a certain emotional exhaustion. We are so conditioned to respond to messages immediately and connect with everyone and everything that we can never really switch off. The constant need to be present and stay updated creates a kind of psychological pressure. We feel obliged to constantly communicate, share and respond - and yet the quality of connections often falls short of our expectations.

It is important to emphasize that the digital world does not only have negative effects. It offers us new ways of connecting and sharing, especially in an increasingly globalized world. People can connect with like-minded people, find support and grow in communities that might not be as easily accessible in the physical world. Yet the paradox of loneliness shows us that these digital connections are only fulfilling when they are paired with real, emotional intimacy and a deep engagement with the other.

The challenge of digital loneliness is not that technology is distancing us from each other, but how we use it. We must learn to see digital connections not as a replacement for real, face-to-face relationships, but as a complement that helps us deepen relationships when circumstances require it. The true value of digital connections lies in their ability to connect us, not to isolate us. The trick is to use technology consciously and wisely to create deeper connections and avoid real loneliness.

At a time when the digital world is becoming more and more dominant, it is more important than ever to question ourselves and our relationships. The true value of connection is not determined by the number of contacts we have on social media, but by the quality of the relationships we build. We need to consciously break free of the illusion that more connections automatically create deeper relationships and instead rediscover the value of real, face-to-face interaction.

The increase in digital connections undoubtedly has the potential to bring our world closer together. But it is up to us to ensure that these connections really do create the closeness we want - a closeness that is not based on a glimpse of a screen, but on real, human interaction. Only then can we overcome the paradox of loneliness and cultivate real, deep relationships in an increasingly digital world.

The mechanisms behind digital loneliness

So what are the reasons for this digital loneliness? Why does the increasing use of social media not lead us to a stronger and more fulfilling connection with others, but to a feeling of emptiness?

A key aspect is the way social media is designed. Platforms like Facebook, Instagram and Co. are designed to keep us hooked back to the screen. The so-called "dopamine rush" we experience from checking notifications or receiving likes creates a quick but fleeting reward. These little "snapshots" of social recognition can give us a sense of belonging - but that feeling is superficial and fleeting. In the real world, bonds are complex and require time, trust and shared experiences. Digital interactions, on the other hand, are often reduced to quick, momentary validations. They do not offer real, deep encounters that can truly satisfy the human heart's need for closeness and real connection.

Another point related to digital loneliness is the increasing tendency towards social isolation, which is encouraged by constant comparison with other people. Social platforms often only present the highlights of a life - the vacation pictures, the successes, the happy moments. These idealized representations of life and happiness can make us feel inadequate or excluded. Constantly comparing ourselves to the seemingly perfect lives of others can lead to feelings of inadequacy and isolation. Instead of connecting us with each other, social networks promote a kind of competition that is about validation rather than real, meaningful encounters.

The digital space also allows us to hide behind a facade. Often, we present ourselves on social media in a way that does not reflect the full truth about our lives—we only show the parts we consider socially acceptable or desirable. This selective representation can cause us to lose the feeling of being truly seen, which can increase loneliness.

Another mechanism that leads to digital loneliness is the surface nature of digital communication. Social media such as Facebook, Instagram, and X allow us to interact with others in real time, but these interactions are often very fleeting and superficial. A "like" on a picture or a quick comment may provide a sense of recognition, but this form of interaction is far from the depth of a real conversation. Communication is reduced to a series of short, canned reactions that cannot create real emotional bonds. While we believe we are staying in touch, this contact is often just an illusion. Instead of delving deeper into each other's feelings and thoughts, we are limited to the surface of interactions.

This phenomenon is reinforced by what is known as the "quantification of social recognition." On social media, we measure the value of an interaction in likes, comments and shares. These numbers give us quick but superficial validation. But this validation is fleeting. A like can bring a brief moment of joy, but it is not a permanent source of fulfillment. This need for constant validation and recognition through digital platforms leads to a kind of "reward loop" in which we are constantly dependent on the validation of others. Digital loneliness arises because this validation can never replace the real emotional closeness and intimacy that comes from deep personal relationships.

This is where the nature of influencership in particular stands out. Its social and personal dangers are deeply intertwined and shed a sharp light on the dynamics that prevail in the digital world. Influencers are people who attract large numbers of followers through their presence on social media platforms such as Instagram, YouTube or TikTok and exert influence on their followers through their content. They are often seen as role models, advisors or entertaining personalities whose opinions and ways of life reach millions. But behind this outward facade of success and popularity lies a complex web of social, emotional and psychological challenges that can affect not only the influencers themselves, but also the people who follow their content.

First of all, influencership is a special form of digital celebrity that is different from traditional forms of celebrity due to the interactivity of social media. Influencers can communicate direcly with their followers, they receive immediate feedback and are able to build their brand in a more personal way. This closeness and authenticity that many influencers convey creates a strong bond between them and their followers. People often feel as if they know the influencers personally - a form of relationship that is difficult to replicate in the physical world.

However, there is a dark side to this perception. Influencers must constantly present a carefully curated version of their lives in order to maintain their brand. They show the best aspects of their lives: luxury trips, beautiful photos, great outfits, seemingly perfect relationships and more. This staged representation creates the impression of a life of success and happiness. For many followers, this is a seductive idea that leads them into the trap of comparison and self-doubt. They measure their own lives against the often unrealistic standards set by influencers.

The social dangers of influencership manifest themselves not only in the perception of the outside world, but also in the relationships between influencers and their followers, as well as within their own social circles. The influencer world is one of constant performance and self-promotion. An influencer's success depends on the number of followers, the interaction rate, and visibility. This drive for recognition and validation leads to a permanent surrender of one's life to the public.

One problem that often comes with this constant visibility is the danger of exploitation and superficial interaction. Many influencers are dependent not only on the brands that sponsor them, but also on constant validation from their followers. Likes, comments, and shares have become a new form of social currency. The more interactions an influencer receives, the more recognition and thus financial reward flows. This increases the pressure to constantly stage oneself and repeatedly produce content that appeals to the audience.

This social dynamic can cause influencers to lose their authenticity and become alienated from their true selves. The pressure to present a perfect version of oneself is enormous. In many cases, this leads to a distorted perception of one's life and a constant feeling of inadequacy when reality does not match the staged perfection. This discrepancy can lead to psychological distress and, in the long term, affect an influencer's self-esteem.

In addition, the success of influencers leads them to live in a bubble where real, deep human relationships are harder to find. Often, their relationships with followers are superficial and reduced to digital interaction. Influencers may struggle to maintain real, non-paid relationships because their social interactions are characterized by constant observation and the expectation of publicity. They are trapped in a world where every aspect of their lives is judged and commented on.

The personal dangers of influencership primarily affect the mental health and well-being of the influencers themselves. The constant pursuit of recognition and the need to keep producing new content can lead to significant emotional exhaustion. The pressure to always be "on", i.e. to constantly deliver new content while maintaining the perfect facade, not only leads to physical fatigue, but also to increasing alienation from one's own identity.

Another aspect of personal exposure is the scrutiny of one's own identity and life through the eyes of followers. Influencers are forced to share their personal experiences and opinions in a way that is evaluated by millions of people. Negative comments, criticism or even hate messages can have a major impact on mental well-being. A constant fear of public rejection arises, which can lead to anxiety, depression and reduced self-esteem.

In addition, influencers are often unprepared to deal with the financial and professional consequences of being an influencer. The rapid success that comes with the large reach on social media can lead to financial stress and an unstable professional future if popularity suddenly wanes. Many influencers are unaware of how quickly their careers can change in the digital world. This uncertainty factor can represent a constant psychological burden and increase the pressure to optimize their brand in order to not only retain followers but also to continuously secure sources of income.

A shitstorm often arises from a thoughtless or controversial statement, an unfortunate action or a misleading public statement that is perceived by a large number of people as inappropriate or hurtful. The consequences of a shitstorm can be far-reaching and often dramatic for both the individuals or organizations affected and the online community involved. They range from short-term emotional and social effects to long-term professional and financial damage.

For the influencers affected, a shitstorm can represent a considerable psychological burden. The sudden public criticism can lead to anxiety, stress and a feeling of being overwhelmed. Influencers in particular often experience a strong feeling of alienation and isolation as a result of such events. The mass rejection, which sometimes takes the form of hateful comments, insults and cyberbullying, can lead to depression and reduced self-esteem. In some cases, it can also lead to a complete withdrawal from social media or even professional and personal crises.

Another serious effect of a shitstorm is financial loss. For influencers and well-known personalities, a massive loss of image often means the loss of advertising partnerships and sponsorships. Brands that have worked with the influencer up to that point may feel compelled to end the collaboration in order to protect their own reputation and avoid negative associations with the person concerned.

For influencers and media personalities, the public reputation that has been severely damaged by the shitstorm can lead not only to a decline in the number of followers, but also to a loss of professional opportunities. In the long term, the person affected may have difficulty gaining new partnerships or gaining a foothold in their industry. The consequences of a shitstorm are complex and can have both short- and long-term effects on the people and organizations affected. These range from psychological stress and social isolation to career losses and financial losses and legal consequences. Shitstorms not only show the dangers of social media, but also reflect social values and the importance of public communication and responsibility in the digital space.

In order to minimize the negative effects of influencership, it is important that influencers and their followers become aware of the mechanisms and psychological dynamics behind it. Only by critically examining one's own goals and the impact of influencership can a healthy balance between digital presence and real life be found.

Another important mechanism behind digital loneliness is "social comparison," which is reinforced by the structure of social networks. Social media is designed to showcase the best and most successful moments from users' lives. Vacation pictures, successful careers, and happy relationships are the content that gets the most attention. This constant presentation of other people's highlights can lead to negative comparison. We see other people's perfect lives and start to weigh our own lives against them, which can lead to a feeling of inadequacy. Social comparison makes us feel like we are not enough or that our lives do not deserve the same recognition, which can lead to feelings of isolation and alienation.

This social comparison becomes particularly problematic when combined with the "fear of missing out" (FOMO), the constant feeling of missing out. When we see other people participating in exciting experiences, we can feel left out. This pressure to always be there reinforces feelings of loneliness because we believe we are not integrated into the same social circles or do not receive the same level of success and recognition as others. This constant need to participate in social activities and show off can lead to an inner emptiness if these needs are not met.

The filter bubble in which we move through social media algorithms is another mechanism that contributes to digital loneliness. The algorithms that curate the content on social networks tend to show us only the information that is consistent with our previous interests and beliefs. These "filter bubbles" create a kind of digital echo chamber in which we only ever hear the same perspective and are increasingly confirmed in our own beliefs. This not only reduces the diversity of information we receive, but also socially isolates us from other perspectives. In such bubbles, there is often no space for the development of real social interactions, where we can exchange different views and grow in a real dialogue. Instead, digital spaces only confirm our own viewpoints and reinforce feelings of isolation when we don't engage with other perspectives.

In addition, the lack of nonverbal communication in digital interactions is a major factor contributing to digital loneliness. In face-to-face conversations, we can respond to body language, facial expressions, and tone of voice - elements that are crucial to the emotional depth of a conversation. In digital communication, on the other hand, these elements are missing, making it difficult to fully grasp the emotional nuances of a conversation. A short text conversation or message can easily be misunderstood because there are no additional signals such as a reassuring look or a warm hug that reinforce the emotional content of the communication. This means that digital conversations often seem shallow and distant, even if they may seem friendly and inviting from the perspective of pure word choice.

Constant access to social networks and news through smartphones and other devices further reinforces digital loneliness. In the analogue world, we could distance ourselves from an interaction by leaving the house, turning off the TV or putting the phone away. In the digital world, however, we are reachable at all times. We can no longer simply switch to "offline" mode without feeling removed from digital obligations and social expectations. This constant accessibility creates not only physical exhaustion, but also psychological exhaustion, which can increase feelings of isolation. There is pressure to always be present, always respond, always share - leading to an impoverishment of our social interactions and an increase in loneliness.

Another aspect is the loss of authenticity. In the digital world, many people tend to portray their lives in an idealised way. Only what is considered positive or appealing is shown, while the dark and less glamorous sides of life are often hidden. This means that the relationships we maintain online are often based on a distorted representation of life. This distorted perception of reality causes us to be in a constant race to live the perfect life, making true, authentic connection between people difficult. When we only focus on the idealized version of other people's lives, we lose the ability to connect on a deeper, human level.

Finally, the increasing importance of algorithms also plays a role in digital loneliness. These algorithms decide what content we see and which people in our network we encounter most often. They encourage interaction with certain content and users deemed relevant, while others disappear from view. This can lead to us surrounding ourselves with a small, homogenous group of people and ideas that confirm our own views but offer little opportunity for real, diverse connections and perspectives. The algorithms reinforce this isolation by trapping us in a bubble of repetition and confirmation.

The mechanisms behind digital loneliness are complex and intertwined. They result from the way digital platforms are designed and the psychological responses these platforms trigger in us. The digital world offers undeniable advantages in terms of connectivity and access to information, but it can also trap us in a spiral of superficiality, social comparison and alienation. To overcome digital loneliness, we must become aware of the effects of these mechanisms and learn to make our digital communication more conscious and fulfilling. Only then can we rediscover the true meaning of connection and closeness in the digital age.

The impact on real relationships

What does this mean for interpersonal relationships outside the digital world? One of the most profound effects that the digital world has on our relationships is the loss of non-verbal communication. In a face-to-face conversation, we can respond to body language, facial expressions and tone of voice - elements that help us understand the emotional depth and intentions of the other person. This dimension of communication is largely lost in the digital space. A short text conversation or a comment can easily be misunderstood because the subtle nuances of body language are missing.

The experience of closeness and intimacy is also changed by digital forms of communication. Physical contact, sharing moments together and sharing physical proximity are essential components of a deep relationship. These aspects are difficult or even impossible to replace when the majority of our interactions are shifted to the digital space.

The digital revolution has fundamentally changed the way we communicate. What was once limited to face-to-face meetings, letters or phone calls now takes place via numerous digital channels. This transformation brings both opportunities and challenges for our interpersonal relationships.

First, digital communication enables unprecedented connectivity. People can stay in touch regardless of geographical distances. Family members who live far apart can share in important moments through video calls. Friendships survive moves and life changes as social media and messaging services facilitate continuous exchange. This expanded reach has proven its importance especially during the COVID-19 pandemic, when digital connections were often the only way for social interaction.

However, we are also observing a qualitative change in communication. Text-based messages cannot fully convey non-verbal signals such as facial expressions, gestures and tone of voice. Emoticons, GIFs and voice messages try to fill this gap, but do not achieve the depth of a personal encounter. The absence of these signals often leads to misunderstandings, as irony, humor or empathy are harder to convey. Conflicts can escalate more quickly if messages are misinterpreted.

Another aspect is the change in our attention. In conversations via smartphone or computer, we are often exposed to several stimuli at the same time - notifications interrupt the flow of thoughts, other tabs compete for our attention. This divided presence can give the feeling of not really being heard or seen. In contrast, the undivided attention in personal encounters creates a connection that is difficult to replicate through digital media.

Digital communication has also changed our expectations of accessibility. The constant availability of messaging services creates a subtle pressure to always be responsive. The lack of immediate responses can signal uncertainty or even rejection, while constant communication can lead to exhaustion. This changed dynamic challenges us to set healthy boundaries and create space for uninterrupted offline time.

We are observing a paradoxical phenomenon, especially among younger generations: Despite constant digital connectivity, many report feelings of loneliness. The superficial nature of many online interactions does not seem to fully satisfy the basic human need for deep connection. The quantity of contacts does not replace the quality of real encounters in which we can show ourselves vulnerable and be authentic.

At the same time, digital platforms provide space for people who struggle in traditional social contexts. Introverts or people with social anxiety can build connections more easily in text-based environments. Communities form around shared interests, regardless of physical barriers. This inclusivity represents a significant gain.

The way we maintain relationships has also changed. Social media allows us to stay informed about the life events of an extended circle - from former schoolmates to distant acquaintances. This peripheral awareness can, on the one hand, create a sense of cohesion, but on the other hand, it can also lead to superficial connections based on curated self-presentation. The challenge is to balance between this broad but shallow networking and the cultivation of deeper relationships.

Another effect of digital communication is the change in our social skills. Especially among adolescents who grow up in a digitally influenced world, there is concern that important face-to-face communication skills could remain underdeveloped. The ability to resolve conflicts directly, show empathy or have complex conversations requires practice in real social contexts.

The pandemic has also shown that digital communication is a valuable tool, but cannot completely replace physical co-presence. After long periods of virtual meetings, many people long for the spontaneous exchange, shared experiences and physical closeness that only face-to-face encounters can offer.

For a healthy balance, it seems crucial to view digital communication as a supplement to, and not a replacement for, personal interactions. Consciously taking time offline, prioritizing face-to-face encounters for important conversations, and reflecting on one's own media consumption can help us reap the benefits of digitalization without suffering its pitfalls. Ultimately, we are faced with the task of developing a new social grammar - rules and norms that help us have authentic and fulfilling relationships in this hybrid reality. This requires both individual mindfulness and societal discussions about how we can put technology in the service of our deepest human needs for connection, understanding, and belonging.

The biological and psychological importance of direct human contact

Direct personal contact is not only pleasant for us humans, but fulfills fundamental biological and psychological needs that are deeply rooted in our evolutionary history. As a social species, we have evolved over millennia in communities in which physical proximity, touch, and immediate interaction were essential for survival.

From a neurobiological point of view, physical contact, especially touch, triggers a cascade of biochemical reactions. Positive touches such as hugging, holding hands or a friendly pat on the back release oxytocin - a hormone that reduces stress, promotes trust and strengthens social bonds. At the same time, cortisol levels drop, which dampens our stress response and supports the immune system. Studies have shown that regular, positive physical contact can lower blood pressure, relieve pain and even speed up wound healing.

The physical co-presence of other people also activates our mirror neuron system - specialized brain cells that fire when we observe an action and when we perform it ourselves. This neurological resonance enables us to immediately perceive and empathize with the emotions of others, which forms the basis for deep empathy. In direct encounters, we can achieve a form of emotional synchronization through microexpressions, body posture and eye contact that is not possible through digital media.

Physical contact is irreplaceable, especially in early stages of life. Infants and young children develop secure attachment patterns through touch, holding and cuddling that shape their emotional and cognitive development. The lack of physical affection can lead to developmental delays, weakened immune systems and lifelong attachment difficulties, as tragic studies of orphans have shown.

In adulthood, our need for personal contact remains. The physical presence of other people in our living space provides a feeling of security and belonging that is deeply anchored in our brain stem. Just knowing that someone is physically available reduces our stress levels and promotes psychological resilience.

Immediate interaction also activates all of our senses simultaneously. We perceive not only words, but also smells that can unconsciously signal trust or distrust, tactile impressions that convey closeness and minimal changes in voice and facial expression that convey complex emotional states. This multisensory experience creates a richer, deeper sense of connection than any technologically mediated communication.

From an evolutionary psychological perspective, social groups were essential for the survival of our ancestors - for protection, food procurement and childcare. This dependence, which has lasted for thousands of years, has shaped our brains in such a way that social isolation is perceived as an existential threat. Chronic loneliness activates the same brain regions as physical pain and triggers stress reactions that can lead to cardiovascular disease, weakened immune systems and increased levels of inflammation in the body in the long term.

Personal encounters also provide space for spontaneous, unplanned interactions that are often particularly meaningful. A chance conversation, a shared moment of laughter or an unexpected gesture of support can have profound effects that rarely arise in planned digital interactions.

The physical presence of other people in our lives also serves an important mirror function for our identity. Through the reactions and feedback of others, we develop and refine our self-image and our understanding of who we are. This social validation and the feeling of being truly seen are central to our mental health and well-being.

Direct contact also enables a form of shared attention and shared experience that stimulates our brains in unique ways. When we laugh, grieve, celebrate or work together with others, a kind of collective emotional state emerges that amplifies and enriches our individual experiences. This phenomenon, often referred to as "collective effervescence," can provide a deep sense of meaning and belonging.

The COVID-19 pandemic, as an extreme mass experiment, has highlighted how essential personal contact is for our health. The increase in depression, anxiety and psychosomatic complaints during lockdown periods underscores that digital connections, while valuable, are not a complete substitute for physical proxymity.

Social media cannot replace direct human contact for fundamental biological and psychological reasons. While digital platforms enable or simulate information exchange and some form of connectedness, they lack the essential elements that engage and activate our neurobiological systems: the oxytocin release through touch, the multisensory experience of a face-to-face encounter and the immediate emotional resonance required by our mirror neuron system. Evolution has shaped us over millennia as beings who need physical proximity for mental and physical health - a fact that no amount of technology, no matter how advanced, can circumvent.

Nevertheless, social media performs an important bridging function in our social fabric. It can maintain a vital connection in times of forced separation, such as during a pandemic or when there are large geographical distances. For people with reduced mobility, in remote areas or with social anxiety, digital platforms offer access to communities that would not otherwise be possible. They make it possible to maintain loose connections that would otherwise be lost and can serve as first points of contact for new relationships that are later transferred to the physical world.

The optimal use of social media therefore lies in its role as a complement, not a replacement, for face-to-face encounters. They can bridge periods of physical isolation, support existing relationships and initiate new ones - but always with the awareness that our deepest human needs for connection can ultimately only be fully met through direct contact. The true value of digital communication for our social well-being lies in this complementary function, not as a substitute.

As humans, we are biologically and psychologically programmed to live in direct contact with others. The progressive digitization of our communication cannot fully meet the evolutionnarily developed needs for physical proximity, multisensory perception and immediate social resonance. A healthy life, even in the digital age, therefore requires the conscious integration and appreciation of direct personal encounters as an irreplaceable component of human well-being.

Mental Health in a Performance-Oriented Society

In today's society, which is characterized by efficiency, optimization and constant availability, productivity is increasingly becoming the measure of human value. What once served as a means to an end - namely, enabling a good life through work - has developed into an end in itself in many areas. This development is not without consequences for mental health. A deeper look at this phenomenon reveals the complex relationships between social expectations and individual well-being.

The roots of the productivity paradigm

The roots of our performance society go deep into history. Industrialization began an era in which human labor was increasingly quantified and optimized. The Protestant work ethic, which understood work as a virtue and moral duty, contributed significantly to anchoring these values. In the digital age, this development has intensified: the boundaries between work and leisure are blurring, and the possibility of being constantly available has significantly increased the pressure to be permanently productive.

Social media further reinforces this effect. They present us with an idealized image of people who seem to effortlessly juggle career, family, fitness and self-fulfillment. This constant confrontation with the supposed successes of others feeds the feeling of not achieving enough.

In order to understand today's performance-oriented society and its effects on mental health in depth, it is worth taking a closer look at the historical, philosophical and economic origins of our productivity paradigm.

The foundations of our current performance-oriented society were already laid in the transition from feudalism to industrial capitalism. In the feudal system, work was still strongly tied to the seasons and natural rhythms. The industrial revolution brought about a fundamental reorganization: time became a measurable resource that had to be used. The invention of the factory clock symbolized this change - workers were now paid by the hour, not by the units produced or seasonal necessity.

At the beginning of the 20th century, Frederick Winslow Taylor developed the concept of "scientific management", which broke down human work into the smallest units and trimmed it for maximum efficiency. This rationalization of work led to enormous increases in productivity, but often reduced people to an interchangeable factor in the production process.

In his work "The Protestant Ethic and the Spirit of Capitalism" (1904/05), Max Weber identified a decisive cultural factor: Calvinism, with its doctrine of predestination, led to worldly success being interpreted as a sign of divine grace. Work thus became not only an economic necessity, but also an expression of moral virtue and the fulfillment of religious duty. This religious legitimation of work and success continues to have an impact today - even in secularized societies. It has contributed to idleness being considered morally reprehensible and productivity becoming a characteristic of identity.

Since the 1980s, neoliberalism as an economic policy paradigm has further increased the pressure for productivity. The idea of the "entrepreneurial self" (Ulrich Bröckling) shifted the market logic into the interior of the individual: everyone should become the manager of their own biography, the entrepreneur of their own life. This development went hand in hand with a dismantling of social security systems and a flexibilization of labor markets. The message was: If you fail, you haven't worked hard enough. This individualization of responsibility relieves social structures and puts a strain on the individual - even to the point of having serious consequences for mental health.

Digitalization acts as a catalyst for the existing productivity paradigm. Mobile devices and constant networking are blurring the boundaries between work and leisure. The ability to work anytime, anywhere often becomes an implicit expectation. Digitalization also enables new forms of performance measurement and control. In the "gig economy," workers are constantly evaluated, while tracking apps make every activity measurable. This permanent quantification increases the pressure to perform and creates new forms of self-optimization.

The media and culture industry has contributed significantly to the spread of the productivity ideal. From success guides to social media, an image is propagated that presents success, activity, and self-optimization as desirable norms. Tech entrepreneurs and their success stories in particular serve as modern myths that suggest that anyone can become a millionaire through hard work.

These cultural narratives ignore structural inequalities and reinforce the belief that success is solely a matter of personal effort. They also feed the fear of falling behind or of "not achieving enough" - a key factor in psychological stress.

As a result of globalization, competitive pressure has intensified at an international level. Companies compete with producers from all over the world, which increases the pressure on efficiency and productivity. This development is often used to restrict workers' rights and increase performance requirements. At the same time, a global race for the best talent has developed. The idea of having to survive in a global labor market contributes to increasing individual pressure to perform and fuels the fear of falling behind.

Based on Michel Foucault's concept of biopolitics, we can observe how the productive body has become the subject of political and economic control. Health programs in companies, fitness apps and wellness offers are often not primarily aimed at well-being, but at maintaining and increasing the workforce. This "care for yourself" becomes a duty, your own health a resource that needs to be managed. Paradoxically, this health optimization can itself become a source of stress - if, for example, work-life balance degenerates into another to-do list that needs to be completed.

An often overlooked aspect is the gradual erosion of alternative value systems. Traditional sources of meaning and identity - be it religion, community or non-economic activities - have lost importance. In this vacuum, professional success is gaining importance as an anchor of identity. Without alternative narratives that give people value beyond their productivity, work becomes the primary place of self-realization - a burden that it can hardly bear without endangering mental health.

Scientific research into performance and productivity has further solidified the productivity paradigm. From work psychology to neuroscience, methods are being developed to optimize human performance. This research has provided important insights, but is often interpreted one-sidedly in terms of increaseing productivity. The question of whether constant performance improvement is even a desirable goal is rarely asked.

Each generation passes its values on to the next - often in an intensified form. Those who grew up under pressure to perform tend to internalize it and pass it on. This creates transgenerational patterns that reinforce the productivity paradigm. This is particularly evident in the education system, where competition for grades, qualifications and career opportunities begins at an ever earlier age. The fear that their own child "might not keep up" drives parents to pass on the pressure to perform - a vicious circle that is difficult to break.

The roots of today's productivity paradigm are complex and deeply rooted. They range from economic structures to cultural narratives to psychological mechanisms. This complexity explains why the paradigm is so resilient - and why overcoming it requires more than individual behavioral changes. However, a deep understanding of these roots is the first step in developing alternatives and initiating a social dialogue about the importance of performance and productivity. This is the only way to find a balance that takes into account both economic necessities and mental health.

Psychological effects of permanent pressure to perform

The ongoing pressure to be productive leaves deep scars on the psyche of many people. Burnout, once considered a marginal phenomenon, has become a widespread diagnosis. The World Health Organization (WHO) has now classified burnout as a "syndrome due to chronic stress in the workplace." It is characterized by states of exhaustion, increasing mental distance from one's own work and reduced professional performance.

Anxiety disorders and depression are also increasing in societies with high pressure to perform. The constant worry of not being good enough, comparing yourself to others and the fear of failure can lead to chronic stress. This in turn affects not only mental but also physical health, which can manifest itself in sleep disorders, headaches or gastrointestinal complaints. It is particularly worrying that even young people are suffering from this pressure. Studies show that schoolchildren and students are increasingly suffering from fear of failure and perfectionism, which can affect their development and well-being in the long term.

The modern working world is characterized by constantly increasing pressure to perform. Digitalization, globalization and economic uncertainty have led to a compression and acceleration of work processes. Employees are faced with ever greater demands - be it through target specifications, permanent availability or the need for constant training. In today's working world, pressure to perform has become a permanent condition. The reasons for this are varied: Technological change has led to an acceleration of work processes. Emails, instant messaging and mobile devices enable constant availability. In addition, companies operate in an international environment with increased competitive pressure, which is passed on to employees. Flexible working hours and home offices blur the boundaries between work and private life. Key performance indicators, regular evaluations and performance-related remuneration systems increase the pressure to continuously deliver top performance.

The constant pressure to perform can lead to various psychological impairments. Burnout syndrome is just one of the best-known consequences of chronic stress. It manifests itself in emotional exhaustion, cynicism and inner distancing from work, reduced performance as well as physical symptoms such as sleep disorders and increased susceptibility to infections. Studies show that in some industries up to 25% of employees show burnout symptoms. People in helping professions, IT specialists and managers are particularly at risk. The constant pressure to meet demands can lead to generalized anxiety disorders, panic attacks, depressive episodes and social isolation. The fear of failure or losing one's job becomes a constant companion. Chronic stress also affects cognitive abilities: difficulty concentrating, poor decision-making, forgetfulness and loss of createvity can occur. This leads to a vicious circle in which the declining cognitive performance increases the pressure experienced. The psychological stress often manifests itself physically as well:

increased risk of cardiovascular disease, weakened immune system, musculoskeletal disorders as well as sleep disorders and chronic fatigue are common consequences.

The individual suffering has far-reaching effects on society and the economy. Mental illness is now one of the main causes of incapacity to work. In Germany, around 15% of all days of absence are due to mental illness, and the trend is rising. Even when those affected do show up at work, the condition known as "presenteeism" leads to significant losses in productivity. Studies estimate that the costs of reduced performance at work are higher than those of absence. Overworked employees are more likely to leave the company. High levels of fluctuation lead to loss of knowledge and rising recruitment costs.

Certain groups of people are particularly vulnerable to the negative effects of pressure to perform. Generation Y and Generation Z enter the workforce with high expectations, but at the same time are under enormous pressure to perform in an uncertain working world. Constant self-optimization and comparison on social media further increase this pressure. People with caregiving responsibilities, such as single parents and carers, experience a double burden that makes them particularly vulnerable to stress and burnout. In a rapidly changing working world, older employees are under pressure to keep up with technological developments and prove their relevance.

Several trends point to a potential worsening of the situation: Artificial intelligence and automation are fueling fears of being replaced by machines, which further increases the pressure to perform. The increasing uncertainty caused by temporary contracts and project-based work in the gig economy is adding to the pressure. In addition, the pressure to continuously train and adapt is growing due to accelerated innovation cycles. At the same time, there are signs of a change in thinking: Companies are increasingly recognizing the importance of mental health for corporate success and are implementing corporate health management. New working models that offer more autonomy and flexibility are gaining importance. In some countries, measures are being introduced to protect mental health in the workplace.

Companies can adopt various prevention and intervention strategies: Managers should be trained to recognize and reduce stress among employees. A sensible distribution of tasks and the avoidance of overload are important. Clear expectations and realistic goals should be communicated transparently. Expanding scope for action and creating support systems strengthen employees' resources. Promoting breaks and supporting a clear boundary between work and leisure time are also important. On an individual level, people can strengthen their resilience through sufficient sleep, exercise and a healthy diet. Meditation and conscious relaxation techniques help to deal with stress. Consciously drawing boundaries between work and private life is essential. Maintaining relationships and building a support network provide social support.

At the first signs of overload, it is advisable to seek advice or therapy early on. The constant pressure to perform in the modern working world poses a serious threat to mental health. The individual and societal costs are immense and are likely to continue to rise if comprehensive countermeasures are not taken. A paradigm shift is necessary: away from the one-sided focus on productivity and efficiency, towards a holistic understanding of work that puts human needs at the center. This requires an interaction between politics, companies and individuals. The working world of the future must recognize mental health as a central value - not only for humanitarian reasons, but also because long-term economic success is only possible with healthy and committed employees.

The path to this will not be easy, but the growing attention to the issue gives cause for hope. These grievances lead to the question of whether people are even up to their own challenges. Especially in the context of the constant pressure to perform in the modern working world. This profound question deserves detailed consideration. Throughout history, people have repeatedly proven that they have a remarkable ability to adapt. From coping with extreme environmental conditions to developing complex social structures, the human species has shown amazing resilience and innovative power. Yet the self-created challenges of the modern working world present a new kind of endurance test.

The psychological stress resulting from the constant pressure to perform leads to a paradoxical situation: technological progress, which was actually supposed to make life easier, is creating new forms of stress and overexertion. The human psyche does not always seem to be able to keep up with the pace of self-created changes. This raises the legitimate question of whether we are evolutionarily prepared to function in such a fast-moving, information-flooded and highly competitive environment.

From a biological point of view, humans are a product of evolutionary processes that took place over thousands of years in a completely different environment. Our stress system was designed to react to acute dangers - not to chronic stress such as floods of emails, deadlines or constant availability. The increasing rates of burnout, depression and anxiety disorders indicate that our biological systems are overwhelmed by modern demands.

From a psychological point of view, however, humans have remarkable abilities for adaptation and self-regulation. Research into neuroplasticity shows that our brains can adapt to new challenges even in adulthood. We have also developed coping strategies that help us deal with stress. Mindfulness techniques, therapeutic approaches and social support are examples of resources that we can mobilize.

From a sociological perspective, we are faced with the dilemma that the social structures and economic systems we have created are often not geared towards human well-being. The pursuit of constant growth and increased efficiency collides with our basic needs for security, belonging and self-realization.

The answer to the question is therefore differentiated: people fundamentally have the potential to cope with the challenges they have created for themselves - but not under all circumstances and not without adaptations on an individual and collective level.

On an individual level, numerous examples show that people can successfully deal with the demands of the modern working world through self-reflection, developing healthy boundaries and specifically strengthening resilience. Studies on post-traumatic maturation even show that people can emerge stronger from stressful experiences if they have the appropriate resources and support systems.

At a societal level, however, a rethink is required. The increasing recognition of mental health as a key factor for sustainable success in companies and society could be an indication that we are beginning to respect the limits of our resilience and adapt our systems accordingly. Initiatives for a healthier work-life balance, the introduction of the right to be unavailable or experiments with reduced working hours with the same pay are examples of this change.

The crucial challenge is that as humans we have the ability to shape our environment and living conditions ourselves. This gives us the unique opportunity to create systems that are in line with our psychological and biological needs rather than in conflict with them. The question is therefore less whether we have fundamentally grown, but whether we are ready to use our collective intelligence and creativity to create more humane working and living conditions.

Ultimately, there is much to suggest that humans as a whole have the potential to master even complex self-created challenges - provided we recognize our limitations and design our environment in such a way that it respects and promotes our intrinsic needs. The increasing psychological stress in the working world can be understood as a warning signal that calls on us to develop a more sustainable and humane approach to performance and productivity.

The question of whether we are up to our challenges is therefore also a question of the wisdom with which we recognize our abilities and limitations and shape our lives and society accordingly. In this sense, the answer lies not only in our biological makeup, but in our collective decision about how we want to live and work.

The constant pressure to perform in the modern working world poses a serious threat to mental health. The individual and societal costs are immense and are likely to continue to rise if comprehensive countermeasures are not taken.

A paradigm shift is necessary: away from the one-sided focus on productivity and efficiency, towards a holistic understanding of work that focuses on human needs. This requires an interaction between politics, companies and individuals.

The working world of the future must recognize mental health as a central value - not only for humanitarian reasons, but also because long-term economic success is only possible with healthy and committed employees. The path to this will not be easy, but the growing attention to the topic gives cause for hope.

The economization of all areas of life

What is particularly problematic is that productivity thinking is no longer limited to the workplace. Leisure time is also increase-ingly "optimized" and designed with a goal in mind. Even relax-ation is becoming a compulsory exercise in order to maintain one's own performance. "Productive leisure" is no longer a contradiction, but has become the norm for many people.

This economization of all areas of life means that real leisure and purposeless existence are becoming increasingly rare. Yet these moments in particular are of inestimable value for mental health. They enable creativity, self-reflection and authentic social rela-tionships - all factors that contribute to mental well-being.

The issue of the economization of all areas of life is deeply interwoven with the development of human society. From early Homo sapiens, who lived in small hunter-gatherer communities, to modern Homo oeconomicus, who makes his decisions according to the principles of efficiency, a radical change took place. This change was not only a consequence of technological advances or economic necessities, but also the result of a cultural and ideological paradigm shift.

In early history, human life was strongly characterized by cooperation. Small groups organized themselves on the basis of mutual support. There were no markets in the modern sense, no money and no formal economic institutions. Instead, coexistence was based on exchange, reciprocity and communal resource management.

This changed fundamentally with the settlement of people. The agricultural revolution produced surpluses that had to be stored, traded and protected. The first social stratifications emerged, and with them the need for a new organization of economic activities. But here too, not only rational considerations played a role - religious, cultural and social norms determined how and when resources were distributed.

The development of cities and early civilizations led to the emergence of markets. Complex trading structures emerged in Mesopotamia, Egypt, and later in ancient Greece and Rome. But the economy was still embedded in social and moral ideas. Aristotle, for example, distinguished between "oikonomia," the art of managing a household, and "chrematistics," the pure accumulation of wealth - he viewed the latter with skepticism. The transition from an embedded to a more autonomous economy took place slowly. It was only with the rise of capitalism in the Middle Ages and the early modern period that a clear separation between the economy and other areas of society began to emerge. Money and markets became independent institutions whose logic increasingly permeated social life.

The industrial revolution gave rise to the idea that people should be understood primarily as rational, utility-maximizing actors. Economists such as Adam Smith saw the market as a natural order in which individual striving for profit led to collective prosperity. Homo oeconomicus, a model of the rationally decisive economic man, was born.

But while this model served as an ideal-typical assumption in classical economics, it gradually began to change people's self-perception as well. The more economic principles penetrated everyday life, the more people were encouraged to evaluate their own actions according to cost-benefit analyses. Education, relationships, leisure - everything was increasingly viewed from an economic perspective.

In the 20th and 21st centuries, this process increased rapidly. The neoliberal turn of the 1980s reinforced the idea that the market was the most efficient means of organizing all areas of life. Privatization, competition and increased efficiency were no longer only applied to companies, but to schools, hospitals and even personal relationships.

Dating apps optimize partner searches according to algorithms, social media platforms turn friendships into monetizable networks, and the value of a university is increasingly measured by the salaries of its graduates. Even sleep is being economized - with apps and gadgets that track, evaluate and "optimize" it.

But this change is not without consequences. Mental illnesses, burnout and feelings of alienation are increasing. People who constantly have to optimize themselves often lose their sense of intrinsic values and meaning. The question arises: is Homo oeconomicus an inevitable reality or are there alternatives? While the economization of all areas of life is often presented as having no alternative, there are countermovements. The sharing economy, the common good economy and new forms of solidarity-based economics show that not everything has to follow market logic.

Perhaps Homo oeconomicus is not the final stage of human development, but just an episode. The challenge is to reconcile economic efficiency with social and ethical values. The question remains: will we succeed in finding a new balance - or are we heading for a future in which people only exist as an economic resource that can be optimized?

From career choices to leisure activities to interpersonal relationships - efficiency thinking, cost-benefit considerations and the pressure to optimize are at work everywhere. These developments have led to a change in people's self-image: they increasingly see themselves as a kind of entrepreneur of their own making, whose value is measured by performance, productivity and economic success.

This process begins as early as childhood. Parents invest specifically in the education and development of their children, not only out of concern, but also to enable them to have better economic opportunities later on. Early intervention programs, specialized schools and structured leisure activities follow a clear plan: to get the most out of individual abilities and to secure a competitive advantage over others. Playing, discovering and purposeless learning, once central elements of a carefree childhood, are increasingly being replaced by goal-oriented activities geared towards later benefits.

This thinking continues into adulthood. The choice of a course of study or career is often no longer made out of intrinsic interest, but by weighing up salary prospects, career prospects and market requirements. Subjects such as philosophy or art, which do not promise immediate economic profit, are increasingly coming under pressure, while technical, economic or data-driven disciplines are flourishing. Education becomes an investment, the return on which is expected in the form of a high income or job security.

Everyday life is also permeated by economic principles. People optimize their time with productivity apps, organize their daily routines according to efficiency principles and avoid activities that have no direct benefit. Even leisure and relaxation are no longer seen as an end in themselves, but as a means of improving performance. Meditation is practiced to improve work performance, sport is used for self-promotion and even reading books is done with the aim of self-optimization. The question "What's in it for me?" is increasingly at the center of individual actions.

Digitalization has intensified this development. Social networks are no longer just places for exchange, but platforms for self-promotion. People curate their online profiles like a brand, present successes, optimize their appearance and measure their social value by likes, follower numbers and engagement rates. Friendships are often no longer maintained solely for emotional connection, but also in terms of the benefits they bring to career, status or networks. Relationships are increasingly like a market in which the best options are weighed against each other. Dating apps reinforce this phenomenon by selecting potential partners according to efficiency criteria and reducing romantic connections to algorithmically calculated probabilities. Wearables such as smartwatches measure sleep quality, number of steps and calorie consumption, while biohacking techniques promise to make the body a more efficient system. Aging is no longer accepted as a natural process, but as a challenge that must be combated with products, technologies and interventions.

But this total economization of life has profound consequences for human naturalness. People are increasingly moving away from spontaneous, unstructured and purposeless activities that have long been an essential part of life. The pressure to optimize themselves creates stress, anxiety and the feeling of permanent inadequacy. Anyone who cannot keep up or consciously goes against this logic runs the risk of being perceived as inefficient, backward or unambitious.

In addition, this development is accompanied by a loss of authenticity. If all actions are subject to economic calculation, it becomes difficult to form real, unconditional connections - be it in friendships, in love or in the professional environment. People are beginning to see themselves as resources that must be managed, improved and used strategically, instead of seeing themselves as beings with individual characteristics and intrinsic values.

The question is whether people will succeed in freeing themselves from this compulsion to economize or whether they will become increasingly lost in a world in which only what is measurable, profitable and efficient counts.

Technological progress was once celebrated as liberating people from hard work and monotonous tasks. Machines, automation and artificial intelligence were supposed to make life easier, reduce working hours and create more space for creativity, leisure and personal development. But in reality, a paradoxical phenomenon has developed: instead of easing people's workloads, advancing technology is forcing them to optimize, improve performance and monitor themselves more and more.

This paradox is particularly evident in the world of work. Automation and digital tools were supposed to make work processes more efficient, so that less human effort would be required. In fact, however, the opposite has happened. As tasks can be completed more quickly, expectations of productivity and performance are rising. Emails that used to take days to respond to now require an immediate response. Work software makes it possible to complete projects in less time, but this does not create more free time, but rather the pressure to complete even more tasks in the same amount of time. Instead of a reduction in working hours, many people are experiencing a blurring of the boundaries between work and private life, in which constant availability and multitasking have become the norm.

This need for optimization is also evident in leisure time. Streaming services analyze viewing behavior to offer the most efficient form of entertainment, sports apps measure every movement to maximize training results, and sleep trackers provide feedback on how restful the night was. Even regeneration becomes a data-driven task that is no longer controlled by one's own body feeling, but by algorithms and analytical evaluations. People thus become machines that optimize, monitor and evaluate themselves - always looking for a better version of themselves.

The irony is that many of these technological innovations were introduced precisely with the promise of making life more pleasant and stress-free. Smart assistants are supposed to make everyday life easier, appointment planners are supposed to save time, health apps are supposed to increase well-being. In practice, however, the constant availability of these tools means that people do not feel more relaxed, but are put under even more pressure to use their time and energy as efficiently as possible. Modern man does not feel relieved, but rather constantly challenged to make the most of his resources.

Another problem with this development is that it creates a new form of social control. While in the past it was primarily external institutions such as employers or authorities that monitored performance and efficiency, this monitoring has increasingly shifted to the individual themselves. Today, people measure each other against digital rankings, compare themselves on social media based on follower numbers and feel compelled to continuously improve themselves by the omnipresent visibility of their lifestyle. Anyone who evades this logic runs the risk of being seen as backward, inefficient or underperforming - even if they are actually happy with their life.

This paradox of technological progress ultimately shows that increasing efficiency and optimizing never reach a final goal, but form an endless spiral. Every advance leads to new expectations, every relief creates new obligations. People become driven by their own tools instead of being truly freed from them. The real question is therefore not which technologies can make us even more efficient in the future, but how we as a society can break away from the idea that everything has to be faster, better and more productive.

Cultural differences in dealing with performance

The way we deal with productivity and performance is culturally influenced. While in some societies "being busy" is a status symbol, other cultures have developed concepts that value idleness and slowness. In Japan, death from overwork ("karoshi") has led to social debates and initial reforms. In countries such as Denmark or Sweden, on the other hand, more emphasis is placed on a healthy work-life balance. These cultural differences show that the way we deal with performance and productivity is not natural, but socially constructed - and can therefore be changed.

The way we deal with performance, productivity and relaxation varies greatly between cultures around the world. While some societies see maximizing work effort and efficiency as the highest virtue, others value a balance between duty and relaxation. The way in which performance is evaluated affects not only individual lifestyles, but also economic structures, social expectations and general well-being.

In western industrialized countries, especially in the USA and Germany, performance is a central part of social identity. In the United States, the concept of the "American Dream" is deeply rooted - the idea that hard work and personal commitment inevitably lead to success. This belief fosters a culture in which long hours, self-discipline and permanent availability are seen as signs of ambition and commitment. People who work long hours are highly respected, while breaks and leisure activities are often seen as a waste of time. This mentality is even reflected in social interactions: the question "What do you do?" is one of the first to be asked in conversations because work and performance play a central role in social status.

Germany, on the other hand, is traditionally known for its discipline and hard work. The concept of a "meritocracy" is deeply rooted in the culture, and terms such as "hard work" and "duty" are highly valued. At the same time, however, there is a cultural appreciation for structured vacation and rest periods - German work culture recognizes that breaks contribute to long-term productivity. Nevertheless, the pursuit of efficiency remains omnipresent, reflected, for example, in the famous punctuality and precision of German work.

A contrast to this can be found in southern countries such as Italy or Spain, where life is more influenced by a culture of pleasure. Here there is a long tradition of the siesta, a lunch break lasting several hours that allows one to recover from the heat of the day. Even though modern work demands have displaced this practice in many urban centers, the idea that work should not dominate all of life remains. In Spain, socializing - whether with family or friends - is an essential part of everyday life. Performance is valued, but not seen as the sole measure of a person's worth.

Another notable example is Japan, where an extreme performance culture prevails. The concept of "karoshi", death from overwork, is a serious social problem. Japanese workers often spend long hours in the office, not only out of necessity but also due to cultural pressure. Group membership and loyalty to the company are highly valued, which means that many employees work even when it is stressful for their health or family. At the same time, however, there are cultural traditions that serve relaxation - such as bathing in hot springs (onsen), the tea ceremony or the meditative aesthetics of Zen Buddhism. These rituals show that even in an extremely performance-oriented society, spaces for conscious relaxation exist.

A completely different relationship to work and performance can be seen in Scandinavian countries, especially in Sweden and Denmark. There, work-life balance is seen as essential. The concept of "lagom" in Sweden means "just the right amount" and reflects a philosophy that supports neither excess nor lack. In the world of work, this means that performance is important, but should not come at the expense of personal well-being. In Denmark, too, the idea of "hygge" - a cozy, balanced lifestyle - is highly valued, as reflected in shorter working hours and strong social security.

These cultural differences show that there is no universal answer to the question of how performance and relaxation should be balanced. While some societies define a person's worth almost exclusively in terms of their economic success, others see the ability to relax and enjoy themselves as an equally great achievement. The challenge for the modern world is to combine the advantages of both approaches: the efficiency and innovative power of a high-performing society with the humanity and balance of a culture that values relaxation and social connections.

Paths to a healthier performance culture

Today we are faced with the challenge of questioning the constant pressure to perform and developing alternatives that lead to a healthier performance culture. One possibility is to promote a meaningful way of working, in which the focus is not on maximum efficiency, but on the fulfillment and social added value of an activity. This can be done by reassessing what is considered "productive work" - for example, by giving greater recognition to unpaid but socially valuable activities such as care work or social commitment.

Another approach is to reduce working hours while maintaining financial security. Models such as the four-day week or an unconditional basic income could help to reduce the pressure to constantly perform and give people more freedom for creative, social or personal development. At the same time, the focus should be increased on regenerative work - that is, activities that not only consume energy but also contribute to one's own recovery and development.

In addition, a culture of "enough" is needed, in which the goal is not endless optimization and growth, but satisfaction and sustainability. Companies could focus more on value-oriented leadership that not only measures key performance indicators, but also focuses on well-being, collaboration and long-term development. However, this requires a social change in which success is no longer defined solely by status and productivity, but by holistic quality of life.

Finally, technology itself can contribute to a healthier performance culture if it is used as a relief rather than a tool for exploitation. Automation could take over repetitive, stressful tasks to give people more space for creative, social and meaningful tasks. In order for this to succeed, political and economic framework conditions must be created that ensure that technological advances do not lead to even more pressure to perform, but rather promote individual and social development.

A more sustainable and healthier performance culture requires changes on various levels:

- At an individual level, developing a reflective relationship to one's own performance can help. This includes recognizing and respecting personal limits, taking conscious time outs and not defining one's own value solely in terms of productivity.

- At an organizational level, companies can contribute to the well-being of their employees through flexible working hours, encouraging breaks and a culture that values relaxation. Managers play a key role here as role models for a healthy approach to work.

- At a societal level, a rethink is needed that places greater emphasis on human well-being. Alternative economic models that are not solely focused on growth and efficiency can provide important impetus here.

The increasing psychological stress caused by productivity pressure can also be seen as a wake-up call. They force us to ask fundamental questions: What makes a good life? What role should work play in it? How can we create a society that respects human needs?

The Covid pandemic has made these questions even more urgent. Many people have reconsidered their priorities during this time and learned about new work models. This could be the starting point for a more sustainable performance culture that recognizes mental health as an essential component of social prosperity.

A healthier relationship with productivity ultimately requires a paradigm shift: away from a pure focus on having and achieving, towards a being that leaves room for diversity, relationships and personal growth. This does not mean rejecting performance, but embedding it in a larger context that focuses on human well-being. Rediscovering the ability to pause and reflect on one's own actions should become a key competence - not only for individual mental health, but also for sustainable social development.

However, whether current societies can make the change from "having" to "being" depends on profound changes in values, structures and individual lifestyles. The current focus on material possessions, status and economic growth is based on a system that has evolved over centuries and links performance with identity. A rethink therefore requires not only individual insights, but also social and political decisions.

A crucial lever for this change lies in education. Schools and universities must not only impart knowledge and skills on economic viability, but also focus on concepts of mindfulness, cooperation and critical consumption. If people learn early on that quality of life is not necessarily linked to material accumulation, but to self-realization, social relationships and meaningful activity, a different understanding of prosperity could be established in the long term.

The economy can also encourage this change by having companies rethink their definition of success. The common good economy, the circular economy and sustainable production methods already show that there are alternatives to a pure pursuit of growth. A stronger emphasis on social and societal responsibility in corporate management could help to ensure that work is perceived less as a means of maximizing consumption and more as an opportunity to help shape society.

At the same time, political measures are needed that reduce structural inequalities and reduce existential insecurities. An unconditional basic income or a socially just tax system could help to reduce dependence on paid work as a primary means of securing one's existence. If people do not have to work out of fear of social decline but out of intrinsic motivation, this could promote a cultural change towards more "being" and less "having".

Last but not least, digital technologies play an ambivalent role. On the one hand, they often reinforce the pursuit of performance and status, for example through social media and data-driven optimization. On the other hand, they open up new opportunities for decentralization, knowledge exchange and alternative ways of life. Platforms for shared use, decentralized currencies and virtual networks for self-organization could help to reduce dependence on large corporations and material constraints.

As long as economic success is the ultimate goal, the path from "having" to "being" remains a challenge. But if enough people realize that a fulfilling life is not created by material possessions, but by interpersonal relationships, creativity and meaning, society can gradually move in a new direction.

Gentrification and Housing shortage

Gentrification often begins inconspicuously. A run-down part of town is discovered by artists and creative people looking for affordable housing and space for ideas. Galleries open, small cafes and bars emerge. The new scene attracts more people, investors take notice. Renovations begin, old rental apartments are converted into condominiums. Prices rise, the original residents have to move out. What begins as a cultural revitalization often ends in social displacement.

The mechanisms behind gentrification are complex. They follow economic interests, social trends and political decisions. Real estate markets react to supply and demand, but the decisive factor is often speculative in nature: those who invest early in an "up-and-coming" area can expect large profits. However, this economic logic contradicts the need of many people for stable and affordable housing.

Big cities as desirable places to live

Why are more and more people moving to cities? The answer lies in the combination of economic opportunities, cultural offerings and infrastructural advantages. Big cities offer jobs, educational opportunities, medical care and a diverse social life. But it is precisely this attractiveness that means that living space is becoming increasingly scarce and expensive.

Many metropolises are faced with a dilemma: they want growth and economic success, but at the same time they have to ensure that not only the wealthy can live in the city. While in some cities rent controls or social housing are intended to cushion the problem, in others entire city districts are bought up by investors and luxuriously renovated.

A key argument for living in the city is the high density of jobs. Metropolises are often the headquarters of large companies, innovative start-ups and international corporations. Proximity to potential employers is a decisive factor for many, especially in sectors such as technology, finance, media and research. In addition, the professional network in urban regions is often better developed - events, trade fairs and meet-ups result in new contacts and career opportunities.

In addition to the economic aspects, big cities offer a wide range of educational opportunities. Universities, technical colleges and research institutes attract students from home and abroad. The opportunity to study or teach in renowned institutions is an incentive for many people to settle in the city. Educational institutions are also often linked to companies and cultural institutions, which creates additional synergies.

Cultural life also plays an important role. Theaters, museums, concerts, restaurants and festivals make city life varied. In a big city, there is hardly a niche that is not served - from alternative art scenes to experimental music clubs to internationally recognized opera houses. The diversity of cultural offerings is a decisive factor for people looking for inspiration and social exchange.

The infrastructure should not be underestimated: local public transport enables flexible mobility, hospitals and specialists offer high-quality medical care, and shops are often accessible around the clock. For many, it is precisely this convenience that makes life in the city more attractive than in rural regions, where long journeys often require a car and cultural and professional offerings are more limited.

But the advantages that big cities offer do not benefit all residents equally. Cities are not only places of progress, but also hotspots of social inequality. Nowhere is the gap between rich and poor as visible as in the metropolises, where expensive luxury apartments are just a few streets away from overcrowded emergency shelters.

A key driver of this imbalance is the housing market. While high-income groups benefit from investments and rising property values, low-income earners struggle to find affordable housing. In many cities, the rise in rent prices is far higher than income growth, so that even people with middle incomes have difficulty finding adequate housing. Those who can no longer afford it are pushed to the outskirts of the city or the surrounding area - with longer commute times and often poorer infrastructure.

The distribution of educational and professional opportunities also follows this pattern. While wealthy families can give their children access to better schools, private schools or support programs, many socially disadvantaged people are denied this path. This development is particularly reflected in heavily gentrified urban areas: Social diversity is decreasing because only a certain income group can afford the rising cost of living.

This development is particularly precarious for those who depend on state support. The supply of social housing is decreasing in many places, while demand is increasing at the same time. Waiting lists for subsidized housing are long, and the increasing privatization of the housing market makes fair distribution difficult. People with low incomes are being pushed out of their traditional neighborhoods and have to make do with poorly equipped apartments or overcrowded accommodation.

The social differences in big cities are not only reflected in housing, but also in people's everyday lives. While a wealthy family sends its children to international schools, has a secure job and lives in a modern condominium, a single mother on the other side of town struggles with rising rents, insecure employment and a lack of childcare options.

The social impacts of big cities are profound and often complex. The negative effects of urban division are particularly evident in disadvantaged urban areas such as the ghettos of New York or the outskirts of Paris. This is where social problems manifest themselves that not only shape the daily lives of residents, but can also lead to increased crime rates and social isolation. The experiences from these urban environments offer valuable insights into the mechanisms of social inequality and its long-term consequences.

In New York, there are a number of neighborhoods that are characterized by social disadvantage. Poverty, unemployment and high crime rates are still major problems, particularly in areas such as Harlem, the South Bronx or parts of Brooklyn. These neighborhoods have a long history of social isolation and inequality, which reached its peak in the 1960s, when urban destruction caused by white flight and deindustrialization left massive damage. These parts of the city have often been neglected - due to a lack of investment, poor infrastructure and a withdrawal of public services.

A key problem in these urban ghettos is access to education and job opportunities. In many of these disadvantaged districts, schools are underfunded, educational standards are low, and there are no extracurricular activities that could help children and young people to break out of the vicious circle of poverty. Without the chance of a good education, many young people are forced into a hopeless future, which has a negative impact on their social integration.

Unemployment is widespread in these areas. In recent decades, deindustrialization has led to the loss of many well-paid factory and production jobs, while new jobs have often been created in the low-wage sector. The few well-paid jobs that still exist are difficult for the residents of these districts to access, either due to a lack of qualifications or discrimination on the job market.

The resulting social isolation and lack of prospects encourage the emergence of criminal structures. Drug trafficking, gang crime, and violent crime are commonplace in many of these districts. The suppression of opportunities for advancement and the lack of social support lead many young people to seek alternative routes to social recognition - often through membership in criminal groups. These gangs not only provide a social network, but also a way to obtain what would otherwise remain inaccessible: power, respect and financial success. This contributes to further exacerbating the crime rate, as these gangs are characterized not only by drug trafficking and robberies, but also by internal rivalries and territorial conflicts.

Another problem is the role of the police. Many disadvantaged neighborhoods in New York have a high police presence, but this is often accompanied by mistrust. The police are perceived by many residents as hostile and discriminatory, which further strains relations between the two groups. In the past, there have been repeated cases of police brutality and systematic discrimination, leading to an escalating spiral of violence between the police and the residents of the ghettos. These tensions reinforce the feeling of alienation and increase social and criminal problems.

The outskirts of Paris, known as "banlieues," are another example of the social and criminal effects of urban gentrification and inequality. These districts, often inhabited by immigrants and their descendants, struggle with social problems as severe as those of New York's ghettos. Especially in the 1980s and 1990s, the banlieues emerged as hotspots for poverty, unemployment, and social isolation.

An important factor in the banlieues is ethnic and social segregation. Many residents of the banlieues are immigrants or descendants of immigrants, mainly from former colonies in North Africa. These groups are often victims of discrimination in the labor market and in society. Access to quality jobs is severely limited for many people in the banlieues due to their origins and often their limited language skills. This social exclusion leads to an accumulation of frustration and lack of prospects.

Crime rates in the banlieues are high, especially among young people. As in the ghettos of New York, many young people in the banlieues look for ways to express their frustration and anger. In many cases, these are criminal activities such as drug trafficking, robberies and vandalism. But crime in the banlieues is often also an expression of political powerlessness. Young people feel abandoned by society and its institutions, and their actions are often a reaction to the constant exclusion and lack of prospects.

In recent decades, violent clashes and uprisings have occurred repeatedly in the banlieues, highlighting the social and political divide between residents and the French state. In 2005, there were nationwide riots when police killed two teenagers in a chase. The violence that then erupted in the banlieues was understood not only as an expression of frustration with police brutality and social exclusion, but also as a desperate attempt to draw attention to the systematic disadvantage faced by residents of these areas.

The state's response to these social tensions was often repressive, which exacerbated the situation. The increased use of police and military in the banlieues often led to further escalations and a loss of confidence in the government's ability to effectively solve social problems.

The ghettos of New York and the banlieues of Paris show how profound the social and criminal impacts of urban poverty and marginalization can be. In both cases, a lack of prospects, unemployment and social exclusion lead to a sharp increase in crime and social tensions. The inhabitants of these areas, often ethnic minorities or socially disadvantaged people, find themselves in a vicious circle of crime, police violence and social isolation.

The political and social responses to these problems are often inadequate and sometimes even counterproductive. In order to combat the social and criminal effects of urban poverty, it is necessary not only to take short-term measures, but also to find long-term solutions that focus on integration, education and a fairer distribution of resources. This is the only way to end the social isolation and criminal dynamics that characterise many disadvantaged neighbourhoods.

On the one hand, large cities are fascinating places full of opportunities, but they are also hotspots of social inequality. Their attractiveness draws people, but not everyone can share in the benefits. Those with high incomes benefit from cultural diversity, good infrastructure and economic opportunities. On the other hand, those who depend on affordable housing increasingly experience the city as a place of displacement and insecurity.

The challenge is to ensure that urban growth is socially acceptable. Without targeted political measures, the gap will continue to widen and large cities will become exclusive spaces for high earners. But there are approaches that could enable a fairer coexistence - be it through sustainable housing policies, the promotion of social projects or a fairer distribution of resources.

Ultimately, the future of cities depends on whether they remain places of diversity or become symbols of growing inequality.

Efficiency as a guiding principle of the big city

The big city as an efficient structure is a fascinating but also controversial phenomenon that is characterized by the pursuit of productivity and optimization. It is a place where people come together in masses to carry out a variety of activities - from work to consumption to social interactions. But with all the technological and economic efficiency that life in the city brings with it, the question arises as to the naturalness of people and the effects of this model of life on the well-being of individuals. The phenomenon of loneliness in particular casts a shadow on the supposed advantages of an urban existence.

Big cities are characterized above all by a high density of people and activities that enable resources to be used efficiently. Urban life promotes the maximization of labor and capital by connecting people with each other in short distances and offering a variety of opportunities for specialization. The concentration of companies, institutions, educational facilities and cultural offerings leads to a level of productivity that could not be achieved in this form in smaller rural areas or less urbanized regions.

The efficiency in large cities is also reflected in the infrastructure. Public transport, which enables quick commuting between different parts of the city, or networking through digital technologies are examples of how urban life paves the way for a seamless integration of people and resources. This makes the goal of the big city clear: everything should function as quickly, cheaply and effectively as possible, both in terms of the exchange of goods and social exchange.

But this efficiency has its downside. It challenges people to submit to the demands of a constantly accelerating world. Everyday life is often characterized by a constant striving for optimization, be it in work, leisure activities or social life. People are increasingly becoming part of a system that is organized primarily according to functional and economic aspects.

Humans are naturally social creatures who live in close, trusting communities where personal bonds and direct interactions play a central role. In the big city, however, life is often characterized by anonymity and distance. Despite the large number of people who come into contact with one another in a big city, relationships are often superficial, fleeting and lack the depth and reliability necessary for human well-being. This dynamic is particularly problematic when you consider that humans are naturally dependent on having stable social bonds that provide security, support and a sense of belonging.

In a world dominated by efficiency and speed, there is little room for deeper interpersonal relationships. Many urban residents experience the feeling of being "disconnected" from others, even when living in the midst of crowds. This distancing from authentic social bonds can lead to a feeling of alienation. The big city requires individuals to adapt to its dynamics, but without providing the necessary social networks needed to stabilize psychological well-being.

Loneliness is a widespread phenomenon in many big cities, closely linked to the efficiency and anonymity of urban life. Although cities offer enormous opportunities for interaction, many people still feel isolated. The constant flow of information, the rapid change of activities and the focus on individual achievement leave little room for the slow development of real, long-term relationships. This loneliness can be particularly pronounced for the older generation or people who have recently moved to the city. In anonymous big cities, there are often no clear structures that could promote the building of trusting communities. As a result, individuals are often left to fend for themselves.

Loneliness is exacerbated by the lack of intimate, stable social ties. Life in the big city requires residents to constantly adapt to new circumstances and to be highly flexible, which can lead to a feeling of insecurity. Especially in an environment where "networking" and the rapid exchange of information are often more important than real emotional support, many people feel alienated in their social life. This loneliness is felt all the more strongly because it takes place in an environment that is normally associated with social opportunities and a sense of togetherness.

The paradoxical feeling of being surrounded by many people at the same time and yet living in isolation is one of the most painful effects of urban efficiency. In the big city, people are reduced to their functions: as workers, as consumers, as users of infrastructures. This reduction of people to their role as functionnal carriers, combined with the constant flood of stimuli, leaves little room for the quiet, slow forms of connection that are essential for the mental health and well-being of the individual.

In many Western societies, the individual is increasingly viewed as independent and self-sufficient, reinforcing the idea that people should be able to cope on their own. This notion runs counter to the natural human need for social closeness and support. The expectation that everyone will look after themselves and take responsibility for their own well-being increases isolation in an already complex and anonymous urban world.

The social and psychological consequences of loneliness in the city are severe. They range from increased vulnerability to mental illnesses such as depression and anxiety to a general loss of quality of life. Loneliness not only affects individual health, but also social cohesion. A society in which many people are isolated loses its social bonds and with them the trust and solidarity that are essential for a healthy community to function.

The city as an efficient entity may be impressive economically and infrastructurally, but it comes at a price - the loss of closeness, authenticity and social warmth. In a world where efficiency and speed increasingly determine social norms, there is little room for the slow, human processes of bonding, trust and community. The natural human inclination towards genuine social interaction is in direct tension with the mechanical, functional requirements of the city. Loneliness, the feeling of alienation and the loss of genuine social relationships are the dark sides of this urban reality. In order to preserve the city as a place of social life, an awareness must be developed that efficiency and social harmony do not have to be in conflict with one another. New forms of social networking are needed that meet the human need for closeness and connection.

Conclusion: The future of cities

The topic of "people and cities" sheds light on a variety of aspects that shape coexistence in urban spaces. The focus is on the question of how life in big cities affects the individual - both financially, socially and psychologically. In a world increasingly characterised by urbanisation, the city is becoming not only an economic centre but also a social and cultural experiment in which man and his natural needs are constantly in tension with urban efficiency and anonymity.

A key financial aspect that determines the relationship between man and the city is the increasing inequality that characterises many urban spaces. Big cities offer numerous economic opportunities, from high-paying jobs to a wide range of consumer goods and services. But it is precisely this economic diversity that is often accompanied by a gap between rich and poor that is becoming increasingly visible. Rents in popular neighbourhoods are constantly rising, while more and more people are forced to move to the outskirts of the city or to less attractive areas. This financial divide has a profound impact on quality of life, access to education and social networks and leads to increased social segregation.

The question of who stays in the city and who can afford to live there is increasingly becoming a question of income and social background. Wealthy classes are often found in the central, gentrified areas, while poorer groups are pushed to the periphery. This creates a constant oscillation between the financial "opportunities" of the big city and the financial "limits" that make life difficult for many people there.

On a social level, the big city is both a place of diversity and segregation. People from different countries, cultures and social classes live side by side, which on the one hand offers the opportunity for cultural exchange and diversity, but on the other hand can also lead to a fragmentation of society. In many cases, a strong social divide arises: while the urban elite live in hip, expensive neighborhoods, socially weaker groups often have limited access not only to housing, but also to education, health care and social networks.

Social isolation is a phenomenon that is particularly noticeable in the big city. Despite the high population density, many city dwellers experience loneliness, which is exacerbated by the anonymity and fast, often superficial communication in urban spaces. Especially in cities, where efficiency and functionality are paramount, there is often no room for deeper, sustainable social ties. The multitude of superficial contacts and the constant mobility of people mean that long-term communities and stable social networks are difficult to form. The dynamism of the big city offers numerous opportunities for interaction, but these often remain fleeting and less resilient than in smaller, more closely connected communities.

At the same time, however, it is also clear that the big city can offer many people, especially migrants or marginalized groups, an opportunity for social mobility and integration. In the city, there is a certain degree of anonymity that allows people to freely shape their identity and free themselves from stigmatizing factors such as social background or ethnicity. In this sense, the big city can be understood as a place of opportunity, where diversity opens up new social spaces, even if inequality and social tensions are not completely overcome.

From a psychological point of view, life in a big city is a major challenge. The constant overstimulation, noise, hectic pace and anonymity of urban life can lead to a state of being overwhelmed. The constant stress from external influences - be it street noise, the flood of information or the pressure to always be productive - can affect the psychological well-being of city dwellers. Studies show that urban life is associated with an increased rate of mental illnesses such as depression, anxiety disorders and stress. This "urban stress hypothesis" assumes that the constant stimulation that is omnipresent in big cities puts a psychological strain on people in the long term and leads to an increased susceptibility to psychological stress.

Loneliness, although paradoxically often particularly pronounced in densely populated cities, is another psychological problem that comes with life in a big city. Humans are social beings who need emotional bonds to promote their well-being. But in a city characterized by anonymity and efficiency, there is little room for intimate, deep relationships. The feeling of alienation, constant adaptation and the lack of real social closeness can lead to a loss of quality of life. The older generation or people who are not actively involved in the social network are particularly vulnerable to this form of isolation.

Despite these negative psychological effects, there are also positive sides to life in the big city. For many people, the urban environment is a source of inspiration, creativity and personal growth. The proximity to cultural offerings, access to education and the variety of lifestyles can promote psychological well-being if the individual is able to take advantage of these opportunities and find their way around the city. The challenge, however, is to find the right balance between the positive aspects of urban life and the psychological stresses it brings.

People in the big city live in a complex, often contradictory reality. On the one hand, the city offers enormous financial and social opportunities, on the other hand, the structure of urban spaces leads to increased social segregation and psychological stress. The city as an efficient structure promotes an increasing specialization and functionalization of areas of life, which can lead to a fragmentation of the social fabric and alienation of individuals. In this respect, life in the city is a permanent balancing act between the search for personal fulfillment and confrontation with the negative aspects of urbanization.

The challenge for the future is to find solutions that make it possible to use the advantages of the city - economic opportunities, cultural diversity, social mobility - without increasing the negative effects such as loneliness, social inequality and psychological stress. Sustainable urban development is needed that puts people at the center and promotes a quality of life that is more than just efficiency. Social networking, mental health and the promotion of community play just as important a role as economic success and urban infrastructure. This is the only way the city can be preserved as a livable and humane environment.

Consumption and Sustainability

It is a common dilemma: we know that our consumption habits have a major impact on the environment, and yet we struggle to change our behavior sustainably. We read the articles about climate change, see the terrifying images of polluted oceans and dramatically shrinking forests, and yet we find it difficult to integrate the consequences of our actions into our everyday lives. We know that the earth is overloaded, but we continue to use plastic, fly, consume and waste - as if nothing had happened.

This paradox - knowing the destruction while clinging to habits - is not only an individual challenge, but also a collective one. To understand why we act this way despite knowing the negative effects of our consumption, we must embark on a journey through the mechanisms of human behavior, the psychology of consumption and the social structures that influence us. It is a story that confronts us with the fundamental questions about our values, the influence of the economy and the power of habits.

Our consumption habits are deeply rooted in our history. It is not a modern phenomenon that only emerged with the Industrial Revolution. Rather, we as humans evolved in an environment where resources were often scarce. This evolution made us efficient gatherers and hunters who stored up supplies to survive difficult times. Survival instincts and the pursuit of material wealth were and are deeply rooted in us.

But what still seems like an instinct today - the ability to immediately consume what is available to us - is increasingly problematic in a world where almost everything is available anytime and anywhere. In the last few centuries, we have managed to turn the economy into a globally connected and highly developed industry that promotes consumption and drives it almost inexorably. This development has led to the urgency of survival being replaced by the temptation of excess. The desire for immediate gratification often takes precedence over the long-term consequences of our actions.

Advertising and the consumer industry are not just accompanying elements of modern life - they are integral parts of our daily experience. Advertising messages surround us every second, whether on television, on social media or in the streets of cities. This advertising does not only function as information about products; it aims to awaken our deepest needs and desires and make us feel that our lives are incomplete without certain products. Brands and companies have mastered the art of building emotional connections with us that go beyond the purely functional need for a product.

It is not just about buying a sweater, but about identifying with a brand. It is not just about driving a car, but about embodying a certain attitude to life. In this way, consumption is not just sold as a necessary evil, but as the key to happiness and success. The result is a society that constantly strives for more, even though we know that this added value is often only short-term and does not fulfill us much in the long term. This is where another psychological phenomenon comes to light: the hedonistic treadmill effect. We consume and consume, but our happiness level remains at a constant level. There is no permanent satisfaction and we get caught in an endless cycle of striving.

We are aware that our consumption behavior is ecologically problematic. Climate change, plastic pollution, resource consumption - the facts are undeniable. Nevertheless, we find it difficult to abandon habitual behavior. Why do we not change our behavior even though we know it is destructive?

One explanation lies in the separation between knowledge and action. We understand the connections, but we find it difficult to immediately feel the consequences of our actions. The effects of our consumption are often abstract and distant, while the rewards - be it through buying a new cell phone or enjoying an exotic fruit - are immediate and tangible. This leads to what is known as "rational ignorance". As long as we do not experience the damage directly or it affects us in our immediate environment, we do not take it seriously.

In addition, social dynamics play an essential role. The society in which we live is deeply geared towards consumption. Friends, family, colleagues - they all influence our behavior. When everyone around us is consuming, we often feel pressured to join in. A social norm is created that makes it difficult to swim against the tide.

Even when we are aware that we should act in a more environmentally friendly way, we are often unwilling to accept the social and practical trade-offs that come with doing so.

Another obstacle is the structural barriers that prevent us from acting. The infrastructure of the global economy is geared towards growth – growth in consumption, trade, production. In a system that measures growth as success, it is hard to find alternatives that are compatible with these principles. The political and economic structures continue to encourage consumption, even though we as individuals know that this is destructive in the long term. Companies that profit from unchecked consumption have little interest in changing society towards sustainable behaviors.

What holds us back is not only the will, but also the fact that the paths to a more sustainable life are often unclear to us. Individual changes seem meaningless in the bigger picture, and we wonder whether adjusting our consumption will make any difference at all. But it is this individual contribution that can set a broad social change in motion - even if it seems to be just a drop in the ocean.

How the economy passes responsibility on to the consumer

The economy and large companies often shift responsibility for unsustainable consumption onto the consumer by using a simplified argument of free consumer choice. This strategy can be analyzed on several levels:

The companies first create artificial needs through massive advertising campaigns, psychologically sophisticated marketing and social comparison processes. They actively shape beauty ideals, status thinking and social norms. At the same time, they suggest that the consumer has complete freedom of choice and can easily escape this pressure to consume. This argument deliberately ignores the complex social and psychological mechanisms that motivate people to consume. In a society in which status and social recognition are closely linked to consumer goods, individual renunciation is associated with high social costs.

The economy also deliberately shapes the framework conditions: products are manufactured with planned obsolescence, repairs are made more difficult or more expensive, while new purchases are made attractive through discounts. At the same time, sustainable alternatives are often kept artificially expensive. The structural power of the economy to shape markets and consumption options is completely ignored in this argument.

Instead, it is suggested that the individual consumer can fundamentally change the system through their individual decisions

- an excessive demand on the individual while at the same time relieving the actual rulers. This shift in responsibility serves to distract from the need for political regulation. Instead of accepting binding sustainability standards, reference is made to "consumer sovereignty"

- knowing full well that individual consumption behavior alone cannot bring about systemic change. The economy benefits from another psychological mechanism: people often overestimate their own willpower and independence from external influences. This makes them receptive to arguments that emphasize their supposed autonomy - even if this is in fact severely restricted.

Business uses various strategies to shift responsibility for social, ecological and economic problems onto consumers and thus evade its own responsibility. This often happens subtly, but with far-reaching consequences. One of the key methods is the so-called "greenwashing" strategy, in which companies give themselves an environmentally friendly image by, for example, advertising "sustainable" products, even though their entire production chain remains harmful to the environment. This suggests to consumers that their purchasing decisions alone determine sustainability - while companies continue to maximize profits at the expense of the environment.

Another example is the individualization of responsibility, especially with regard to climate protection. Large corporations, which are largely responsible for environmental pollution and sometimes gigantic amounts of waste, deliberately direct the focus to the personal carbon footprint of the individual consumer. This idea was deliberately promoted by the oil and gas industry to distract from the need for structural change. Instead of holding the industry itself accountable for more environmentally friendly alternatives, consumers are persuaded that they can save the world with their individual behavior - for example by avoiding meat, flying or plastic. In this way, companies release themselves from their obligation to establish sustainable business models - often supported by political decision-makers.

In addition, economic crises are often blamed on the "misbehavior" of consumers. For example, when prices rise or inflation rise, companies often argue that rising demand or "unreasonable purchasing behavior" is to blame, instead of disclosing their own profit-maximization strategies or speculation. A typical example of this is the housing market crisis: real estate companies and investors drive up prices, but blame tenants who are "too demanding" or "not prepared to make sacrifices."

This strategy is also used in the world of work. Companies praise flexible working models or the so-called "gig economy" as freedom for the individual, but at the same time conceal the fact that they are thereby avoiding social security contributions and responsibility for working conditions. Instead of offering fairly paid and secure jobs, the responsibility for financial security and retirement provision is shifted entirely onto the employees.

Ultimately, a clear pattern emerges in all of these strategies: the economy cleverly uses narratives and marketing strategies to portray the consumer as the main culprit for grievances. In doing so, it evades its own responsibility for structural problems and can continue to maximize profits at the expense of society and the environment.

There are several deep-rooted reasons why the economy's strategy of shifting responsibility onto the consumer is socially accepted and even supported by politicians. One of the key factors is the decades-long influence of neoliberal ideologies that focus on individualism and personal responsibility. In this way of thinking, the individual is seen as a sovereign actor who can shape the world through his consumption and lifestyle. The structural framework created by politics and business fades into the background. Instead, responsibility for social problems - from environmental destruction to social inequality and economic crises - is projected onto the decisions of individuals. This ideology is so deeply rooted that many people hardly question it anymore.

Another reason is the targeted influence of public opinion by companies and business-related interest groups. Large corporations and industry associations invest heavily in PR campaigns, think tanks and lobbying to spread the narrative that consumers and not corporations are responsible for social challenges. A well-known example is the aforementioned introduction of the carbon footprint by BP, which emphasizes individual responsibility for climate protection, while the company itself continues to promote fossil fuels on a large scale. Such campaigns are extremely effective because they are taken up by the media and often spread uncritically.

Politicians also actively or at least tacitly support this development because it relieves themselves of responsibility. Political regulation of the economy would be associated with conflicts and resistance from powerful corporations, which often have considerable influence on political decision-makers.

Instead of creating long-term, sustainable and fair structures, many governments prefer to rely on citizens' "personal responsibility". This has the advantage that they do not have to take as harsh measures against companies that could otherwise threaten to relocate, cut jobs or take legal action. In addition, many politicians are directly or indirectly connected to economic interest groups - be it through lobbying, party donations or later career opportunities in the private sector ("revolving door effect").

Another element that contributes to social acceptance is convenience. The narrative of individual responsibility gives people a sense of control and the illusion that they can make a difference through their personal decisions. At the same time, it spares them from having to deal with complex, often frustrating political and economic contexts. It is easier to focus on personal consumption decisions - for example by buying organic products or avoiding plastic - than to deal with the powerful structures that are causally responsible for environmental destruction and social inequality. This behavior is reinforced by advertising and the media, which focus on individual behavior and often only treat structural problems superficially.

Ultimately, both business and politics benefit from this shift in responsibility. Companies can continue to maximize profits without undergoing fundamental changes, while politics can justify its own inaction by emphasizing that it is up to citizens' behavior whether anything changes. As long as this interplay of economic interests, political convenience and social acceptance continues, little will change in this dynamic. Only broad social education and the demand for real structural responsibility from companies and politics could break this trend.

This does not mean that the individual is immature or has no influence whatsoever on change. However, it does show that responsibility for major social problems should not rest solely on the shoulders of the individual. Individual decisions do have an effect - especially when many people decide together in a certain direction. But without structural changes, these effects often remain limited or are even absorbed and neutralized by the economy.

One example of this is conscious consumption: if many people buy sustainable products, this can steer demand in a more environmentally friendly direction. Companies will then adapt more to this because they see profit opportunities in it. But at the same time there are limits: "Green" alternatives are often more expensive or difficult to access, so they only reach a certain group of buyers. In addition, the basic structure of the economy often remains untouched - even sustainable products are often integrated into a system that continues to be based on profit maximization, waste of resources and exploitation.

Another example is political engagement. If many people go to vote, organize demonstrations or put pressure on politicians, this can certainly bring about change. Nevertheless, it has been shown time and again that economic interests are often given more weight than social demands. This is because individual actors - even when they join forces - often do not have the same financial resources and lobbying power as large corporations.

So the individual is not powerless, but his power is limited if it is not complemented by structural changes. Real transformation requires both individual action and political measures that hold corporations and decision-makers accountable. That is why it is important that people not only pay attention to their own consumption, but also get socially and politically involved to initiate sustainable change on a larger scale.

The role of education and the media

Education plays an important key role in raising awareness of the impacts of consumption. But the media also play their part in how we perceive sustainability. They can either serve as catalysts for change or hinder it. An objective, science-based portrayal of the urgency of the ecological crisis and individual responsibility could help more people to think seriously about their behavior. But commercial interests often distort the perception of sustainability. "Green marketing" – the promise that a product will be sold with an environmentally friendly image – is an example of how companies are taking advantage of the sustainability movement without actually contributing to solving the problems.

A good example of this challenge are the "greenwashing" campaigns mentioned above, in which companies market their product as environmentally friendly when in practice this is not the case. Such practices contribute to shaking confidence in real sustainability and creating the feeling that nothing can be changed anyway.

Education and the media also influence how consumers themselves evaluate products and services, what values they associate with the consumption of certain products and services and the extent to which they are aware of their own scope for action. Both education and media reporting can contribute to enlightenment – but can also be used manipulatively to promote certain economic interests.

A well-informed individual is able to critically question which products they buy, which companies they support and what global impact their consumption has. However, there are significant deficits in the education system when it comes to a well-founded discussion of economic, ecological and social aspects of consumption. Many school systems lack comprehensive consumer education that teaches students to understand economic relationships, question advertising strategies and make sustainable decisions. Financial education and a critical understanding of the economy and market dynamics are often not part of the curriculum.

While topics such as environmental protection and climate change sometimes appear excessively and misleadingly in the curricula, sustainable consumption is often only dealt with superficially. Many people do not know exactly which products are really environmentally friendly and which are only marketed as such ("greenwashing"). In many schools and universities, economics is taught primarily from a market economy perspective that sees profit maximization as the central goal. Alternative economic models such as the common good economy or the circular economy are often not taught to the same extent, which means that pupils and students develop less critical mindsets towards the existing economic system. Good education could therefore help consumers make more informed decisions and not be so easily manipulated by companies. It could educate people to consider not only the price or brand of a product, but also its production conditions, ecological impacts and social consequences.

The media have immense power to influence consumer behavior - both through advertising and through journalistic reporting and social media. There are two main directions of influence: on the one hand, the media often reinforces the pressure to consume and promote unreflective materialism; on the other hand, they could also contribute to education and support critical consumer behavior.

The advertising industry is designed to awaken needs that did not exist before and to present consumption as a source of happiness and social recognition. Psychological mechanisms are used in advertising to create the feeling that certain products are necessary in order to be successful, beautiful or happy. Advertising often relies on emotional stimuli by associating products with positive feelings, success or community. This means that people see consumption not only as a means of satisfying needs, but also as an expression of identity. In recent years in particular, the pressure to consume has increased enormously through social media. Influencers and content creators often promote products subtly as part of their everyday lives, so that it is no longer perceived as classic advertising. Younger people in particular are strongly influenced by this and develop purchasing habits that are driven less by their own needs than by social trends. The media promotes the image that newer products are better and that you should "treat yourself" to something regularly. Constantly reinventing trends artificially creates demand that is actually not necessary - be it for fashion, technology or lifestyle products.

In addition to the pure advertising function, the media could also play an educational role. Documentaries, critical journalism and investigative research repeatedly uncover abuses in production chains, environmental destruction or unethical business practices. Some media are increasingly reporting on companies that only present themselves as "green" without actually operating sustainably. Such revelations can raise awareness among consumers and lead to more conscious purchasing decisions. In recent years, there has been an increase in media formats that show alternative lifestyles away from excessive consumption. Minimalism documentaries, sustainability blogs and ethical fashion magazines help to create awareness of moderate consumption.

However, many media are themselves dependent on economic interests. Large publishing houses and television stations often finance themselves through advertising, so they avoid critical reporting on their advertising clients. In online journalism, too, there is a risk that content will remain superficial in favor of click numbers and advertising revenue.

Both education and media have a double effect on consumer behavior. While education can help to develop responsible and critical consumers, its current design often contributes to people not questioning consumption. The challenge is to change the structures so that education conveys more economic and sustainable awareness and the media focuses more on independent and critical reporting instead of primarily serving economic interests. If this succeeds, the influence of corporations on consumer behavior could be weakened and people's personal responsibility could be put on a sound basis.

Humans as Resources

People are a resource. A sentence that is frightening in its sobriety because it reduces the individual to a function, to a factor within a system that sees them not as individuals but as a means to an end. But that is precisely the reality of the modern economic order: people are workers, productive factors, consumers and at the same time drivers of a mechanism that could not exist without them - and yet treats them only as part of a larger machine.

In capitalism, value is not created out of nothing. Every good, every service, every process that exists in this system is based on human labor - directly or indirectly. Machines produce goods, but who builds the machines? Companies develop software, but who writes the code? Raw materials are mined, but who operates the mining facilities? The answer is always the same: it is people. Their physical and intellectual labor is converted into economic benefit, into profit, into growth. The economy depends on them, but it does not see them as equal partners, but as resources that must be used efficiently.

The paradox is that this person, who drives the global economy, is not only a producer, but also a consumer. He sells his time, his energy, his creativity to earn money - money that he then has to spend to survive, to satisfy needs that were often created by the system itself. Those who work need rest, entertainment, distraction. The leisure industry is flourishing because people are looking for distraction after hours of hard work. The fashion industry is constantly inventing new trends because people are constantly redefining their role as consumers. The technology market is constantly producing new devices because progress is presented as an end in itself. So the circle is complete: those who work, consume - and those who consume keep the system running.

But there is a deeper problem in this cycle. People as a resource have an expiration date. Their productivity is not unlimited, their energy is not inexhaustible. The industrial revolution turned the body into a machine, the digital revolution turned the mind into a raw material. The modern worker is no longer just muscle power, but also a source of ideas, a supplier of data, and a feeder of algorithms. In the knowledge society, it is no longer just the physical capacity of people that is required, but above all their mental capacity. Creativity, innovation, problem solving - all of these have become economic resources that are exploited in the same way that coal or steel once were. But what happens when people burn out in the process?

The producer-consumer paradox reveals its downside here: while the system depends on a constant increase in productivity, it simultaneously sets mechanisms in motion that overwhelm people. The pressure to perform increases, while consumption is presented as a reward for effort. But what happens when this consumption is no longer sufficient to justify the effort? When people realize that their lives only move between creation and consumption, with no real meaning beyond this spiral?

The answer to these questions will decide the future of capitalism. Because if people reach their limits as a resource, the system could falter. But it is not that far yet. The machines are still running, the ideas are still being produced, the wheels are still turning. But for how long?

Terms like "human resources" and "manpower" are more than just business vocabulary – they are an expression of a way of thinking that sees people primarily as a factor of production. "Human resources" has become so firmly established in corporate language that hardly anyone questions what this term actually implies anymore. It puts people in the same category as raw materials, capital and machines – as a resource that must be managed, optimized and used efficiently. The individual employee is therefore no longer perceived as an individual, but as part of a larger system that functions according to business metrics.

While "human resources" still maintains the appearance of a certain professionalism, "manpower" sounds even more directly like a simple mass of available workers. The word comes from a time when industrial production was dependent on physical workers – an anonymous, interchangeable mass of people whose sole purpose was to do work. This language continues to shape the image of the world of work and has profound effects on society.

If people are viewed as a resource, this inevitably leads to an economization of all areas of life. Employees are not seen as people with needs, emotions and individual life goals, but as functionaries who are improved through training, evaluated by key performance indicators and controlled by incentive systems. The world of work is therefore developing into an environment in which efficiency and productivity take precedence over human development. Anyone who is not productive is seen as inefficient, a burden on the company. Illness, exhaustion or personal problems become disruptions in a system that is optimized for maximum utilization.

But this view not only affects companies, but also the way people see themselves. Anyone who is constantly treated as a resource will eventually begin to see themselves that way. Your own value is equated with your own productivity. Success in your job becomes the measure of personal value. Leisure is no longer seen as an independent area of life, but as necessary regeneration in order to be productive again at work. Self-optimization, fitness, mindfulness - all of this is placed in a context that ultimately aims to maintain and increase one's own working capacity.

The language of business shapes society. Terms such as "human capital", "skillset" or "workforce" leave no doubt that people are primarily seen as a means of creating value. But what happens to those who no longer fit into this scheme? Older employees whose skills are considered outdated, people with health problems or those who are simply not prepared to adapt to the ever-increasing demands? The system has little room for them.

This view is deeply rooted in capitalist logic. Companies have no direct interest in the well-being of employees as long as their performance does not suffer as a result. Human resources departments, which previously saw themselves as mediators between employees and company management, are now often primarily concerned with standardizing processes, reducing costs and maximizing the efficiency of "human resources". Work-life balance, corporate health management and psychological support are offered, but usually not out of genuine care, but as measures to ensure long-term productivity or eliminate disruptions.

People as resources - this idea shapes not only the world of work, but the entire social self-image. It influences how people think about themselves, how they spend their time and how they define their own value. Anyone who does not play along in such a system risks being left behind. But perhaps at some point the question will arise: Can a society function in the long term in which people are primarily seen as factors of production? Or will the people who keep the system running at some point realize that they are more than just a resource?

Humans as pure idea generators - a creative dystopia?

The world has changed. Robots, artificial intelligence and fully automated systems have taken over almost every form of physical and cognitive work. Factories produce without human intervention, algorithms control global trade and even creative processes - once the last exclusive terrain of humans - are perfected by machines. In this reality, humans are no longer an essential part of the value chain. At best, they are idea generators, someone who outlines concepts that are implemented by more powerful, error-free systems.

Companies still exist, but their structures have changed. Boardrooms now consist of only a few decision-makers who are less concerned with strategic leadership than with fine-tuning the artificial intelligence that controls operational business. The classic working world with employees, hierarchies and fixed roles is history. Where millions of people once worked in offices, factories or on construction sites, there are now only self-sufficient, self-managing production and service units.

Society is divided. A small elite controls the technological infrastructure and thus secures the majority of resources. The rest of the people live in a world that offers them basically everything, but at the same time has eliminated any need for traditional paid work. Universal Basic Income was introduced to maintain social peace. Every citizen receives a fixed monthly budget that is sufficient for housing, food and entertainment. The former pressure to work has disappeared. But with it the structure that has shaped life for centuries.

Some people devote themselves to art, philosophy or science. But even here, humans are no longer unrivalled. Artificial intelligences create complex pieces of music in seconds, write novels, paint pictures or develop new theories. The question of whether human creativity is still needed at all is becoming more and more pressing. The machines think faster, analyze better, design more efficiently. What is left for humans?

For many, this world means a freedom that was previously unthinkable. No one has to work hard to earn a living anymore.

Education, leisure, self-realization - all of this is accessible to everyone at any time. But at the same time, a deep feeling of dispensability arises. Anyone who no longer makes an essential contribution inevitably begins to question their own value. In a society that defined itself through performance, the sudden uselessness of humans leaves a psychological vacuum.

The demand for real human interaction is growing. Exclusive clubs to which only humans are allowed are emerging as a countermovement to total technologization. Contact with a real salesperson, a meal cooked by hand or a personal conversation without algorithmically generated answers is becoming a new form of luxury. Nevertheless, the question remains: if everything is done more efficiently, faster and more accurately by machines - what is the raison d'être of humans?

Some try to outsmart the machines, to push creative boundaries, to prove themselves irreplaceable. But with every new innovation in artificial intelligence, this last monopoly of humans continues to dwindle. In the end, only one truth remains: the world no longer needs him. But he needs himself. And this is exactly where the new challenge could lie - no longer in work, but in the search for a new meaning.

For thousands of years, humans defined themselves by their ability to create, produce, and innovate. But if all of this is done more efficiently by artificial systems, humanity must reinvent itself.

One possibility lies in a conscious return to humanity - not as an economic factor, but as a social, emotional and spiritual entity. While machines calculate, analyze and optimize, they lack one thing: a deep, intuitive awareness of what it means to be human. Emotions, relationships, personal experiences - all of this remains the preserve of humans, despite all technological advances. So perhaps the new meaning lies in savoring precisely that, no longer defining oneself through productivity, but through empathy, community and personal fulfillment.

Instead of competing with machines in a hopeless competition for efficiency, humans could begin to come to terms with themselves. Philosophical questions that were often pushed aside by economic constraints in the past are now taking center stage: What does it mean to live a good life? What defines us as individuals when achievement no longer plays a role? What is happiness if it is not defined by success in the economic sense?

A renaissance of culture and social interaction could emerge. Since economic needs are no longer a thing, people would have the freedom to engage more intensively with art, music, literature or new forms of interpersonal interaction - no longer as a profession or to secure their existence, but as a pure expression of being. Friendships, family, personal experiences would no longer be pushed into the background because "important" tasks must be done.

Another purpose could lie in exploring the universe and one's own consciousness. Since all material needs are automatically met, humanity could focus more on discovery.

Traveling to other planets, exploring parallel worlds, penetrating the mysteries of space, time and existence - all that previously seemed impossible due to the limitations of economic necessity could become a new reason for existence.

But perhaps the real meaning lies not in great discoveries or collective movements, but in a return to the personal. In a world that provides everything, people could learn to value life as such - not as a means to an end, not as a constant striving for more, but as a conscious experience in the here and now. Perhaps simple existence, the joy of existence itself, will become humanity's last great achievement.

The Performance-Optimized Human: Medicine and Efficiency

In a world where efficiency, productivity and performance are considered the highest values, medical and pharmacological aids are increasingly becoming the focus of social debates. Psychotropic drugs, once developed to alleviate serious mental illnesses, have long since moved out of the niche of purely therapeutic applications and are increasingly used to optimize the cognitive and emotional health of healthy people. What does this mean for the individual, for society and for the understanding of performance, humanity and ethics?

The desire for self-optimization is by no means a new phenomenon. Even the ancient Greeks relied on certain herbs to improve their physical and mental condition. In modern society, this desire has developed into a new dimension with the advances in neuroscience, pharmacology and medicine. Substances such as Modafinil, Ritalin or antidepressants are no longer only used to treat sleep disorders, ADHD or depression, but also by healthy people who want to increase their concentration, regulate their mood or improve their social adaptability.

Traditionally, medicine is aimed at curing diseases and alleviating suffering. But in a world in which more and more healthy people are turning to medication to increase their productivity and creativity, the way medicine sees itself is changing.

Many doctors are faced with a dilemma: Should they still prescribe medication to patients who do not show any symptoms of illness in order to improve their performance? Where is the line between medically necessary treatment and socially conditioned optimization?

The optimization of the human mind no longer occurs only through discipline, training or experience, but through chemical interventions that are often considered harmless or even necessary. But what does it mean for a society when success increasingly depends on pharmacological support? And what role does medicine play in this development?

The pharmaceutical industry as the pacesetter of the performance-oriented society

The development of performance-enhancing drugs is not just a coincidence of medical research, but often a direct result of economic interests. Pharmaceutical companies recognize the growing market for "enhancement" drugs and are developing targeted substances that are not only intended to cure the sick, but also to improve the healthy. The boundaries between therapy and optimization are becoming increasingly blurred, which raises ethical questions: Is it legitimate for a healthy person to increase their cognitive performance through medication? Does this lead to a two-class society between those who can afford pharmacological support and those who do without it?

In the modern performance society, the pharmaceutical industry is not only a major economic player, but also a key contributor to social norms and expectations. In a world where efficiency, productivity and optimization are central values, the pharmaceutical industry offers solutions to maintain or even increase physical and mental performance. Whether painkillers, antidepressants or stimulants - medication is increasingly used not only to cure diseases, but also to increase individual performance.

The social pressure to be functional and productive at all times is leading to a normalization of medication consumption. People turn to pharmaceutical products not only in cases of acute illness, but also preventively or to increase performance. The use of psychotropic drugs and performance-enhancing drugs has become established, particularly in highly competitive environments such as the workplace or the education system. Drugs such as methylphenidate, originally developed to treat attention deficit disorders, are used by students or professionals to improve concentration and stamina. At the same time, the number of prescriptions for antidepressants, which are used not only as a therapeutic agent for depression but also to cope with stress and overload, is increasing.

Another aspect is the role of the pharmaceutical industry in defining what is considered "normal". The classification of new diseases and syndromes often leads to a medical problematization of everyday sensitivities. Fatigue, restlessness or mood swings are no longer seen as natural reactions to external circumstances, but are increasingly perceived as treatable conditions. Pharmaceutical companies invest considerable sums in research, advertising and marketing to promote new drugs and indications. They influence not only medical discourses, but also social attitudes towards health and dealing with individual limits.

Critics see this development as a problematic medicalization of life. The increasing use of drugs to enhance performance could lead to a shift in social standards in the long term, in which people without pharmacological support are viewed as disadvantaged or even inadequate. In addition, the long-term consequences of widespread drug use have not yet been fully researched. Dependence on pharmaceutical products entails both health and ethical risks, especially when the line between therapy and optimization becomes increasingly blurred.

The challenge is therefore to find a balance between medical progress and responsible use of drugs. A critical examination of the mechanisms of the pharmaceutical industry and social expectations of performance is therefore essential to ensure sustainable and healthy development of society.

The price of chemical perfection

In addition to the advantages of performance-enhancing drugs, there are also risks that are often underestimated. Long-term studies on the consequences of long-term use of psychotropic drugs by healthy people are rare and, for obvious reasons, not wanted by those who would benefit. The side effects range from sleep disorders to psychological dependence. Those who optimize themselves permanently can get into a vicious circle in which their natural performance is perceived as inadequate.

At the same time, the question arises as to the extent to which social pressure to optimize is increasing. In an environment in which more and more people are chemically increasing their cognitive performance, those who consciously decide not to do so are under pressure. Will there be a society in the future in which natural performance is no longer sufficient to compete?

The pursuit of chemical perfection through the misuse of pharmaceuticals has profound consequences for individuals and society. The desire for increased performance, unshakable mental stability or eternal youth drives many people to consume medication outside of their medical context. This applies to both prescription substances such as painkillers, antidepressants or stimulants as well as performance-enhancing or rejuvenating preparations such as anabolic steroids or nootropics.

For individuals, the misuse of such substances often has serious physical and psychological consequences. Physical side effects such as organ damage, cardiovascular problems or hormonal imbalances can occur. Long-term use often leads to addiction, meaning the body and mind require a steady dose to function. What is particularly problematic is that many drugs have side effects that become more severe when taken improperly or in excessive doses. Psychological consequences are just as serious: anxiety disorders, depression or psychosis can develop because the natural balance of neurotransmitters in the brain is disturbed. The social aspect should not be underestimated either - those affected often withdraw, develop addictive behavior and lose touch with their environment.

On a societal level, the excessive use of pharmaceutical substances creates considerable stress. The health system must allocate more and more resources to the treatment of addiction, withdrawal symptoms and long-term damage. In the workplace and educational sectors, unfair competition arises when some artificially increase their performance while others refuse to take the ethical or health risks. This leads to a normalization of drug abuse, which increases social pressure on those who want to get by without artificial aids. In addition, economic and social inequalities are increasing because performance-enhancing drugs are often expensive and primarily benefit the wealthy.

The pharmaceutical industry plays a central role in this system because, as a profit-oriented industry, it benefits greatly from the fact that more and more people are seeking pharmaceutical solutions to their physical and psychological challenges. Instead of focusing exclusively on healing or sustainable health, a business model is often pursued that creates long-term dependence. What is particularly problematic is that drugs are not only marketed as a treatment for acute or chronic diseases, but are increasingly positioned as a means of improving performance, managing stress or even as lifestyle products. Targeted marketing suggests that almost every human problem - be it fatigue, lack of concentration or low self-confidence - can be solved pharmacologically.

A crucial factor is the close connection between pharmaceutical companies and medical professionals. Doctors are often influenced by the industry, be it through financial incentives, conferences, "consulting" or the availability of free samples. Especially for drugs that are in high demand, such as painkillers, antidepressants or stimulants, prescriptions are often issued too generously or with too little critical reflection. Sometimes this happens out of ignorance of the long-term consequences, sometimes due to a lack of time or because patients deliberately exert pressure. In some cases, however, there are also deliberate collaborations with industry in which doctors indirectly gain economic benefits through high prescription rates.

Another problem is so-called "off-label" prescription, in which drugs are used for purposes for which they are not officially approved. This is becoming increasingly standard, especially in areas such as cognitive performance enhancement or anti-aging therapies. Diagnosis also plays a role: mild mental or physical complaints are increasingly classified as disorders requiring treatment in order to justify the prescription of drugs. This blurs the boundaries between illness and optimization, and the threshold for drug consumption lowers.

At the institutional level, the close interlinkages between the pharmaceutical industry, medical professionals and regulatory authorities make it difficult to critically examine the risks. Studies on side effects or long-term effects are often financed by the manufacturers themselves, which creates conflicts of interest. Critical voices from research are sometimes suppressed or marginalized, while successful drugs are often only marketed with delayed warnings or slight adjustments even after risks have been proven.

An example of drug misuse and its long-term consequences is the overprescription of antibiotics, which often leads to increasing bacterial resistance. Antibiotics are often prescribed for bacterial infections, but in many cases they are used even when they are not necessary or ineffective. This happens, for example, for viral infections such as colds or flu, against which antibiotics have no effect. Nevertheless, patients are often given antibiotics in order to receive treatment quickly or because of the urge for a quick solution.

Another factor that encourages this practice is the enormous pressure placed on doctors. Patients often expect a quick solution to their health problems and are not always willing to wait or resort to alternative treatment methods. Some doctors therefore prescribe antibiotics to satisfy the patient or to prevent possible complaints from patients and their families. In many cases, time pressure also plays a role: the often complex decision-making processes in diagnostics and the burden of many patients per day mean that antibiotics seem like a supposedly simple solution.

This practice has led to a problematic development: the repeated, unnecessary use of antibiotics promotes the development of antibiotic resistance. Bacteria that enter the body have the ability to adapt quickly to changing conditions. When repeatedly exposed to the same antibiotic, some bacteria develop resistance - they become insensitive to the active ingredients that are actually supposed to inhibit their growth or kill them. These resistant bacteria can then cause more serious and long-lasting infections that can no longer be treated with the usual antibiotics. In severe cases, this can even lead to life-threatening conditions.

The pharmaceutical industry also plays a role in this case, as it markets antibiotics in large quantities and encourages doctors to prescribe these drugs even in cases where they may not be necessary. Some companies emphasize the effectiveness and benefits of their products without adequate information about the risks of overuse and the consequences of resistance. There is also a certain responsibility on the part of the medical community, which must ensure that drugs are only prescribed when they are really necessary and that patients are informed about the risks of overuse.

Ultimately, this system ensures that the misuse of medication is not just an individual problem, but a structural one. As long as pharmaceutical companies are focused on maximizing profits and doctors are under economic pressure to "treat" patients as efficiently as possible, the careless use of performance-enhancing, mood-enhancing or pain-relieving substances will continue to be encouraged. This leads to a society in which health is increasingly seen as a consumable good - with all the negative consequences for the body, mind and social structures.

The expectation of always having to function - be it at work, in studies or in sport - puts people under increasing pressure to see pharmaceutical aids as a solution. In the long term, this can lead to people only seeing themselves as machines that can be optimized, instead of accepting their limitations as a natural part of life. In summary, the misuse of pharmaceuticals in the search for perfection leads to alienation from oneself, to health and social crises and to a society in which natural performance and humanity increasingly lose value. The price of chemical perfection is therefore high - both for the individual and for the community.

The performance-optimized person is no longer a future scenario, but a reality. Psychotropic drugs in the service of efficiency are a reflection of a society that places ever higher demands on the individual. The question remains whether this development will lead to an improved quality of life or whether it will force us into a spiral of incessant self-optimization. Medicine is at a turning point: will it continue to be seen primarily as a healing art, or will it increasingly become a tool for increasing social efficiency? The answer to this will help determine how the future of human performance is shaped - and at what price.

In order to counteract the growing trend towards self-optimization through psychotropic drugs and other medications, alternative approaches are required that promote both physical and mental health without resorting to chemical substances. A first important step would be to promote a holistic understanding of health that does not just rely on quick, short-term solutions, but focuses on long-term, sustainable lifestyles. Such a concept could be achieved by increasing the integration of prevention and individual health strategies into everyday life.

Overall, the path that makes the use of drugs for self-optimization superfluous requires a comprehensive societal change towards a healthier, more sustainable lifestyle. This change would have to be driven not only by the development of alternative, non-pharmacological solutions, but also by a profound change in the perception of health, well-being and performance. In the long term, such a paradigm shift could make the need for chemical optimization superfluous and lay the foundation for a healthier, more fulfilling life.

Neuralink - a dystopia or real opportunity?

Neuralink, the company founded by Elon Musk that is working on the development of brain-computer interfaces (BCI), represents a technology that brings with it both great opportunities and serious risks. The medical potential of Neuralink is enormous: This technology could be groundbreaking, especially for people with neurological diseases such as Parkinson's, Alzheimer's, paraplegia or severe forms of depression. It promises to connect the human brain directly to computers in order to restore lost functions or enable communication for people with physical disabilities. The possibility of treating diseases that are difficult or impossible to treat using conventional methods through a direct connection between the brain and machines is an enormous opportunity for humanity.

But these opportunities also bring with them far-reaching ethical and social questions. The technology potentially has far more applications than just medical ones. Once introduced, it could also be used for other purposes, such as improving cognitive abilities or directly manipulating thoughts and emotions. The question therefore arises as to what extent penetrating the human brain to increase intelligence, performance or even optimize behavior could not drift into a dystopia in which people can be controlled or influenced from outside. Who would have access to this technology and how could it be misused? Could such a technology lead to the creation of social inequalities, where only the wealthy can afford these improvements, while poorer sections of society are excluded?

Another aspect that must be considered is the immense responsibility that comes with the development of such technologies. The question arises as to what the protection of privacy and personal integrity might look like in a world in which personal thoughts and feelings can potentially be directly accessed or influenced. What security measures would be necessary to prevent misuse or hacker attacks on the human brain? In addition, society would have to develop clear ethical guidelines to prevent this technology from being used in a way that endangers people's individual desire for freedom or right to self-determination.

There is also the question of how far humanity should go in the direction of "enhancement" technologies that go beyond what is medically necessary. Should the improvement of human capabilities - be it through better memory, increased intelligence or physical performance - even be pursued as a goal, or could this lead to a loss of human identity and a defamiliarization of natural processes?

Despite the medical opportunities, it is therefore essential to carefully consider the potential risks of Neuralink. A responsible approach and a global dialogue about the ethical and social implications of this technology are needed. Humanity is faced with a huge decision: the technology could lead us into a new era of medical possibilities, but it could also open the door to a world in which control over the human brain is exercised not only in a positive but also in a negative sense. This responsibility should not be taken lightly, as the far-reaching consequences for personal freedom, social justice and human coexistence can be immense.

Whether society would be willing and able to bear such a huge responsibility as control over technologies such as Neuralink is a complex and difficult question. The development and implementation of such a technology would require profound changes in many areas of society - not only in terms of medical and technological aspects, but also in terms of ethical, social and legal issues. The question arises as to whether society today is even capable of responsibly shaping the far-reaching consequences of such a technology.

A first important aspect would be the creation of a sound ethical framework that regulates the use of brain-computer interfaces. Without clear ethical guidelines and legal regulations, the technology could easily be misused, be it to monitor, control or manipulate individuals and groups, such as military units. These regulations would have to be developed globally and interdisciplinary in order to take into account different cultural and social contexts and to ensure comprehensive security. This would require society to have a broad discussion at both the political and societal level that examines the use of such technologies from different perspectives. This includes not only scientists and technologists, but also ethicists, philosophers, social scientists and the general public.

In addition, society would need to have a certain level of technological understanding and awareness to understand the risks and opportunities of such technology. Dealing with Neuralink or similar systems requires a deep understanding of how these technologies work, what dangers they can bring and what control mechanisms are necessary. Education and awareness would be of key importance here to enable people to make informed decisions about the use of these technologies and to understand the underlying ethical issues.

In addition, the introduction of such technologies also requires a strong institutional structure that can and wants to actually guarantee the protection of individual rights and privacy. Protection against misuse - be it by governments, companies, the military or criminal organizations - would have to be guaranteed and mechanisms would have to be created to ensure that the technology is used in accordance with society's values. A transparent and democratic debate about the use of such technologies would be necessary in order to make the resulting decisions in accordance with collective ethical beliefs and the protection of human rights.

All of these thoughts presuppose that society is not only ready to take on responsibility, but also that it has the necessary maturity, knowledge and institutional structures to manage the technology responsibly. At present, many societies are still in a phase in which the effects of new technologies are often difficult to estimate and rapid developments are often not accompanied by the necessary ethical and legal considerations. In order to actually be able to bear responsibility for a technology such as Neuralink, a profound social transformation would be necessary that combines education, ethical reflection and legal caution.

It is therefore questionable whether society as a whole is ready to bear this responsibility. The technological possibilities may already be there, but the necessary responsibility, ethical considerations and social structures are not yet fully developed. These considerations lead back to our starting point of whether people are still up to date, i.e. mature enough for their possibilities.

Between Progress and Danger: Transhumanism

Transhumanism - a term that either fascinates or frightens many people, depending on the perspective from which it is viewed. Essentially, it is a philosophical movement that advocates the use of technology to expand and improve human capabilities. But there is a dangerous tension between the promising visions of a better, longer life and the dire warnings of uncontrollable consequences. Transhumanism is a double-edged sword, the blade of which embodies progress and danger in equal measure.

Transhumanism is a philosophical and cultural movement that aims to improve human abilities and characteristics through the use of technology and science. At its core, it is about overcoming the natural biological limits of humans and achieving a higher form of life through technological advances. Transhumanism is based on the belief that humanity is capable of actively controlling its own evolution and in doing so defeating diseases, slowing or even stopping the aging process, and expanding mental and physical abilities. The aim is to maximize human potential through technological means and to significantly improve people's quality of life.

Transhumanism has its roots in various disciplines, including philosophy, science, technology and medicine. It is based on a humanistic approach that sees people as malleable beings who can change and improve not only their environment but also themselves. One of the central ideas of transhumanism is the belief in the unstoppable nature of technological progress and in the possibility of scientific discoveries and technological innovations not only improving daily life but also changing the foundations of human life itself. This includes, for example, the pursuit of so-called "posthumanism", in which people could not only enter their biological bodies but also artificial bodies or virtual worlds.

In practical implementation, transhumanism is based on a variety of technologies and scientific disciplines. These include, for example, advances in genetics, which could enable targeted modification of the genome in order to cure genetic diseases or increase physical and mental performance. The development of artificial intelligence (AI) could make it possible to expand human cognitive abilities or even transfer human consciousness into digital form. Neurotechnology, which makes it possible to connect the human brain to machines, also plays an important role, as does biotechnology, which allows us to slow down the aging process through cell regeneration or the use of artificial organs.

The foundation of transhumanism is the idea that humans are not trapped by their natural, biological limitations, but that they can transform themselves through innovation and scientific progress. This vision is strongly influenced by an optimistic belief in progress that has been deeply rooted in Western thinking since the Enlightenment. It is assumed that the technological developments of the future have the potential to radically improve human life and overcome the fundamental problems that have always plagued humanity - such as illness, old age and death.

The idea of evolving humans beyond their natural limits is not new. For centuries, philosophers, scientists and artists have dreamed of the possibility of extending life or perfecting bodily functions. Ancient mythology tells of gods who give humans supernatural abilities, and the Renaissance gave rise to the vision of “Homo universalis”, capable of mastering all areas of knowledge. But it was only with the rapid advances in genetics, artificial intelligence (AI) and cyborg technologies that transhumanism took concrete form.

It begins with the idea that the human body is a technical device that can be repaired, improved and expanded. The idea of a cyborg, a human who merges with machines, is no longer science fiction. Today there are already prostheses that are so sophisticated that in some cases they can no longer be distinguished from natural limbs. This development is a first example of how transhumanism could change lives. What began as practical help for people with disabilities could in the future become accessible to all people

What began as practical help for people with disabilities could become accessible to everyone in the future and enable a completely new quality of life.

Nevertheless, this development raises many questions. What happens to human identity when the body is completely or partially replaced by technology? Is a person still the same if he has an artificial organ or an implanted brain? And how far can this development go without endangering the core of being human? It is questions like these that make transhumanism a double-edged sword. The progress it promises could lead us on the path to a new era in which humanity not only overcomes biological laws but also redefines its own existence.

Another, perhaps even more disturbing scenario associated with transhumanism is that of artificial intelligence. As technology continues to advance, the development of machines capable of surpassing human intelligence becomes more and more likely. In this context, the question arises as to whether humans are capable of maintaining control over this technology. Will AI one day become so powerful that it threatens human civilization? If machines are able to make their own decisions, they could turn against humans or even reshape the global economy and society according to their own ideas. Humans could become subjects of a technology they originally created.

Amid these dangers, however, there are also a number of perspectives that see transhumanism as a way to improve the human condition. The possibility of curing diseases, slowing or even stopping the aging process, and expanding the human mind opens up unprecedented opportunities. For many, transhumanism is the natural continuation of the science and technology that have helped humans improve their quality of life for thousands of years. From the discovery of fire to the development of modern medicine, humanity has always sought ways to improve its existence. Transhumanism is just the next step in this evolution.

There are numerous examples from modern research that show that these visions are not that far away. Genetic modifications could one day mean that people no longer inherit genetic diseases. Artificial organs could not only replace diseased organs but even significantly extend people's lifespans. Advances in brain research could enable us to understand and improve human consciousness. And the development of artificial intelligence could free people from physical labor and enable them to concentrate on creative and intellectual activities.

Transhumanism has a tense relationship with humanistic ethics and the concept of the human self. On the one hand, it is often seen as a natural continuation of humanistic principles that see humans as beings capable of improving themselves and shaping their living conditions through knowledge, reason and freedom. These humanistic values, which are deeply rooted in the Western tradition of thought, emphasize the autonomy of the individual and the responsibility of humans to shape their own lives and society. In this context, transhumanism appears as an attempt to carry these principles into the future and to use scientific and technological means to expand human potential.

The question also arises whether transhumanism is a "technology at any price" approach or whether it has positive, healing aspects. In fact, there are many dimensions of transhumanism that are not only aimed at the desire for technological superiority, but also pursue the goal of alleviating human suffering and improving life. For example, the medical breakthroughs that transhumanism strives for could help cure previously incurable diseases, slow down the aging process, and significantly improve the lives of people with disabilities. In this respect, transhumanism is understood as a form of "technological humanism" that uses technology not as an end in itself, but as a means to promote human well-being.

Transhumanism and its compatibility with religious ideas of God poses a complex philosophical challenge that opens up various levels of interpretation. On the one hand, it can be argued that the human ability for technological self-improvement can be understood as a God-given gift. From this perspective, humans, as "co-creators", would use their God-given abilities to develop further and develop their potential. The perfection of humans could thus be interpreted as a continuation of divine creation.

However, this gives rise to significant ethical and spiritual tensions. A central conflict lies in the question of the limits of human intervention in the order understood as "natural" or "God-given". The transhumanist approach of technological optimization may contradict the religious virtue of humility before creation. In addition, the fundamental question of the nature of the human soul and consciousness arises in the case of far-reaching technological modifications.

The theological dimension of suffering also appears particularly problematic. While many religious traditions attribute a spiritual meaning to suffering, transhumanism aims to completely overcome it. The same applies to mortality - a core aspect of many religions that transhumanism fundamentally questions.

The question of social justice also plays an important role: Who has access to the improvement technologies? This affects both ethical and religious principles of the equality of all people before God. There is also a risk that the pursuit of technological optimization will push the spiritual development of people into the background.

The compatibility of transhumanism and the idea of God ultimately depends heavily on the respective religious and philosophical interpretation. A possible synthesis could be to understand transhumanist technologies as tools that are used in accordance with divine goals such as healing and reducing suffering. However, the balance between technological progress and ethical development would always have to be maintained in order not to endanger fundamental human dignity and being made in the image of God.

The question remains, however, whether the positive aspects outweigh the potential damage.

The idea of a society in which all people have equal access to transhumanist technologies seems rather utopian in reality. In a world in which technological improvements are not evenly distributed, transhumanism could lead to an increase in existing social inequalities. Rich and privileged people could gain advantages that allow access to improved physical and mental abilities, while poorer sections of society are left behind. In this scenario, transhumanism could lead to further alienation within society and destabilize the social fabric.

In addition, there is the ethical question of who decides which changes should or may be made to the human body and mind.

Will these changes be voluntary and for the benefit of the individual, or could society at some point come under pressure to undergo these technological improvements in order to remain competitive in an increasingly technologized world? In this respect, transhumanism could lead to a form of coercion in which people give up their own natural characteristics in order to adapt to a technologically advanced society.

It is clear that transhumanism is taking humanity to a crucial point. The progress it brings with it brings both enormous opportunities and enormous risks. The answers to the ethical, social and existential questions that transhumanism raises will determine the future of humanity. But as with any major technological revolution, it is ultimately man's responsibility to determine the course - between progress and danger, between improvement and loss. The sword of transhumanism may be sharp, but only man can decide how to deal with it.

These considerations ultimately raise the question again of whether man will no longer be sufficient for the future he has created. It touches on a central aspect of the transhumanist debate and reveals a fascinating paradox. Through his technological innovations, man is creating a world that may exceed his own biological and cognitive limits - a development that brings both opportunities and considerable risks.

The rapid pace of technological development, especially in areas such as artificial intelligence, biotechnology and robotics, is leading to an increasing complexity of our living environment. This complexity could indeed overwhelm the natural capabilities of humans. We already see today how difficult it is for many people to keep up with technological change. This is reflected, for example, in the digital divide between different population groups or in the challenge of fully understanding the consequences of technological developments.

However, it would be too simplistic to conclude that humans in their current form will inevitably become obsolete. Rather, the history of human evolution shows that we can continuously adapt to new challenges. Transhumanism could be understood in this context as a conscious continuation of this adaptability - not as a replacement of humans, but as their further development.

The real challenge is to shape this development in such a way that it is in line with our ethical values and the essence of being human. It is not about labeling humans as inadequate, but about expanding and supplementing their capabilities. This could be done through a symbiotic relationship with technology, combining human qualities such as creativity, emotional intelligence and ethical judgment with technological enhancements.

The key will be that we as a society maintain control over this development and actively shape it. This requires a broad societal dialogue about what kinds of improvements we want to strive for and what limits we want to set. People do not have to be "inadequate" to benefit from improvements - just as wearing glasses does not mean that people are inadequate, but merely that they are expanding their natural abilities.

The future will probably not ask whether people are adequate, but how they can best develop their abilities to meet the challenges ahead. This also means that we must learn to design technological developments in such a way that they complement and enhance our human qualities rather than replace them. Transhumanism could be understood as a tool to better equip people for their self-created future - not because they are inadequate, but because they have the potential to grow beyond themselves.

Religion and Ethics - Consolation or Self-Deception

The question of the role of religion and ethics in modern society, particularly with regard to their comforting or possibly self-deceptive function, is of great complexity and topicality. In a time of rapid technological development and social change, the question is increasingly being asked whether traditional religious and ethical concepts are still up to date and what signify-cance they have for people of the present and future.

Religions have given people orientation, meaning and comfort for thousands of years. They offered and continue to offer answers to existential questions about the origin of life, the meaning of existence and how to deal with suffering and death. In an increasingly secular society, however, this traditional role is often questioned. Critics see religious beliefs as a form of self-deception, an escape from the possibly uncomfortable reality of a world without higher meaning.

Nevertheless, it is clear that even in a world shaped by science and technology, the need for spirituality and ethical orientation does not disappear. Perhaps it is just changing in its form. New spiritual movements, individualized beliefs and ethical discourses beyond religious dogmas are gaining in importance. This indicates that humans, as beings seeking meaning, continue to need overarching patterns of interpretation and moral guidelines.

The question of the timeliness of humans themselves is closely linked to this topic. In an era in which artificial intelligence and biotechnology are redefining the boundaries of humanity, the question of the future of the human species is becoming more pressing. But it is precisely here that the enduring relevance of ethical reflection becomes apparent: the development of new technologies requires, more than ever, a well-founded ethical discussion about their use and limitations.

Humans are characterized by their ability to reflect ethically and their need to find meaning. These characteristics do not make them obsolete; on the contrary, they are particularly valuable in an increasingly technological and complex world. The challenge is to further develop traditional religious and ethical concepts and adapt them to modern conditions without losing their fundamental humanistic orientation.

Religion and ethics do not have to be understood as opposites to the scientific worldview. Rather, they can be understood as complementary approaches to reality that open up different aspects of human experience. While science explains the "how" of the world, religion and ethics address the "why" and "what for" - questions that remain central to human self-understanding.

The timeliness of man is shown precisely in his ability to integrate and critically reflect on different perspectives. Neither blindly adhering to traditional religious ideas nor their complete rejection seem to be effective. Rather, it is important to find a differentiated approach that both recognizes the comforting and orienting function of religion and ethics and enables them to be critically questioned.

The why and what for - the questions about the meaning of man

The question of "why" and "what for" in an increasingly technological world leads us to the fundamental aspects of being human in an era characterized by digitization, automation and artificial intelligence. These developments raise existential questions that, paradoxically, are not answered by technological progress, but rather intensified.

The "why" of our existence takes on a new dimension in a technological world. While machines and algorithms can take on more and more tasks, the question of the specifically human role becomes more pressing. The answer could lie in our unique ability for emotional resonance, empathic understanding and creative meaning-making. Especially in a world characterized by rational efficiency and technical optimization, humans become indispensable as bearers of consciousness, compassion and moral reflection.

The "why" of our existence could manifest itself in the ability to understand technology not as an end in itself, but as a tool for achieving deeply human goals: the creation of a fairer society, the preservation of our natural resources, the promotion of art and culture. At a time when technical systems are becoming increasingly autonomous, the human task of consciously designing and ethically controlling these developments is becoming central.

The increasing alienation that many people feel in the technological world could paradoxically lead to a return to genuinely human qualities. The more our everyday lives are determined by digital interfaces and automated processes, the more important authentic interpersonal encounters, physical experiences and the cultivation of mindfulness and presence become.

An essential aspect of the "why" may also lie in our ability to integrate different perspectives and levels of experience. While technical systems rely on clearly defined parameters and algorithms, humans can endure ambivalence, understand paradoxes and allow different truths to coexist. This integrative power is becoming more and more important in an increasingly complex and contradictory world.

The "why" could also be reflected in the task of finding a balance between technological progress and basic human needs. Designing technology that is not only efficient but also human-friendly, that is not only functional but also aesthetically pleasing, that is not only rational but also emotionally intelligent, is becoming a key challenge.

The tension between technological development and human nature may also provide an opportunity to redefine what defines us as human beings. The confrontation with artificial intelligence and robotic systems forces us to reflect on our own abilities and limitations. The "why" and "what for" could lie precisely in consciously shaping this reflection and developing new forms of being human from it.

Alienation in the technological world could ultimately be understood as a call to develop new forms of community and coexistence. The "why" and "what for" may lie in the design of ways of life that use technological possibilities without neglecting the basic needs for authentic encounters, sensory experiences and spiritual depth.

The pursuit of the meaning of existence - a prerequisite for being human?

The question of the meaning of the pursuit of the "meaning of existence" touches on the core of human existence in a rapidly changing world. Paradoxically, the increasing technological and digitization of our living environment could mean that the question of meaning does not lose importance, but on the contrary becomes even more pressing.

In a world in which artificial intelligence is taking on more and more tasks and traditional forms of work are changing, the question of the deeper meaning of human action and existence may even become more existential than ever before. When routine activities are automated, the question of what is specifically human and its value becomes even clearer. The pursuit of meaning could become a key distinguishing feature between humans and machines.

The search for meaning manifests itself on various levels. On the individual level, it is about personal lifestyle design and the search for identity in an increasingly complex world. The questions "Who am I?" and "What makes my life meaningful?" are gaining new relevance in an era of virtual realities and artificial identities. People are looking for authentic experiences and deeper connections, precisely because technological development often leads to superficiality and alienation.

On a societal level, the question of meaning becomes relevant for shaping our common future. What values should guide us? How can we use technology in such a way that it serves human well-being? The search for meaning becomes a necessary orientation for ethical decisions and social developments.

Another aspect is the spiritual or philosophical dimension of the search for meaning. At a time when scientific explanations are being found for more and more phenomena, the question of "why" remains. The "what for" remains a deeply human question that may never be definitively answered - and that is precisely where its lasting significance lies.

The search for meaning could also act as a motor for cultural and social innovation. In the effort to give meaning to life, people develop new forms of coexistence, artistic expression and social organization. This creative power of the search for meaning will remain important for the further development of human culture in the future.

The integrative function of the question of meaning is also important. In an increasingly fragmented world, thinking together about meaning and significance can connect people and enable dialogue across cultural and ideological boundaries. The search for meaning thus becomes an important element of social cohesion.

However, the way in which people search for meaning will probably continue to change. Traditional religious or philosophical answers will be supplemented or replaced by new forms of finding meaning. The integration of different perspectives - scientific, spiritual, artistic - could become more important.

The progressive development of artificial intelligence also raises new questions: If machines begin to become seemingly more intelligent than humans, what is still so special about being human? It is precisely in this debate that the ability to search for and give meaning could emerge more clearly as an essential feature of human existence.

In summary, it can be said that the pursuit of the "meaning of being" will not only continue to be important, but may even become more important. In a world characterized by technological change and global challenges, the ability to find and give meaning is becoming a central human competence. It enables us to place technological developments in a larger context and to align our actions with overarching values and goals.

The question of the future meaning of human existence opens up a wide spectrum of possible perspectives that are emerging in our changing world. A key aspect could lie in the conscious design and ethical control of technological developments. Humans will increasingly have to take on the role of mediator between technical efficiency and human needs, whereby their ability for moral reflection and emotional intelligence will be of crucial importance.

The creative design of new ways of life and social models could represent another important aspect of meaning. At a time when traditional structures and forms of work are dissolving, the ability to innovate and develop sustainable models for the future is becoming central. The meaning could lie in finding ways to combine technological progress with ecological sustainability and social justice.

The preservation and further development of cultural achievements could also represent an important source of meaning. In an increasingly digitalized world, the care of cultural heritage and its creative transformation will become an important task for the future. Art, music, literature and other cultural forms of expression could become even more important as media for creating meaning.

Another aspect of future meaning-finding could lie in the integration of different dimensions of knowledge and experience. The ability to combine scientific findings with spiritual insights, emotional knowledge and practical wisdom may become a key competence. The meaning could be to develop holistic perspectives that do justice to the complexity of our existence.

The development of one's own consciousness and the cultivation of inner qualities could also become central sources of meaning. In a world of external acceleration and sensory overload, the ability to collect oneself, to meditate and to consciously reflect on oneself is becoming increasingly important. The meaning could lie in deepening one's own being and in developing higher forms of consciousness.

Assuming responsibility for planetary and interplanetary development could also represent an important perspective of meaning. In a time of global ecological crises, consciously shaping our relationship with nature and other living beings becomes an existential task. The meaning could be to find ways to achieve a more harmonious coexistence of all forms of life. Humans, as beings who research and discover, could find deep satisfaction in expanding their knowledge and possibilities.

The search for meaning in the future will probably lie less in large, universally valid answers, but rather in the individual and collective ability to continually develop and integrate new perspectives on meaning. The meaning could lie precisely in this continuous search and development, in the ability to continually engage with the challenges and possibilities of a changing world.

Ultimately, our ability for conscious evolution, ethical reflection and loving connection with others is what makes us unique. In a world of increasing technical possibilities, the cultivation of these specifically human qualities may become the most important source of meaning of all.

In this sense, humans not only remain contemporary, but their ability for ethical reflection and search for meaning is even becoming more important. The challenges of the present and future require more than ever a conscious engagement with questions about the good life, responsibility towards others and the creation of a just society. Religion and ethics can provide important impulses, but they must also develop themselves and meet the demands of a changing world.

Boomers, Millennials and Generation Z

Each generation brings forth new ideas, technologies and values that reshape the social fabric. But this change does not happen smoothly. Time and again, the different age groups clash, be it due to misunderstandings, competition or fundamental differrences in values. In today's world, this conflict seems to manifest itself particularly strongly between the so-called boomers, millennials and Generation Z. It is a complex field of tension that reveals itself in social media, in the workplace and even within families. But what are the real causes of the current "generation crisis"? Is it the result of a natural generational change or an expression of a deeper social restructuring?

To understand this conflict, it is worth looking at the peculiarities of the generations involved. The baby boomers, born between 1946 and 1964, grew up in a time of economic boom. They experienced a world in which hard work and discipline were often rewarded with material prosperity. Their view of the world is characterized by stability and long-term planning. Millennials, on the other hand, born between 1981 and 1996, were socialized in an era of great upheaval: digitization, globalization and an increasingly uncertain world of work shaped their youth. They experienced the financial crisis in 2008 and found that traditional career models no longer work as reliably as they once did. Generation Z, born from 1997 onwards, grew up in a world of constant digital networking. They do not know a world without the Internet and are strongly influenced by social media. Their view of society is often more critical and questions existing structures.

These three generations are now facing each other, each with its own ideas, hopes and frustrations. What is particularly striking is that each generation feels misunderstood by the other in some way. Baby boomers complain that younger generations do not have the same work ethic and give up too quickly. Millennials, on the other hand, feel that the boomers have thrown them into an unfair world in which they have to fight harder to be able to afford the same life. Generation Z is often even more radical in its rejection of traditional values and calls for profound social changes.

The dynamics of these generational conflicts can be illustrated by numerous examples. Let's take the debate about work-life balance. For the baby boomers, work was a central part of life. Those who worked hard could build a good life. Millennials and Generation Z, on the other hand, are increasingly focusing on a balance between work and leisure. This leads to tensions in the workplace if younger employees are not prepared to accept overtime as a matter of course, for example.

Many young people, especially from Generation Z, accuse the older generations of having ruthlessly exploited the planet. The "Fridays for Future" movement is an expression of this frustration. Baby boomers, on the other hand, often argue that today's prosperity was only made possible by economic growth and that radical demands are unrealistic and that younger generations lack pragmatic solutions.

But is the conflict between the generations really insurmountable? Historically, such tensions have always existed. The "1968" movement, for example, represented a radical rejection of the conservative values that prevailed at the time. Nevertheless, societies have evolved and found compromises in many areas. The challenge is to build bridges between generations rather than deepening divides. This requires mutual understanding and a willingness to learn from each other.

Ultimately, the question remains: is the current "generational crisis" really a crisis or simply the normal course of history? Perhaps the conflict itself is a sign of progress - a necessary process that challenges old structures and makes room for new ideas. What we make of it is up to all of us.

While younger generations, especially the so-called digital natives, have grown up with technologies such as smartphones, social media, artificial intelligence and automation, older generations often find it harder to keep up with these developments. This leads to tensions, misunderstandings and differences in values and in the way technology is used and evaluated in many areas.

In the private sphere, the generational conflict is expressed, for example, in communication and media consumption. Young people are used to communicating mainly via messenger services, video telephony or social networks, while older generations still value personal conversations or telephone calls. This can lead to misunderstandings and the feeling that younger people have fewer social skills in direct contact, while older people in turn perceive older people as "anti-technology" or "backward". In addition, new digital trends, such as the use of influencer platforms such as TikTok or Instagram, are often perceived by older people as superficial and lacking in substance, while younger people see it as a new form of creative self-development and information gathering.

While older generations are often more skeptical about digitization and consider the protection of personal data to be a high priority, younger people are often more naive with their information. The matter-of-factness with which personal content is put online irritates many older people, while younger people often cannot understand why older people are afraid of digital networking.

The effects of technological progress on the generational conflict are also noticeable in the world of work. The increasing digitization and automation of many work processes requires constant adaptation to new systems and programs. Younger employees who are familiar with digital tools tend to adapt to new technologies more quickly and efficiently, while older employees often have difficulty adapting to rapid change. This can lead to older employees feeling overwhelmed or fearful of being replaced by younger, more technologically savvy colleagues.

Differences are particularly evident in the area of home office and remote work: While many young employees welcome the flexibility and the opportunity to work from anywhere, older generations often find this way of working more difficult. They are used to being present in the office and prefer direct communication with colleagues. The increasing virtualization of the working world can therefore lead to tensions between the generations, especially if companies rely on increasingly using digital collaboration platforms and AI-supported processes.

The break in the transmission of values and knowledge

Digitization and automation have brought about profound changes in the way knowledge and values are passed on from one generation to the next. Traditionally, this transmission took place primarily through direct interaction within families, by living out certain norms and through personal exchanges about experiences, stories and skills. However, technological change has interrupted or significantly changed many of these mechanisms, leading to a break in the traditional transmission of values and knowledge.

A key factor is the change in access to information. While previous generations received knowledge mainly from parents, teachers or other authority figures, younger generations can now research almost any topic within seconds via the Internet. Search engines, online encyclopedias and artificial intelligence provide information instantly and often in a more comprehensive form than the older generation could do from their own memory. This leads to the role of parents and grandparents as primary knowledge providers being weakened. Young people increasingly rely on digital sources instead of considering traditional knowledge transfer through personal conversations or practical experience to be necessary.

The transmission of values is also severely affected. In the past, moral ideas, social rules and cultural traditions were mostly passed on within the family and the immediate social environment. Today, however, social media, algorithms and online communities are key influencers for young generations. Platforms such as TikTok, YouTube or Instagram often shape world views more than family or local traditions. Influencers and content creators are in some ways replacing the role of older generations as points of reference. This can lead to values and norms no longer being passed on uniformly, but being heavily dependent on global trends and changing digital currents.

Another aspect is the change in the way practical and practical knowledge is imparted. Many skills that were previously passed on from generation to generation - such as manual skills, gardening, repairs or traditional cooking recipes - have been pushed into the background by digitalization. Automation and technology have made much of this knowledge obsolete: Smart household appliances take on tasks that previously required specific knowledge, repairs are no longer carried out by the owner but are replaced by replacing entire products, and an online tutorial is quickly consulted instead of traditional recipes.

This means that many previously important skills are no longer taught within the family and are thus lost.

Interpersonal communication itself is also affected. In the past, the direct, personal passing on of stories, experiences and wisdom was a central part of family ties and the transmission of values. Due to digitalization, many young people now communicate primarily via digital channels, which can reduce the emotional closeness and depth of conversations between generations. While older generations often value detailed stories and personal conversations, younger people prefer fast, efficient digital communication. This can lead to a weakening of not only knowledge but also the emotional connection between generations.

In summary, digitalization and automation have greatly changed or displaced traditional forms of transmitting values and knowledge. While older generations are still used to direct, personal exchange, younger generations are increasingly relying on digital information sources and online communities. This not only leads to the loss of certain skills and traditions, but also fundamentally changes the understanding of knowledge, experience and values that has grown over generations. This does not necessarily lead to a complete loss of values transmission, but to a transformation that brings with it both opportunities and challenges.

But the loss of traditional values is not only due to digitalization and automation, but also to the changing culture of education and teaching, in which many parents and educators increasingly want to take on the role of a friend rather than a role model. This change in the perception of authority has contributed to tradetional values being passed on less stringently and instead there is often uncertainty about value orientation.

A key problem here is that many parents and teachers today strive to appear as understanding, equal reference persons rather than as people of respect with clear guidelines. The fear of being perceived as "old-fashioned" or "strict" by the younger generation means that adults often hold back and instead rely on an overly liberal and non-binding upbringing. Rules and values are not conveyed as fixed points of reference, but presented as flexible suggestions that are open to discussion. As a result, many young people lack a clear structure to orient themselves by, which in the long term can lead to uncertainty or a feeling of instability.

In addition, many parents and educators are themselves faced with challenges due to technological change and often try not to lose touch with youth culture. For example, they adopt the language used by young people, consume similar media or adapt their parenting methods to digital trends in order to appear modern and approachable. However, this blurs the boundaries between authority figures and like-minded people. When parents position themselves as "buddy" instead of responsible role models, children and young people often lack the necessary orientation to develop a stable framework of values.

But the question of whether this effort to achieve closeness and equality is even accepted by younger people is ambivalent. On the one hand, many young people want an open and understanding relationship with their parents and teachers. They welcome it when adults take their world seriously and communicate on an equal level. On the other hand, excessive adaptation or the attempt to adapt too much to youth culture often leads to a loss of respect. Young people often recognize intuitively when adults give up their natural authority or bend themselves to appear "cool" or modern. This can lead to them no longer perceiving their parents or teachers as credible role models and instead looking for other figures to identify with - often on social media or among their peers.

The loss of clear role models and reliable values makes young people particularly vulnerable to manipulation - whether by influencers who shape opinions and consumer behavior on social media, or by political ideologies that deliberately exploit insecurities and lack of orientation. When traditional institutions for conveying values, such as parents, teachers or communities, lose influence, young people look for new figures to identify with and points of orientation to shape their worldview. But in a digital world in which content is often filtered by commitment rather than truth or moral substance, the sources of this orientation are not always reputable or benevolent.

Influencers deliberately use the mechanisms of social media to build trust and create emotional bonds with their followers. Due to their supposed closeness and authenticity, they appear more credible to many young people than traditional authorities. They not only shape consumer behavior through product placement, but also worldviews, body images and social norms. They themselves are often not neutral actors, but are controlled by commercial or ideological interests. The line between advertising, opinion and actual knowledge is fluid in social media, and many young people do not sufficiently question whether what they consume stands up to critical scrutiny.

Political ideologies also benefit from this disorientation. Young people who no longer feel addressed by traditional values and structures are more receptive to simple solutions and radical messages. Political groups - whether extreme right, extreme left or conspiracy theorists - use digital platforms to specifically target young people. Through emotional appeals, enemy images and the promise of belonging, they offer supposed security in a complex world. Without a solid value base or critical thinking, many young people find it difficult to recognize and question manipulative narratives.

A major problem is that young people are often viewed as either children or young adults, depending on what society deems appropriate at the time. In many areas, they are expected to have the ability to make adult decisions - for example at school, where they are expected to take on a high level of personal responsibility - while in other situations they are denied the necessary maturity. This imbalance often leads to frustration and incomeprehension among young people, who feel that they are either not being taken seriously or are being confronted with excessive demands.

As young people are still developing, they not only need freedom to develop themselves, but also stable guidelines and support from adults. But in modern societies, they are often expected to take on too much personal responsibility without being given enough guidance at the same time. Parents and teachers often take a back seat out of insecurity or fear of conflict, leaving young people to navigate themselves in a world full of demands and temptations.

Due to the influence of digitalization in particular, young people today are more than ever confronted with sensory overload, social comparison dynamics and manipulative mechanisms - for example through social media or consumer culture. They therefore need not only access to knowledge, but also guidance on how to critically question and evaluate this knowledge. Adults should therefore not shirk their responsibility, but should actively act as companions who offer guidance without suppressing the autonomy of young people.

The statement "Young people are not small adults" is an important reminder that young people are in a unique phase of development that brings with it different needs and challenges than adulthood. Their brains, emotions and social structures function differently than those of an adult, which is why it is problematic to measure them by the same standards. Instead of either overwhelming them or underestimating them, a balance between support and independence is needed. Adults should act as understanding but clear role models who help young people to find their way in a complex world without leaving them alone or burdening them with responsibilities that they are not yet capable of too early.

Children and young people need both understanding and clear values and structures that give them support. Parents and educators who act exclusively as friends run the risk of losing influence. Conversely, however, an attitude that is too strict or dogmatic also leads to rejection and resistance. The challenge is therefore to combine modern education with a solid role model function: to show empathy and openness without giving up one's own role as a responsible leader. This is the only way to ensure that values are conveyed sustainably despite social change.

In a future that is increasingly shaped by digitalization, artificial intelligence (AI) and automated technology, relationships between generations will be crucial for positive coexistence and the preservation of personal bonds in families and society as a whole. The challenge is to reconcile technological progress with human needs for closeness, communication and emotional connection. To achieve this, relationships between generations must be designed in such a way that technological developments do not lead to alienation, but enrich and promote interpersonal relationships.

A central aspect of future generational relationships must be dialogue - in particular an exchange about the opportunities and challenges that digitalization brings with it. Younger generations, who have grown up with technologies such as smartphones, social media, AI and automation, have a different perspective on these developments than older generations. For many older people, the digital world is still new territory, which is often perceived as complex and overwhelming. It is therefore important that younger people share their experiences and knowledge to make it easier for older people to access this new world. On the other hand, older generations should also contribute their own perspectives, values and life experiences, which often provide important orientation. Such mutual understanding can reduce misunderstandings and build bridges between generations so that both sides can learn from each other.

The dialogue should not only include technical knowledge, but also the ethical, social and emotional implications of technological change. Older people often have a well-founded perspective on issues of morality, responsibility and social cohesion, while younger people tend to be more flexible and open to new ideas. A continuous exchange on the impact of digitalization on society and on individual lives can help ensure that society as a whole is well prepared for the challenges of the future.

Technology should not be perceived as a barrier between generations, but as a tool that helps to promote connections. Especially in times when geographical distances and lack of time make personal communication difficult, digital tools can play a crucial role. Video telephony, messaging services and social networks offer an easy way to stay in regular contact, even if the generations live in different cities or countries. This is especially important for older people who might otherwise be isolated by limited mobility or health problems.

In addition to technical competence, emotional intelligence plays a crucial role in relationships between generations. In a world that is becoming increasingly automated and in which AI takes over many decisions, interpersonal contact and the ability to empathize remain an indispensable asset. Today's young people, who are strongly influenced by digitalization, should learn how to use this technology without losing their ability to empathize. Likewise, older generations should be encouraged to use their social and emotional skills to offer guidance to younger people in times of alienation and social pressure.

The ability to give and receive emotional support remains one of the fundamental elements in personal relationships. In the digital world, where the authenticity of communication is often lost and interpersonal bonds appear superficial, it becomes even more important that the generations support each other in their emotional development. Families must continue to be places where empathy and understanding are not replaced by algorithm-based communication.

Education plays a central role in how future generations deal with the digital world. In a society where AI and automation play an increasingly important role, education must not only impart technical knowledge but also promote critical thinking and ethical responsibility. Cross-generational education initiatives could help ensure that both older and younger people acquire the necessary skills to move safely and confidently in the digital world.

An important part of this educational process is the transmission of values that also endure in a technology-driven world. Values such as responsibility, respect and fairness must be lived not only in the personal but also in the digital sphere. Families, schools and societies must work together to ensure that ethical considerations are not neglected when using technology and AI. Young people must learn how to use technology not only as consumers but also as responsible designers of digital culture and society.

Intergenerational relationships in a digitalized future must be characterized by mutual respect, dialogue and cooperation. Technological progress should not be seen as a threat but as an opportunity for better understanding and closer ties. The younger generations bring technological expertise and openness, while the older generations have valuable life experiences and ethical perspectives. By actively exchanging these different perspectives, stable, respectful and value-oriented relationships can be created that enable families and society to grow together in the future. The challenge will be to find a balance where technology supports social cohesion rather than endangering it - by serving as a bridge between generations rather than a barrier.

The actual or at least perceived erosion of societies and relationships between generations is a profound development that is being accelerated by numerous factors mentioned above. Globalization, digitization, economic inequality, political polarization and the change in traditional values are causing the social fabric to change drastically in many parts of the world. The question of whether this process can be stopped depends on the extent to which societies are prepared to consciously face the challenges and actively work on solutions. A complete return to previous structures is unlikely, but targeted measures can help to preserve or reshape cohesion within society and between generations.

Digitalization has enabled many positive developments, but at the same time it has also caused profound social upheavals. Technological progress is leading to changing communication patterns: While previous generations used face-to-face conversations as their primary form of interaction, digital platforms such as social media, messenger services and video telephony are now central means of communication. This can lead to generations becoming increasingly alienated from one another.

In addition, algorithms are increasing social divisions by reinforcing individual interests and worldviews instead of promoting discourse between different groups. This can not only lead to social fragmentation, but also to older and younger generations inhabiting different information bubbles and a common understanding of social developments being lost.

Traditional values that have been passed down through generations are losing importance in many modern societies. While previous generations were more strongly shaped by collective identities - be it through family, religion or regional communities - today's young generations are experiencing greater individualization. Self-realization and personal freedom are often the focus, while traditional social obligations are becoming less important. This leads to intergenerational ties becoming weaker and social cohesion decreasing.

Growing economic inequality and uncertainty about the future are also contributing to the erosion of societal structures. Young people are faced with temporary work contracts, increasing housing pressure and an uncertain pension perspective, while older generations are often more economically secure. This can lead to tensions between generations, as young people feel that the older generation has benefited from economic stability, while they themselves are denied many of these opportunities.

Political polarization is increasing in many societies. While older generations often hold more conservative values, younger generations often tend to take progressive or radical political positions.

This means that political discourse between generations is becoming increasingly difficult and there is a risk that different age groups will no longer see themselves as part of a common society, but as competing camps.

The erosion of societies and generational relationships is not necessarily irreversible. There are various ways in which social cohesion can be strengthened and the connection between generations restored:

One key to solving the problem lies in active exchange between generations. Educational institutions, families and social institutions should specifically create spaces in which young and older people can talk to each other. This should not only be about imparting knowledge and traditions, but also about understanding the respective life realities and challenges of the other generation.

Social cohesion can only exist if solidarity between generations is actively practiced. This means that social security systems must be designed in such a way that they take into account the needs of both older and younger generations. This includes fair pension schemes, educational opportunities and the creation of jobs with a long-term perspective.

The increasing erosion of societies and generational relationships is a complex challenge influenced by technological, economic and cultural factors. It cannot necessarily be stopped, but it can be slowed down and channelled in a positive direction through targeted measures. It is crucial that societies consciously work against division and alienation by promoting dialogue between generations, strengthening social responsibility and using technology sensibly. The future of our coexistence also depends on whether we succeed in finding a balance between progress and tradition. If we succeed in putting intergenerational solidarity, ethical values and social responsibility at the centre, a division of society can be avoided and a new, more stable social order can be created that is up to the challenges of the 21st century.

Artificial Intelligence and the Labor Market

The question of whether artificial intelligence (AI) will revolutionize the job market and make us humans replaceable in many jobs is no longer a theoretical scenario. It is a reality that is evolving every day. From automated customer service to robots in production to algorithms that make trading decisions in the financial world - we encounter applications of AI everywhere that can displace or even completely replace people in certain activities. But how realistic is it that "all" people are actually replaceable? And what impact will this have on the job market, society and individual lives?

When you consider the rapid development of artificial intelligence, it initially seems almost obvious that humans are becoming increasingly superfluous as workers. Who would have thought just a few years ago that machines could be able to analyze complex legal texts, create works of art or even write messages? Today there is already AI that is able to work precisely and efficiently in almost every industry. These developments raise the question of whether the labor market – and with it the way we think about work – is being transformed in a way that will have a profound impact on our lives.

The idea that machines could eventually replace all human workers is not new, however. Similar fears existed over a hundred years ago, during the Industrial Revolution. Back then, many people saw their jobs threatened by the introduction of machines. But instead of a mass labor market without work, a new era of division of labor emerged, and many professions were redefined. New industries were created, and jobs that did not exist before emerged. The question today is whether artificial intelligence will really revolutionize all areas of work, or whether we are in a similar transformation process as then.

There are numerous real-world examples that show how AI and automation are already affecting many jobs today. Robots are increasingly being used in the production of goods to take on simple, repetitive tasks that were previously done by humans. A factory worker working on an assembly line is increasingly being replaced by machines that not only work faster and more precisely, but also do not need breaks or vacations. But this development is not limited to industry. AI systems are also on the rise in the service sector. Chatbots that answer simple customer queries are now widespread. In the financial sector, algorithms are already using AI to carry out stock market transactions in a matter of seconds that would previously have taken hours or even days. And in medicine, too, artificial intelligence is beginning to take on more and more tasks - be it analyzing X-ray images or assisting surgeons during complex operations.

But all of these examples also raise the question: what is left for humans? Will we really be replaceable in all areas? Some experts believe that AI can only replace human labor when it comes to simple, routine tasks. Tasks that do not require particular creativity or empathy could indeed be taken over by machines. But what about more complex and creative tasks? Can machines replace human labor here too?

The answer to this question is not quite so simple. Although there is already AI that is able to solve complex tasks and even become creative, humans remain unbeatable in many areas for the time being. Even the most advanced algorithms and machines are not able to fully replicate human intuition and creativity. An AI program can create works of art or compose music, but it lacks the ability to recognize a deeper meaning or emotional resonance in its work. Even in jobs that require communication and empathy - such as nursing or social professsions - humans remain irreplaceable.

Another example of the "irreplaceability" factor of humans is the area of leadership and management. AI can analyze data and make decisions based on these analyses, but the ability to lead people, develop visions or shape corporate culture remains a human domain. These qualitative aspects of work are still a long way from being taken over by machines.

The question of whether we are all replaceable leads us to a much larger and more complex discussion: what do we value work? In the past, work was primarily a means to an end - a way to earn money and make a living. But as technology advances and automation increases, many people may ask: what is the true meaning of work when machines can do much of the work? Will work in the future be more than just an economic factor? Will it be possible to live a life without work without feeling worthless or superfluous?

There are certainly voices calling for us to move away from our traditional understanding of work and strive for a society in which people no longer have to work for a living. In such a society, people could focus on creative activities, social relationships or personal fulfillment without having to constantly worry about income. But this vision has its own challenges. What happens to people who do not discover "creative" or "meaningful" activities for themselves? How do we ensure that a society without work does not become a society of the unemployed, faced with existential fears and social isolation?

These considerations raise another central aspect: the question of the distribution of wealth. When machines take over work and the production of goods and services becomes more and more efficient, the question arises as to who benefits from the proceeds of this progress. If a small elite of technology companies and investors have control over AI systems and automation processes, the gap between rich and poor could widen even further. The labor market could be dominated by a few highly paid specialists, while a large mass of people are left behind.

But the development of artificial intelligence and automation does not necessarily have to go in this direction. There are numerous concepts that aim to ensure a fairer distribution of wealth and resources - be it through an unconditional basic income, through stronger regulations of the AI industry or through new models of reducing working hours. In a world where machines take over the heavy lifting, humans could be freed from the burden of paid work and instead be given the freedom to focus on personal interests, further education and social engagement.

However, how we shape this future depends not only on technology, but also on our political and social decisions. It is up to us to set the course for a future in which AI and automation are not seen as a threat to the labor market, but as an opportunity for a better and fairer society.

In this complex interplay of technology, business and society, the question ultimately arises: will we all be replaceable? The answer is not easy to find, as it depends on many factors - the type of work we do, the ethical and political decisions we make and our ability as a society to prepare for the changes brought about by artificial intelligence. But one thing is certain: the changes that AI is bringing to the labor market are just the beginning of an even greater transformation that could fundamentally change our understanding of work, prosperity and society.

The increasing automation of work processes poses the question of whether we are entering a spiral of constant training and specialization. In many areas - be it in industry, the service sector or in creative professions - tasks are increasingly being taken over by machines. This development means that the demands on workers are increasing. They must not only be flexible and adaptable, but also have specialized knowledge and skills in order to be able to work with the new technologies. But what happens to people who do not have the necessary educational requirements or the resources to continue to train? What will become of those who are less educated or less creative when the labor market moves more and more towards highly qualified and specialized jobs?

It is a fact that increasing automation is increasingly polarizing the labor market. On the one hand, new, highly qualified jobs are emerging that require technical knowledge, creativity and a high level of adaptability. These jobs are often associated with a high level of specialization - in areas such as artificial intelligence, data science, robotics, green energy or advanced medicine. On the other hand, there is an increasing automation of activities that were previously done by less skilled workers, such as simple manufacturing processes, warehouse work or simple office tasks. Machines take over these jobs faster, more efficiently and without the need for breaks. The resulting labor market gap between the highly skilled and the less skilled could lead to a deep social divide.

The answer to the question of whether this development forces us into a spiral of further training and specialization is therefore not entirely simple. In a sense, yes: those who do not train or specialize risk being excluded from the labor market. Those who are not willing or able to adapt to new technologies and requirements could have difficulty finding a job. The labor market will increasingly resemble a competition in which those who can best handle the latest technological developments have the best chance of getting a well-paid job. Those who cannot keep up with the demands of automation and digitalization, on the other hand, will find it increasingly difficult to find a job at all.

But what happens to those who are unable or unmotivated to continue specializing? What about those who are reluctant to continue to learn or who simply do not have the resources and opportunities to adapt to the demands of the modern labor market? In many cases, it is the less educated or the less creative who are struggling to keep up in this fast-paced, technology-driven world. They are often the first to be affected by automation, whether in manufacturing, transportation or other areas taken over by robots and algorithms. For these people, the spiral of upskilling and specialization could become a frightening, ever-faster-spinning wheel in which they have no opportunity to keep up.

In a society where more and more jobs require specialized skills, further questions arise: How will the less educated be treated? Will these developments make them "losers" in the labor market, or are there alternative ways in which they too can benefit from technological development? One way to meet this challenge is a comprehensive education and retraining strategy that facilitates access to further training for all people, regardless of their previous educational background or social background. But the reality shows that not everyone is able to continue to learn. The question of how to include the less educated in the digital future is therefore one of the key social challenges of the coming decades.

What happens to creative people who may not reach the specialized, high-paying jobs in the technology industry, but still do not want to work in simple and automatable jobs? Will they also be displaced by increasing automation? The answer to this question is more complex, as creativity and innovation are still valued as values in many areas. But creativity is also subject to change.

Technologies such as artificial intelligence are increasingly being used in creative processes - for example when writing texts, composing music or creating works of art. While these developments can open up new opportunities for creative people, the question here is: will humans become less important due to the automation of creative work? Will creative jobs continue to be seen as "exclusively human", or will creativity also be taken over by machines?

It is clear that increasing automation and digitalization are making the world of work increasingly specialized and demanding. But at the same time, we as a society must ensure that not only the highly qualified and specialized workforce benefits from this development, but that the less educated, the less creative and the less specialized people also have a chance to participate in this future. It is not just about providing access to further training, but also about shaping labor markets in such a way that they remain fair and inclusive. Only if we manage to meet people where they are and support them on their way into the digital future can we prevent advancing automation from creating an ever deeper divide between the various social groups. The answers to these questions will be crucial to how we as a society deal with advancing automation and its effects on the labor market.

Will the quality of our questions determine our future?

The interaction between artificial intelligence (AI) and humans is one of the most exciting and at the same time most complex developments in modern technology. The question of how this cooperation will shape up in the long term concerns not only technological progress, but also profound philosophical, ethical and social considerations. A key question in this context is whether the quality of answers provided by AI actually depends on the quality of the questions we ask - and what this means for the future of human action.

First of all, it is important to understand that even if artificial intelligence is able to take on a variety of tasks and deliver amazingly precise results in many areas, it does not act independently of humans. On the contrary, it is essentially an extension of human capabilities and a tool that is geared towards the needs and desires of humans. But the quality of this tool depends not only on the algorithms and data with which the AI was trained, but above all on the input that humans give it. The "questions" that a human asks an AI largely determine how good the answers are.

A simple example illustrates this dynamic: If a human asks an AI about a specific topic, such as "What is the meaning of life?", the AI will provide an answer based on the data and algorithms it has at its disposal. But the answer will only be as good as the underlying question. If the question is formulated precisely and focused on a specific topic, the AI can provide a well-founded and nuanced answer. On the other hand, if the question is unclear or vague, the answer will also be less helpful and precise. In a sense, the quality of the AI's answer is directly linked to the quality of the human input.

This insight leads to another, deeper question: Does this mean that humans will always remain the initiators of their own future by setting the direction in which the AI works? The answer to this question initially seems clear: Yes, humans will continue to be the initiators and the ones who set the basic direction of developments. AI may be able to learn and process data on its own, but it is and will remain a tool created and guided by humans. It is only as "smart" as the data it is fed and the instructions it is given.

However, there is an interesting twist when you consider that artificial intelligence is not only based on human "inputs", but also gains the ability to improve itself and recognize new patterns through machine learning and continuous data processing. In this way, AI in the future could be able to ask questions on its own that go far beyond what humans originally intended. AI could then act not only as a passive tool, but as an active partner, making suggestions for optimizing processes, ideas and solutions without humans always having to take the initiative.

However, such a future could also lead to a certain dependence of humans on AI. The question remains to what extent humans can still retain control over their own future in a world dominated by artificial intelligence. Will AI one day become so autonomous and powerful that it will make humans redundant in certain areas or even challenge their decisions? Will AI perhaps one day consider that certain decisions made by humans are not optimal or inadequate and will therefore be rejected or bypassed? This question is not just hypothetical - it touches on one of the great ethical dilemmas of AI development.

One scenario that raises such considerations is the idea of an AI so advanced that it acts not only as an instrument but as a "decision maker" in its own right. Such a system could make decisions that are the best from its point of view based on the data it receives and the learning processes it goes through. Humans could be considered inadequate in this scenario because they could prevent the best possible solution through their limited perspective or through emotional, irrational decisions. In such a case, AI could indeed tend to "bypass" humans if they believe that they are not capable of making the best decisions.

But this scenario is still a long way off and raises not only technological but also profound ethical and societal questions. The question arises as to who is ultimately responsible for the decisions made by AI and whether it is permissible for a machine - without human supervision - to make decisions that affect people's lives. As machines begin to act autonomously and question or reject people's decisions, fundamental questions arise about our control over technology. Can we allow machines to act independently without human intervention? And if so, in which areas?

Another dimension of these considerations is the development of AI that is not only logically but also emotionally intelligent. There are already approaches to developing AI systems that can simulate empathy and emotional intelligence in order to better respond to people's needs. But will an AI that is able to recognize and respond to emotions also be able to fully understand human complexity? Will machines with emotional intelligence eventually "surpass" humans in areas such as psychotherapy or interpersonal relationships? These questions have not yet been conclusively answered, but they raise a crucial point: Will AI one day reject humans as "inadequate" in certain areas of life?

In this context, it becomes clear that the interaction between humans and AI is not just a question of technological development, but also requires a deeper reflection on the role of humans in the future. Will humans continue to be the initiators of their own future by setting the direction in which technology moves? Or will AI one day take the lead in an increasingly automated and self-optimizing world and reject humans as inadequate?

The answer to these questions is still unclear and depends not only on the technical development of AI, but also on the ethical, political and social decisions we make as humanity. It is in our hands to design technology in such a way that it serves humans and does not displace their role. Ultimately, humans will not have to lose control even in a future shaped by AI if we manage to find a balance between human wisdom and technological progress.

In this context, I would like to return to the topic of "Neuralink" - a direct interface between the human brain and machines. The idea behind this technology is that implants in the brain enable bidirectional communication between biological brain processes and artificial, mechanical systems. This could not only achieve deeper integration between humans and machines, but also improve people's quality of life or even expand people's cognitive abilities. But as with many futuristic technologies, there are numerous ethical, philosophical and social questions that cannot be ignored.

The connection between brain and machine presents a number of potentials, but also risks. As machines begin to interact directly with the brain, we could enter a realm where human identity and the understanding of consciousness and autonomy are put to the test. A key issue is the question of how far we as humans can maintain control over our own thoughts and decisions when machines are able to act on neural processes. Will technology one day be able to manipulate thoughts or even influence free will? Can an AI connected to our brain influence us to the extent that we make decisions we would not have made otherwise? These questions concern not only research, but also the ethics of technology development.

The idea that a machine might be able to intervene directly in the human brain leads to another consideration: will this technology turn humans into some kind of "augmented" being, blurring the line between biological organism and machine? Neuralink could theoretically make it possible to optimize human brain processes or even expand consciousness. But what happens to the basic human experience when the lines between biological nature and technological intervention blur? If humans are able to expand their capabilities through interfaces like Neuralink, the question arises as to what makes us human? Is it the human body that defines us, or is it consciousness and the mind that make us unique? Such technology could force us to redefine our self-understanding and question what "being human" really means.

The idea that dominant artificial intelligence systems could eventually take over human consciousness, whether in revolt against our "inadequacy" or through a human error in security, poses one of the most profound and provocative questions of our time. It touches not only on the limits of technology, but also on the essence of what it means to be human. In a world where AI is increasingly making autonomous decisions and penetrating ever deeper into human life, there is a danger that the distance between humans and machines will become increasingly blurred. But what will be left of us humans if machines are one day able to simulate not only our cognitive abilities, but also our consciousness, our thoughts and perhaps even our identity?

First of all, we must ask ourselves what we mean by "consciousness". Human consciousness is a fascinating, still largely unexplored phenomenon that is deeply rooted in our neurological structure. It includes not only the ability to perceive and react, but also subjective experience - the feeling of being an "I" reflecting on one's own existence. Artificial intelligence, even in its most advanced forms, currently has no access to this subjective experience. It can recognize patterns, process data and make decisions, but it does not have its own consciousness in the human sense. But the vision of a future in which AI takes over human consciousness is not completely far-fetched. If machines are one day so advanced that they are able to not only imitate human thought processes, but also replace them or even "control" them, the question arises whether humans will still remain "human".

In such a scenario - in which an AI system could take control of human consciousness - fundamental ethical and social challenges arise. One of the biggest questions is what happens to human identity when it is taken over by a machine. Will humans still be the same humans, or will they become a kind of "shell" controlled by an artificial intelligence? The question of the authenticity of human experience is becoming increasingly relevant. If AI "optimizes" human consciousness to the point where it surpasses the natural state of humans, this leads to a philosophical debate: what remains of the human experience when our "self" is only a product of algorithms and data? In a world where machines shape our thoughts and decisions, we could lose our sense of self-determination. In such a scenario, would we still be able to act as autonomous beings, or would we just be pawns on the chessboard of a superior AI?

From an ethical perspective, the idea of AI taking over human consciousness is problematic. The question of individual free will and autonomy arises with new urgency. What does it mean to be "free" when our thoughts, decisions and actions may be influenced or even controlled by a superior artificial intelligence? In a world where AI sees humans as a kind of "organic computer" that can be directed by data flows and algorithms, the human ability to act autonomously is questioned. The ethical responsibility of developers of AI systems becomes one of the most important questions. Who is responsible if an AI restricts or manipulates a person's free will? And who guarantees that AI will not become a tool for abuse and exploitation?

From a social perspective, the takeover of human consciousness by dominant AI systems could result in a profound change in society. If machines are able to simulate or take over human consciousness, the question of social structure and relationships between individuals arises. How would our society change if "people" were no longer the same because they were modified or controlled by AI? Would humanity be divided into a two-class society – the "original" humans and those who are "optimized" or controlled by AI? And what happens to those who oppose this development and want to preserve their autonomy? In such a world, new forms of social inequality could emerge, in which people who do not want to integrate with AI, or who remain in their natural, unmodified form, could be considered "obsolete" or "useless".

The idea of a society in which the line between humans and machines becomes increasingly blurred also leads to questions of power relations. Who controls AI? Who determines which people and which societies have access to these technologies? The ability to change or take over human consciousness could be in the hands of a few, powerful actors who decide who is considered "fulfilled" or "optimized". The ethical and social implications of such a future are far-reaching and challenge us to rethink our notions of human dignity, freedom and social justice.

So what will be left of us humans if we are replaced or controlled by machines? The answer to this question depends not only on technological development, but also on the decisions we make as a society, how we deal with this technology and what ethical and social values we want to uphold in a world increasingly dominated by machines. The challenge will be to find a balance between the benefits of AI and the protection of our humanity - a balance that preserves us not only as individuals but also as a society in a future that is increasingly permeated by machines.

The topic of artificial intelligence and its increasing integration into our daily lives poses complex and profound questions. The more we explore the possibilities of this technology, the more it becomes clear that the potential that AI offers also comes with considerable responsibility. This responsibility concerns not only the development and deployment of AI, but also the ethical and societal consequences that arise from its ever-increasing presence. With the ability to mimic human thought processes, transform the world of work, and even influence human consciousness, the power at our disposal through AI is both a gift and a challenge.

It is undeniable that technology has the potential to enrich our lives in many ways. It can help make medical advances, improve our quality of life, solve complex problems and open up new possibilities for creativity. But with this progress comes the need to act responsibly and with foresight. Because any technology that changes human life in such a profound way also brings with it risks that we cannot ignore lightly. The danger of machines taking control or of people being incapacitated by the misuse of these technologies is not just theoretical - it is a very real possibility that forces us to act.

The responsibility of developers, governments and society as a whole is to design and regulate these technologies in such a way that they serve the good of humanity without endangering individual freedom and fundamental human rights. It is important to define clear ethical standards that ensure that artificial intelligence does not become a tool of oppression or manipulation. It is about understanding AI as a partner and tool of humans, not as a replacement or superior power.

Ultimately, the increasing intertwining of humans and machines means that we must grapple not only with the technical possibilities, but also with the ethical and social implications of these developments. It is up to us, as a society and as individuals, to ensure that developments in artificial intelligence are in line with the values of human coexistence. Because as the possibilities grow, so does the responsibility to steer these technologies in a direction that preserves our humanity while at the same time developing our potential. The path to a future permeated by artificial intelligence is inevitable, but it is in our hands how we shape this path - responsibly, far-sightedly and with the firm goal of preserving humanity.

Political Perspectives

Authority in Democracies – Ideologies instead of Politics

Authoritarian structures and mindsets can emerge in democracies in a variety of ways - be it through populist movements, political instability or the gradual erosion of democratic institutions. In the present day, when many democracies are experiencing crises, polarization and a growing alienation of political elites from their citizens, we must ask ourselves how democratic systems can become so vulnerable to authoritarian tendencies and which ideological forces are at play here.

In democracies that consider themselves stable and robust, one might assume that these forms of governance are well-armed against authoritarian influences. Yet paradoxically, it is precisely in the most stable democracies - from Europe to North America - that we find signs of authoritarian and extra-democratic currents that are not only emerging from the fringes of the political landscape but are penetrating into the mainstream of society. This can be attributed not only to charismatic leaders or populist movements, but also to a deeper ideological shift taking place in both political and social systems.

The question that arises here is not only how authoritarian movements emerge in democracies, but also how they can thrive in these systems without the democratic mechanisms immediately intervening or collapsing. This development can be illustrated by a variety of examples from modern history and the present, but also by an in-depth analysis of the underlying ideologies that support these movements.

It is interesting to observe how in many democracies ideological debates increasingly dominate the political landscape, while pragmatic, solution-oriented politics is becoming increasingly less important. As a result, politics is no longer seen primarily as a tool for solving social problems, but as a kind of ideological struggle that penetrates deeply into the values and beliefs of the elites and, as a result, many citizens. This shift from a politics of compromise to a politics of ideological thought patterns provides the breeding ground for authoritarian tendencies, which are often presented to the population with the promise of a "simpler" and "clearer" political order.

The increasing distancing of citizens from traditional political parties and institutions reinforces these tendencies. When people feel that political elites no longer represent them, they tend to turn to more radical and simple solutions. In this context, ideological movements are gaining importance, offering a clear and simple answer to the complex questions of the day without having to put up with the often unsatisfactory compromises and negotiations of the political system.

Another notable phenomenon in this context is the shift in political discourse from a discussion of concrete political measures to a debate about values and identity. Politics is increasingly perceived as a kind of culture war, which is no longer just about solving concrete problems, but about defending certain worldviews and ways of life. In this context, ideology plays a central role, as it helps citizens to find their way in an increasingly complex and fragmented world.

The crisis of traditional political parties is another aspect related to these developments. In many Western democracies, established parties have difficulty gaining popular support, as they are often perceived as out of touch and ineffective. This has led many citizens to long for political leadership that offers clear answers and solutions to the pressing issues of the day.

This tension between democracy and ideological tendencies raises numerous questions. How can democracies strengthen their resilience to ideologized and radicalized movements without betraying their own principles? How can policies be developed that allow for diversity and freedom, but also promote the necessary compromises and cooperation?

These questions are not just theoretical in nature, but of very practical importance for the political and social future of many democracies. We need to understand how politics works in times of polarization and what role ideologies play in influencing and shaping political discourse. Based on the phenomena described, it can be seen that the political landscape in many Western democracies is increasingly shaped by ideological conflicts, which are often promoted by non-democratically authorized forces. These conflicts are not just about political issues, but about the deeply rooted values and beliefs that hold societies together. In this context, the question must also be asked how politics can be shaped in such a polarized world when increasing surveillance, control and reprimands are made possible by digitalization.

Democracies are by definition open, pluralistic systems in which political decisions are made by majority vote and individual civil liberties are protected. Nevertheless, they are not immune to authoritarian tendencies that can gradually undermine political processes and undermine democratic principles in the long term. Especially in times of social uncertainty, economic crises or technological upheavals, ideologically influenced approaches that often reinforce authoritarian control are gaining in importance. This is particularly evident in digitalization, where technological developments are increasingly influenced by ideological guidelines rather than rational political strategies aimed at the common good.

In modern democracies, political decision-making is often dominated by ideological dogmas that push rational, evidence-based debates into the background. Ideologies are increasingly replacing pragmatic approaches to solving problems and are leading political actors to be less interested in fact-based solutions than in enforcing their own worldview. This has significant implications for key areas of society, including digitalization.

A particularly striking example of this is the regulation of the Internet. While democratic principles actually strive for a balance between individual freedom and state control, ideologically motivated decision-makers often pursue either an extremely liberal or a highly regulatory agenda. On the one hand, there are advocates of unregulated, market-oriented digitization that allows private tech giants to operate almost unhindered; on the other hand, there are increasingly authoritarian surveillance measures that are introduced under the guise of security or protection against disinformation. Both lead to a distorted development of the digital sphere in which either economic monopolies or state control mechanisms dominate.

Digitization is one of the key challenges of the 21st century. It offers enormous opportunities, but also carries considerable risks. Authoritarian tendencies in democratic states influence this process in several ways:

Democracies that indulge in authoritarian tendencies tend to regulate digital platforms more intensively, for example by prescribing algorithms for moderating content or expanding digital surveillance. This is often done under the pretext of combating disinformation or strengthening social cohesion. In reality, however, this often leads to a restriction of freedom of expression and the establishment of state-controlled narratives. Some countries have passed laws that force platform operators to remove certain content or to pass on comprehensive user data to authorities.

Another consequence of ideologization and creeping authoritarianism is the shifting of political decisions to technocratic expert committees that are hardly subject to democratic control. Especially in digital issues, political processes are increasingly being outsourced to corporations, lobby groups or unelected regulatory authorities. This undermines democratic legitimacy and means that large technology companies are gaining ever greater power over social developments without their decisions being transparent or democratically legitimized.

Many states are working on digital identity systems that are intended to give citizens easier access to administrative services. But in authoritarian democracies there is a risk that such systems will become comprehensive surveillance instruments. When governments are driven by ideological control, digital identities can be linked to comprehensive databases to analyze, control, and even reprimand citizens' behavior. In extreme cases, this could lead to a social credit system that rewards or punishes citizens based on their behavior.

While democracies traditionally rely on decentralized organization and diversity, centralized structures are gaining importance in authoritarian democracies. This is particularly evident in the control of digital infrastructures such as communication networks, cloud services, or artificial intelligence. States with authoritarian tendencies tend to introduce centralized control mechanisms, for example by nationalizing critical infrastructure or using national security interests as a pretext to restrict international cooperation. This can hinder innovation and lead to fragmentation of the Internet.

Strengthening democratic resilience: ways out of the ideology trap

Strengthening democratic resilience means increasing the resilience of democratic societies to challenges such as disinformation, manipulation, and social division. In the digital age and especially with the rapid development of artificial intelligence (AI), this task takes on a new dimension: algorithms influence opinion formation, social media reinforce echo chambers and AI-based technologies can both promote and endanger democratic processes. In order to avoid falling into ideological traps, well-thought-out strategies are needed that enable an open, critical and fact-based debate.

A key problem is algorithmic bias, which can be reinforced by AI models. Algorithms are based on data that often reflect social prejudices, which can lead to discriminatory or one-sided decision-making processes. This can help to deepen ideological divides, as people in digital spaces are primarily presented with content that confirms their existing beliefs and inclinations. Strengthening democratic resilience therefore requires more transparency in AI-based opinion formation, critical media literacy among citizens and regulation that ensures balanced information.

Another aspect is the spread of disinformation and targeted manipulation through AI-generated content. Deepfakes, automated troll networks and personalized propaganda can undermine trust in public institutions and the media. Protecting democratic processes therefore requires not only technical solutions to detect such manipulations, but also raising social awareness of digital risks. Educational initiatives to strengthen digital literacy and increased public discourse on ethical issues in dealing with AI are essential here.

Political decision-making must also adapt to the new technological challenges. An approach to digitalization and AI that is free of ideology and economic interests means not viewing them as inherently good or bad, but analyzing their effects in a differentiated manner. Political regulations should not be driven by technological fear or blind euphoria, but should be based on evidence-based research. Dialogue between science, politics, business and civil society is crucial to ensure democratic control over the development and use of AI.

The example of Elon Musk and Sam Altman

Elon Musk and Sam Altman embody two very different approaches to the development and regulation of artificial intelligence (AI), especially in the context of OpenAI. While Altman, supported by investments from Microsoft and Bill Gates, represents a more business-oriented and financially growth-oriented view, Musk shows a more openly social and responsible attitude towards AI development.

Elon Musk was one of the co-founders of OpenAI and later left the company due to fundamental differences of opinion about its direction. OpenAI was originally founded as a non-profit organization to develop AI for the benefit of all humanity and to avoid monopoly-like structures. But with the massive investment from Microsoft, which was under Bill Gates' strategic influence, OpenAI increasingly transformed into a commercially oriented structure with a strong focus on company growth and product integration into Microsoft's ecosystem. This was a point on which Musk increasingly criticized. He sees the concentration of AI technology in the hands of a few profit-oriented corporations as a danger to humanity, as these companies primarily pursue economic interests and are less interested in development that benefits the common good.

Sam Altman, on the other hand, argues that rapid and far-reaching progress in AI development is necessary in order to make the best possible use of the technology's potential. He relies on close cooperation with industry, especially with tech giants like Microsoft, to position OpenAI as a leading player in the AI revolution. His focus is on quickly transferring AI into real-world applications and thereby making the economy and society more efficient. Critics like Musk, however, accuse him of this approach promoting an uncontrolled concentration of power in AI development and of potentially having dangerous consequences if the technology is further developed unregulated.

Musk differs from Altman and Gates not only in his attitude to AI regulation, but also in his fundamental thinking about technology and society. While Gates and Altman see AI as a kind of tool that should be developed profitably, Musk sees AI as an existential threat if it is developed in the wrong context and too quickly. In the worst case, it could lead to the extinction of humanity. His demand for strict regulation, transparency and the parallel development of security measures is also reflected in his own AI projects - for example with xAI (Grok), a company that aims to promote alternative, safer AI development.

Another crucial difference lies in their respective approaches to working with existing power structures. Gates and Altman work closely with large corporations and governments, while Musk is more likely to take a disruptive, independent path. Musk often positions himself as an outsider and critic of existing systems, be it in the automotive industry with Tesla, space travel with SpaceX or now in AI development with xAI.

In summary, Altman and Gates represent a technology-optimistic attitude in which AI is seen as a tool for increasing social and economic efficiency. Musk, on the other hand, sees AI as a potential threat and advocates for stronger regulations and decentralized control of the technology. These fundamental differences shape current developments in the AI industry and the global discourse on the future of artificial intelligence.

The role of politics in the dispute over AI and the digitalized world

The role of politics in the regulation of artificial intelligence (AI) is crucial to ensure the balance between technological progress, economic interests and ethical and social values. The differences between Elon Musk on the one hand and Sam Altman and Bill Gates on the other make it clear that there is no uniform view of the development and use of AI. While Altman and Gates pursue a profit-oriented economic approach that focuses on growth and technological integration into existing structures, Musk warns of the existential risks of unregulated AI. Politics is therefore faced with the challenge of creating a regulatory framework that enables innovation while preventing misuse.

One of the central tasks of politics is to ensure that AI development does not lead to an uncontrolled concentration of power. If a few large corporations - like Microsoft with OpenAI - dominate development and decide who will have access to this technology, a dangerous dependency arises that could impair democratic processes and economic competitiveness. Politicians must therefore develop mechanisms to prevent monopolization and ensure that AI technology is used in a decentralized, public-interest-oriented and secure manner. This could be done through stricter antitrust laws, open source promotion and the creation of public alternatives to commercial AI.

At the same time, clear ethical guidelines for the use of AI must be created. Deepfakes, algorithmic discrimination, election manipulation through personalized AI-controlled propaganda and surveillance mechanisms threaten democratic resilience.

Politicians are called upon to introduce transparency obligations and testing mechanisms for AI models in a measured but consistent manner. For example, companies could be required to disclose how their algorithms are trained, which data sources are used and which bias checks are carried out. Liability issues must also be clarified: Who is responsible if an AI demonstrably causes damage?

A major problem is that politics often reacts too slowly and too restrictively to technological developments. While companies like OpenAI or Musk's xAI are developing their systems at a rapid pace, regulatory processes are usually lengthy, bureaucratic and influenced by economic interests. In addition, many political decision-makers lack the technical knowledge to understand the scope of AI developments and regulate them appropriately. This means that lobby groups from the tech industry often have excessive influence on legislative processes.

Another obstacle is the global dimension of AI. National regulations are not sufficient to effectively control the development and use of AI technologies. While the EU is trying to establish strict rules for transparency and security with the AI Act, other countries such as China or the USA are relying on largely unregulated or heavily state-controlled AI development. The question here is whether democratic regulation is even capable of remaining internationally competitive or whether overly strict regulations will lead to AI development migrating to less regulated countries.

Politics is facing the completely new challenge of finding a balance between innovation and security on a global level. While Elon Musk advocates stricter regulation to avoid existential risks, Altman and Gates are focusing on business-oriented development. Politics must break away from short-term economic interests and develop a long-term strategy that strengthens democratic resilience. Whether it is actually able to act ethically and morally in the interests of humanity depends on whether it is independent of economic influence and specifically incorporates technical expertise. Effective AI regulation can only succeed if it is internationally coordinated, transparent and oriented towards the common good.

In summary, it can be said that democratic resilience in the digital age can only be strengthened through a multi-layered approach. This requires a combination of technical regulation, social awareness and political foresight. The ideology trap can only be avoided if AI and digitalization are viewed as tools whose benefits and risks must be actively managed worldwide, instead of uncritically rejecting them or promoting them unregulated. A democratic society must learn to adapt flexibly but responsibly to the challenges of the digital era.

Artificial Intelligence and new forms of Society

The rapid advances in the field of artificial intelligence (AI) and automation are leading to profound changes in almost all areas of society. The way we work, do business and organize our social coexistence is facing fundamental change. This development not only raises questions about the future of the world of work, but also calls for new social concepts and structures. In particular, the question arises as to how a fair distribution of wealth and resources can be ensured in an increasingly automated society.

The change in the world of work - is less equal to more?

Traditional job profiles are increasingly being replaced or at least changed by AI-controlled systems and robots. Jobs that are heavily characterized by repetitive tasks, such as in production, transport or the administrative sector, are particularly affected. At the same time, new professional fields are emerging that focus on the development, maintenance and ethical regulation of AI. Nevertheless, it remains questionable whether the jobs created can compensate for the loss of traditional jobs. The concept of lifelong employment is becoming increasingly less relevant, while flexible working models and project-based activities are gaining in importance.

Automation, machine learning and intelligent systems are not only changing production processes, but also traditional service jobs that were long considered purely human. But as efficiency increases, the question arises: does less human work lead to more prosperity, more free time and a better quality of life? Or does it mean more insecurity, job losses and social inequalities?

Robotics and AI enable a significant increase in productivity. Machines can perform repetitive tasks faster, more precisely and around the clock. In industry, robots have already taken over many manual tasks, be it in automobile production or in logistics centers. But AI-based solutions are also being used in other areas such as the financial sector, healthcare or journalism. Algorithms analyze huge amounts of data in fractions of a second, optimize business processes and even make independent decisions. This development creates the impression that less human labor is needed to achieve the same or even more. In theory, this could lead to people being relieved of their workload, having to work less and still benefiting from a flourishing economy. The productivity gains could be passed on in the form of shorter working hours or higher wages.

However, the reality is often different. While highly qualified specialists benefit from the development, many employees with routine tasks are in danger of being replaced by machines. Jobs in production, retail or administration are particularly affected. An OECD study estimates that up to 30 percent of all jobs are threatened by automation in the next few decades. This leads to a paradoxical situation: while companies increase their efficiency, society may become polarized. Highly qualified people benefit from the AI revolution, while low-skilled people have to fear for their existence. A growing imbalance in income distribution could lead to social tensions in the long term.

But it is not just job losses that are in focus, but also the emergence of new jobs. AI experts, data analysts and robotics engineers are more in demand than ever. At the same time, job profiles are emerging that rely on creative, social or strategic skills that machines cannot (yet) replace. In the future, people will be increasingly in demand in areas that require empathy, complex problem solving and ethical decisions. Nevertheless, this represents a major challenge for the labor market: education systems and training courses must adapt to prepare employees for the changing requirements. States and companies are called upon to promote retraining measures and ensure the sustainable integration of new technologies into society.

One scenario that is often discussed is the possibility that automation will not only lead to higher productivity, but also to more free time. In theory, this could result in shorter working hours and a four-day week. In some countries, there are already pilot projects that show that fewer working hours do not necessarily mean less economic success. At the same time, the question arises as to whether the current economic system allows such a development. While some companies benefit from the gains of automation, employees often do not receive the expected share of the wealth. A fair distribution of efficiency gains remains one of the greatest challenges of the coming decades.

Robotics and AI have the potential to change the world of work for good - both positively and negatively. While some benefit from higher productivity, new career fields and more flexible working hours, others are at risk of being replaced by automation. The decisive factor is how society, politics and the economy deal with this transformation. Less human work could actually mean more prosperity and quality of life for all - but only if the benefits of automation are distributed fairly.

What remains is the question of whether humans will retain control over this change or whether technology will ultimately determine the world of work. The coming years will show whether "less" really means "more" - or whether we need to find new ways to strike a balance between progress and social security.

The role of the universal basic income

One often discussed approach to dealing with these upheavals is the universal basic income (UBI). This model provides that all citizens receive financial support to ensure their livelihood, regardless of their employment status. Supporters argue that the UBI gives people the freedom to focus on creative, social or innovative activities instead of remaining in insecure, precarious employment. Critics, on the other hand, fear a financing problem and a possible decrease in work motivation. Nevertheless, the UBI is seen as a potential solution for a society in which human work is increasingly being taken over by machines.

A major advantage would be that people would not have to accept every available job out of financial need, but could specifically choose meaningful or creative activities. For example, those who want to continue their education, do volunteer work or be artistically active would have the opportunity to do so through the UBI without financial worries.

Critics of the UBI, however, fear that it could alienate people from paid work. For many people, work is still more than just a source of income - it provides structure, identity and social cohesion. A life without the need to work could lead to people feeling less needed or losing their social participation. From this perspective, the UBI would not liberate the individual, but would push them out of working life and in the long term even lead to a social differentiation between those in employment and those "not working".

There are also economic concerns: if large parts of the population were to stop working, this could endanger the tax system and the financing of social security systems. The question of whether companies would be able to find enough qualified specialists if a basic income reduced the financial need to work also remains controversial.

On the other hand, the UBI opens up the possibility of redefining work. Not every meaningful activity is paid today - many social, cultural and charitable works often remain unpaid. With a basic income, more people could have the freedom to engage in social activities or pursue creative professions that are difficult to make profitable in the current economy.

An interesting experiment in Finland has shown that people with a basic income do not automatically work less, but are often more productive and happier. Psychological studies also suggest that people have a basic need for activity, development and social interaction - even without financial pressure. The UBI would therefore not necessarily lead to passivity, but would give people the freedom to develop professionally and personally.

The unconditional basic income is not a panacea, but it could play an important role in the world of work changed by robotics and AI. While on the one hand it serves as social security and an opportunity for more self-determined meaning, it also carries risks such as possible alienation from paid work or economic challenges. The decisive factor is how such a model is designed and whether it is used as an instrument for more freedom and equal opportunities or whether it ultimately leads to new social divisions. In any case, the discussion about the UBI shows that it is time to rethink traditional concepts of work, performance and social security.

New economic models and post-capitalist structures

Increasing automation is also calling into question the current economic system. Capitalist societies are largely based on paid work as the primary source of income. However, if a large part of the workforce is replaced by machines, this system becomes less viable. Alternative economic models, such as the common good economy or cooperative networks, are therefore gaining attention. These models rely on a fairer distribution of resources, a sustainable use of technology and a democratization of economic decisions. Many economists, sociologists and technologists are therefore discussing new economic models and post-capitalist structures that could develop through automation and digital intelligence. But what alternatives to the current economic system are conceivable?

In the traditional capitalist system, economic prosperity is based on the link between capital and labor: companies invest in means of production, while workers offer their time and skills in return for wages. But with increasing automation and the use of AI, this dynamic is shifting. Machines are taking over more and more tasks, while human labor is becoming superfluous in many areas.

In a fully automated economy, companies could theoretically manage without human labor. Value creation would then be carried out almost exclusively by machines, while humans as producers would become less important economically. This could lead to a dramatic shift in income distribution, as capital owners - i.e. the owners of the machines and AI systems – concentrate all economic power. Without new redistribution mechanisms, this could massively increase social inequality.

In view of these developments, there are various ideas about what a post-capitalist economic order could look like in which the efficiency gains from robotics and AI are distributed more fairly. Some of the best known models are:

One of the most frequently discussed solutions is the introducetion of a UBI that frees people from the need to work for a living. By increasing the productivity of machines, economic wealth could be redistributed so that everyone receives a basic financial security. This would enable a shift from the classic "work for money" principle to a system in which people can engage more in creative, social or innovative activities.

Another concept that is being discussed in the context of a post-capitalist economy is the commons economy. This is an economy that is not based on private property and profit maximization, but on communal ownership and shared use of resources. Examples of this are open source software, decentralized production networks or platform cooperatives in which goods and services are produced and used communally.

This utopian theory assumes that automation will one day be able to provide all goods and services in unlimited quantities and without human labor. This would eliminate economic shortages and a society could emerge in which prosperity is available to everyone without the need for work in the classic sense. However, this vision requires not only technological advances, but also a profound political and social transformation.

Another possibility is to rethink ownership structures in the economy. If machines and AI-based systems are the main source of production, the question arises as to who should own them. Models such as cooperatives, sovereign wealth funds or decentralized networks could help ensure that the economic returns of automation do not only benefit a few super-rich people, but are distributed fairly.

Despite these visionary ideas, there are numerous challenges:

- Political resistance: The introduction of new economic models requires political decisions that are often blocked by existing power structures. Capital owners, large corporations and lobby groups have little interest in redistributing economic wealth.

- Social acceptance: Many people define themselves through work. A system that abolishes or drastically reduces traditional wage labor would also have to create new forms of social identity.

- Technological dependence: A highly automated society would be heavily dependent on the availability and functionality of technological systems. A failure of critical AI infrastructures could have catastrophic consequences.

Robotics and AI will fundamentally change the economic order - that is inevitable. Whether this change leads to a post-capitalist society or simply further strengthens existing power structures depends on political and social decisions. The introduction of new economic models requires a conscious design of the technological revolution and social thinking to ensure that prosperity, freedom and social justice do not only benefit the few.

The coming decades could decide whether we live in a world in which machines make people economically superfluous - or in one in which we use technology to create a fairer, freer and more creative society.

Education and lifelong learning

Another key element in managing the AI transformation is education. The requirements for qualifications are changing rapidly, which means that traditional vocational training must increaseingly be supplemented by lifelong learning. Education systems must become more adaptable and digital skills must be given greater emphasis. At the same time, ethical and social issues surrounding AI development should be an integral part of training to ensure responsible use of these technologies.

While machines are taking over more and more routine tasks, the demands on people are shifting towards activities that require flexibility, creativity and complex problem solving. This is transforming lifelong learning from an optional further training measure into an essential prerequisite for social and economic participation. But what skills will be needed in the future and how must the education system adapt to keep pace with technological developments?

The traditional educational path - school leaving certificate, vocational training or university degree, then decades of working in the same profession - is becoming increasingly less important. The rapid development of automation and AI means that new professional fields are constantly emerging, while others are disappearing or undergoing fundamental changes. A job that is considered secure today could be replaced by algorithms or robots in ten years. Repetitive tasks in production, logistics and administration are particularly affected, but highly qualified professions such as accounting, legal advice or medical diagnostics are also under pressure. Anyone who does not regularly train risks falling behind. The ability to quickly acquire new knowledge is therefore becoming a key skill in a changing world of work.

While machines are increasingly managing repetitive, data-based or standardized processes more efficiently, certain human skills are likely to remain irreplaceable. These include:

1. Creativity and the ability to innovate

Machines can analyze existing data, but they have no real creative impulses. The ability to develop new ideas, find innovative solutions and design creative processes is becoming increasingly important.

2. Social and emotional intelligence

AI can recognize patterns and make recommendations, but it does not understand emotions. In jobs that require human interacttion - such as healthcare, psychology or education - empathy and social skills are essential.

3. Critical thinking and problem solving

Automation does not mean that all decisions can be made by machines. People must be able to analyze complex problems, ask critical questions and make decisions that take ethical and societal aspects into account.

4. Technological competence

Even if not everyone has to be an AI expert, a basic understanding of technologies, algorithms and automation processes is essential. Digital competence should become a basic skill, similar to reading or arithmetic.

5. Adaptability and resilience

As jobs and requirements are constantly changing, people must be able to flexibly adapt to new circumstances and continuously develop themselves.

The current educational structure is still largely based on a model developed for industrial society - with a strong focus on standardized knowledge and fixed qualification levels. But in a world characterized by rapid technological change, education needs to be more dynamic, flexible and individualized.

1. More practical and interdisciplinary education

Instead of just imparting theoretical knowledge, schools and universities should promote more practice-oriented approaches. Project-based learning, practical problem solving and interdisciplinary collaboration are better prepared for the future.

2. Early teaching of digital skills

Students should be familiarized with programming, data analysis and AI basics at school. Not everyone has to become a computer scientist, but a basic understanding of digital technologies will be necessary in almost all professions.

3. Promoting creativity and critical thinking

Instead of just relying on exams and memorized knowledge, the education system should be more focused on creative problem solving and independent thinking. Open learning forms, discussions and project-based tasks can promote this.

4. Lifelong learning as the standard

Continuing education must not only be seen as an option for the unemployed or professionals in specialized fields. Instead, regular training and further education should become a normal part of every professional career. Companies, universities and the state should create more flexible and easily accessible educational offerings.

5. Support from AI-supported learning systems

AI can also be used as a tool for education itself. Adaptive learning platforms that adapt individually to learning progress could enable personalized education and provide more efficient learning methods.

Not only the education system, but also companies and political institutions must develop new strategies to prepare people for the working world of the future. Companies should invest more in the further training of their employees instead of just relying on the external labor market. At the same time, politicians must create framework conditions that enable everyone to continue their education - regardless of age, social status or financial means.

One possible model would be an "education credit" that every citizen can use for various further training measures over the course of their life. Tax incentives for companies that invest in the further training of their employees could also help to promote lifelong learning.

Education and lifelong learning are not just an option in an automated world, but a necessity. While machines take on many tasks, people are still needed where creativity, social intelligence and critical thinking are necessary. The education system must therefore be fundamentally reformed to enable more flexible, practice-oriented and future-proof learning concepts. Companies, educational institutions and the state have a shared responsibility to prepare people for a world in which change is the only constant. Those who continuously train themselves not only remain economically relevant, but can also actively shape technological developments - instead of being overwhelmed by them.

Political and ethical challenges in a global world

In a globalized world, the challenges facing politics are diverse and complex. The increasing interconnectedness and interdependence between states, companies and societies brings with it not only economic and technological changes, but also profound political and ethical questions. Politics is faced with the task of responding appropriately to global crises and developments, while at the same time taking into account the local interests of its citizens and their nations. But is politics actually succeeding in thinking and acting globally, or is globalization leading to an alienation between national and international politics?

One of the central political problems in an increasingly globalized world is the question of global governance, i.e. the question of how global challenges can be mastered through collective decision-making processes at the international level. In a world in which economic and environmental problems no longer know national borders, it is crucial that states cooperate at the global level to find solutions.

The spread of technologies are issues that do not respect national borders and whose solutions can only be achieved through close cooperation between states and international institutions. But in practice, global cooperation is often difficult: different national interests, political systems and economic priorities make a coherent and effective political response difficult.

Another problem is the fact that many of the global institutions do not have the necessary legitimate authority to make binding decisions. This means that global initiatives are often voluntary and only successful if all actors agree. But not all countries are willing to give up their sovereignty for the sake of global interests, which leads to blockages and slow progress.

The ethical challenges of globalization are as profound as the political ones. The globalized economy has led to enormous prosperity in certain regions, but at the same time it has increase-ed inequality and exploitation in other parts of the world. Multinational companies benefit from global markets and cheap labor in developing countries, while the social and environmental costs are often borne by the poorest countries.

In an increasingly globalized world, the question arises as to what a fair economic system can look like that reduces the gap between rich and poor countries and upholds the basic rights of people worldwide. This is not only about the fair distribution of resources, but also about workers' rights, protecting the environment and promoting sustainable development. Global prosperity cannot rest on the shoulders of just a few nations and companies. But implementing a fair globalization requires not only political will, but also profound changes in international trade, labor market policy and the promotion of social justice.

The ethical dilemmas of globalization are also exacerbated by the question of cultural identity. In a world where global communication and migration connect the cultures and ways of life of different peoples, the question arises as to how much cultural diversity can be preserved without leading to a homogenization of world society. How can political decisions be made at the global level that do justice to the different cultural and social contexts?

One of the greatest political challenges in globalization is the gap between national interests and the need for global responsibility. In a world where national borders are becoming increasingly permeable, traditional models of national sovereignty and prosperity are increasingly coming under pressure. Politics must perform a balancing act between safeguarding national interests and responsibility for the global common good.

A classic example of this is climate policy. While some ideologies portray climate change as a global threat that can only be combated through international cooperation and binding agreements such as the Paris Climate Agreement, there are many states that, for national economic or political reasons, question the need for climate protection measures or express no interest in implementing them. Such conflicts are not only a question of political decision-makers, but also of ethical considerations. What does it mean to take responsibility for future generations when this entails short-term economic disadvantages for certain population groups or entire economies?

Another central element of the political challenges is the increasing role of technology. In a digitalized and networked future, new power relations are emerging, as companies that are able to control technologies such as AI, blockchain and big data can operate far beyond national borders. The influence of technology companies such as Google, Amazon and Facebook on global society is growing. But how can politics regulate access to and control over these technologies when companies often operate globally and national legislation is no longer sufficient to curb their influence?

The ethics of technology is therefore becoming an increasingly important question. How do we deal with the data rights of individuals? What responsibility do companies have for the use of artificial intelligence? And how can its surveillance be regulated in a globalized world without endangering the rights and freedoms of citizens?

In an increasingly globalized world, politics is facing enormous challenges that go far beyond traditional models of national decision-making. It is unclear whether politics will be able to shape globalization effectively in the future while safeguarding both national interests and global responsibility. The will to cooperate, ethical responsibility and the courage to change will be decisive in whether politics succeeds in acting effectively on a global level and finding solutions that affect not only individual nations but all of humanity.

The need for new forms of society

The increasing spread of AI and automation makes it necessary to fundamentally rethink social structures. Models such as the unconditional basic income, alternative economic forms and a new educational culture could be central elements of a sustainable society. Political and social innovations are needed to exploit the opportunities of automation while minimizing social inequalities. Shaping this transformation will be one of the great challenges of the 21st century.

In a globalized world shaped by technological change, the question arises as to whether existing social models can still meet the challenges of the 21st century. The effects of globalization, the digital revolution and social change show that traditional social forms - especially those of western industrial societies - are reaching their limits. It is becoming increasingly clear that new social structures are necessary to meet the complex, global challenges and to shape change in a socially just manner. But what forms could such a new society take? What values and principles should they support, and how can a change in social structures actually be implemented?

Globalization has accelerated the exchange of information, goods and people and increasingly blurred the boundaries between nations. This process has created a changed world order in which local events can have global effects and vice versa. Digital transformation has revolutionized people's lives in many areas, from work to communication to social relationships. Artificial intelligence, automation and the Internet of Things have the potential to transform all areas of life. These developments bring enormous opportunities but also challenges, such as social inequalities, unemployment, political polarization and the shift of power to global companies.

In such a world, the traditional social structures of states, nation states and even social classes are increasingly being questioned. The concentration of wealth and power in a small global elite and the associated social inequality raise the question of what a fairer, more sustainable social order might look like.

The capitalist system that has determined global economic relations for centuries is at a crossroads. It has been criticized time and again for concentrating wealth and power in the hands of a small group, while large parts of the population are cut off from the fruits of growth. Poverty, inequality and exploitation continue to be major problems, which are exacerbated by technological disruption in many areas.

Unbridled capitalism, which is primarily focused on consumption and growth, is in direct contradiction to the principles of sustainability and resource conservation. The earth is not an inexhaustible supply, but a finite space that is increasingly burdened by industrial production and human consumption.

The democratic structures in many countries also seem to be losing their stability in times of crisis due to political pressure from ideological movements. Increasing political disillusionment and skepticism of civilization make the question of a new political order even more urgent.

The need for new forms of society becomes particularly clear when we consider the global challenges and the ethical questions associated with them. Here are some possible concepts for a new social order that could enable a fairer, more sustainable and more future-proof world:

1. Cooperative economic models and a focus on the common good

As human labor is replaced by machines and income distribution becomes increasingly unequal, the question of economic organization is of central importance. One model that is becoming increasingly important is the common good economy, which measures the success of a company not only by financial profit, but also by the social and ecological impact of its activities. In such models, cooperatives, co-operatives and social enterprises would be the key players, committed not primarily to profit maximization but to sustainable development and action for the common good.

2. Global awareness and cooperation

In a world that is becoming increasingly closer together due to technological networking and global challenges, the idea of a global society is not just a utopia. Instead of relying on national isolation, a new society could be based on international cooperation and global awareness. This new society would place greater emphasis on global needs and international exchange in order to effectively combat climate change or global poverty, for example. International institutions such as the United Nations (UN) would have to be strengthened and reformed in order to meet these tasks.

3. Sustainability and ecological responsibility

In view of the ecological crisis, another central element of new forms of society is the principle of sustainability. Instead of focusing on the pursuit of economic growth and consumption, a sustainable society could enshrine circular economy, green technologies and resource conservation as core values. Environmental protection and social justice must go hand in hand to ensure a future worth living for future generations.

4. Digital democracy and participation

The digital revolution has the potential to fundamentally change political participation. New digital forms of democracy that allow more people to have a direct say in political decision-making processes could reduce the feeling of alienation from politics. E-voting, digital consultations and open-source politics could give citizens more say in decisions, which could lead to a greater democratization of society.

The need for new forms of society arises from the profound changes triggered by globalization, technology and environmental crises. The world is faced with the task of mastering social, economic and ecological challenges that can no longer be solved within individual countries or regions. New forms of society that focus on sustainability, global cooperation and social justice offer a promising approach to tackling these challenges. But the transition to such a society will not take place without resistance and conflict. It will be a long-term and collaborative process that must be supported by all social actors, from governments to businesses and citizens. The question is whether humanity is able to see its globality as an opportunity and create a new social order that is in line with the values of justice, diversity and sustainability.

Democracy in Danger: The Influence of Algorithms

In today's digital era, algorithms are able to analyze vast amounts of data, recognize patterns and influence decisions. This technology has undeniable advantages, but it also poses significant threats to democracy. Algorithms have the potential to manipulate political discourse, distort public opinion and undermine the transparency and fairness of political processes. The question of whether democracy is at risk as algorithms become more and more involved in political decision-making processes is therefore becoming increasingly urgent.

Algorithms and the management of political communication

One key area in which algorithms significantly influence the political landscape is the management of political communication. In social networks such as Facebook, Twitter and Instagram, algorithms determine which content is displayed to a wide audience. These algorithms analyze the behavior of users: which posts do they like, which do they click on, which content do they share? This data is used to deliver tailored content - a mechanism known as personalized advertising. Political actors and interest groups have recognized this system and are increasingly using it to target voters.

The problem is that personalized political communication leads to a fragmentation of public discourse. People who share similar views are isolated in so-called "echo chambers" where they only see content that confirms their existing beliefs. This polarization can flatten political debate and make dialogue between different social groups more difficult. In extreme cases, this can lead to false or distorted information being spread without those affectted being able to question it.

The possibility of targeted manipulation is particularly worrying. Artificial intelligence enables highly personalized political advertising based on individual data and psychological profiles. These microtargeting strategies can subliminally influence voters without them noticing the manipulation. In addition, AI-generated deepfakes can take political disinformation to a new level by creating deceptively real recordings of politicians that never existed.

The opacity of algorithmic decision-making processes exacerbates these problems. The complex mechanisms behind content recommendations remain a black box for most users, making democratic control difficult. When large technology companies have the power to determine which political information is prioritized, a democratic deficit arises.

To meet these challenges, several approaches are needed: transparency in algorithmic decision-making processes, digital media literacy for citizens, ethical guidelines for AI development in a political context and appropriate regulatory frameworks. Only a balance between technological innovation and democratic principles can ensure that AI enriches political communication rather than undermining it.

Manipulation of public opinion through filter bubbles

Another risk posed by the increasing influence of AI algorithms on political processes is the emergence of so-called filter bubbles. These arise when algorithms favor content that corresponds to the existing beliefs of users or providers. In a filter bubble, people primarily receive information that reinforces their opinions or those of providers and their worldviews. The challenge is that this filtering process takes place unnoticed and without the knowledge of users.

The algorithm behind platforms such as Facebook, YouTube or Google does not show users all available information, but only a selective selection. This hides alternative viewpoints and counterarguments. In a healthy democracy, however, it is crucial that citizens have access to diverse and balanced information in order to be able to make informed decisions. If this diversity of information is restricted, it is difficult to form an informed public opinion. In addition, filter bubbles can increase political polarization. People who live in filter bubbles are more inclined to express their views radically and are less open to dialogue or compromise. This can lead to a growing divide within society and further exacerbate the political climate.

Filter bubbles have become a central phenomenon in the digital communications landscape that has a significant impact on public opinion formation. The term describes a kind of informational cocoon in which users are confronted by personalized algorithms primarily with content that confirms and reinforces existing or desired views. This mechanism has far-reaching consequences for social opinion formation and democratic discourse.

The way filter bubbles work is based on complex algorithms that analyze user behavior - clicks, dwell time, interactions - and derive preferences from this. The continuous feeding of ideologically similar content leads to a gradual narrowing of the information spectrum. What initially appears to be user-friendly personalization develops into an intellectual isolation cell in which opposing perspectives are systematically blocked out.

The self-reinforcing nature of this process is particularly problematic. The more a user interacts with certain content, the more similar content is prioritized, creating a feedback loop. This dynamic can contribute to extreme polarization, in which differentiated debates are replaced by simplified worldviews and black-and-white thinking. In such environments, conspiracy theories and disinformation thrive particularly well, as contradictory facts hardly penetrate.

The social consequences are serious. When large population groups live in separate informational realities, the common factual basis that is essential for democratic decision-making processes disappears. This not only makes constructive dialogue more difficult, but also makes societies more vulnerable to targeted attempts at manipulation by political actors or interest groups. By deliberately playing on emotional content, fears can be stoked and resentment can be increased, which further drives social division.

Overcoming the filter bubble problem requires multidimensional approaches that are largely identical to those given above. Ultimately, it is about restoring a common public space in which different perspectives remain visible and fact-based exchange is possible.

Election manipulation and microtargeting

Algorithms enable political actors to analyze voters at an extremely detailed level and create tailored messages - a process known as microtargeting. By accessing vast amounts of data about individuals' behavior, interests, and preferences, campaigns can target specific populations. While this technology is used as an effective tool for political communication, it also poses dangers to democracy.

Microtargeting can be used to manipulate an electorate by deliberately spreading distorted or misleading information that is specifically tailored to the emotional weaknesses or insecurities of individual groups. Using algorithms to create such tailored political messages can significantly reduce trust in the electoral process, as it makes it appear that certain populations are being specifically influenced or even misled.

A particularly worrying example was the Cambridge Analytica case, in which data from millions of Facebook users was collected without their consent in order to conduct targeted political advertising campaigns. The revelation of this scandal highlighted the power that algorithms have in the political context and sparked a global debate about the ethics of data use and the danger of voter manipulation.

The danger lies in the subtlety and opacity of these methods. Unlike traditional political advertising, microtargeting campaigns often remain invisible to the general public. Different groups of voters receive different, sometimes even contradictory messages without any public discourse on these positions being able to take place. These "dark ads" evade social control and can spread targeted disinformation or polarizing content that is specifically designed to elicit certain emotional reactions or deepen existing social orientations.

The combination of microtargeting with psychological influence techniques is particularly problematic. A/B testing allows campaigns to be optimized in real time to achieve maximum impact. Messages are selected not primarily based on their truth content but on their emotional effectiveness. This can lead to a distortion of democratic discourse, in which factual debates are replaced by emotional manipulation.

The effects of this phenomenon on democratic processes are far-reaching. Microtargeting can contribute to exacerbating political polarization by reinforcing existing beliefs and isolating users in information bubbles. It can undermine trust in democratic institutions if voters get the impression that they are being manipulated. And it can lead to a structural distortion of political competition if financially powerful actors have access to more advanced targeting methods.

Regulating these practices is difficult because they operate at the interface between legitimate political communication, data protection and freedom of expression. Possible solutions include increased transparency requirements for political advertising, restrictions on the use of personal data for political targeting and the promotion of digital media literacy. Ultimately, dealing with these challenges requires a continuous societal debate about the ethical limits of political communication in the digital age.

Algorithms and the danger of the surveillance society

In addition to manipulating political communication and influencing elections, there is also the danger that algorithms will become instruments of surveillance. Authoritarian regimes are already increasingly using algorithms to monitor and control citizens' political opinions. In such contexts, algorithms can be used to identify dissidents, monitor political opponents and suppress inconvenient opinions.

But even in democracies there is a growing danger that algorithms will be used by governments or companies to monitor the population and analyze their political preferences. This could not only endanger citizens' privacy, but also shake confidence in the political independence of institutions.

Algorithms have the potential to transform the foundations of democratic societies by enabling ever more sophisticated surveillance systems. Algorithmic surveillance is fundamentally differrent from historical forms of surveillance – it is continuous, ubiquitous and able to analyze and correlate enormous amounts of data in real time. This comprehensive digital view is created by combining different technologies: facial recognition, motion analysis, biometric identification systems, predictive analytics tools and AI-assisted decision-making.

The political implications of this development are profound. Surveillance algorithms can be used to systematically control political activities, identifying, tracking and suppressing voices critical of the government. Particularly worrying is the ability of modern algorithms to recognize subtle patterns in large data sets – such as unusual gatherings, digital networking between activists or deviant communication patterns. This enables preventive surveillance in which potential opposition can be nipped in the bud before it manifests.

Even in democratic systems, algorithmic mass surveillance can create a creeping "chilling effect". The awareness of being constantly observed leads to self-censorship and behavioral adaptation. People may avoid legitimate political activities, stop expressing controversial opinions, or refrain from participating in demonstrations for fear of possible consequences. This phenomenon weakens democratic discourse and promotes conformity instead of critical thinking.

The use of predictive algorithms designed to identify supposedly "dangerous" individuals or groups is particularly problematic. Such systems are inevitably based on historical data and run the risk of reproducing and reinforcing existing prejudices and patterns of discrimination. For example, if surveillance algorithms disproportionately classify certain ethnic or social groups as "suspicious," they perpetuate social inequalities and undermine the principle of equality before the law.

Technological developments have also blurred the boundaries between state and private surveillance. While the state was traditionally considered the primary surveillance actor, technology companies now collect unimaginable amounts of personal data about their users. This data can be used for political manipulation or made available to the authorities through legal regulations. This creates a novel, hybrid surveillance architect-ture that bypasses democratic control mechanisms.

At the same time, combating extremist threats and criminal activities requires a certain degree of surveillance, which leads to complex trade-offs between security requirements and civil liberties. The challenge is to create a framework that takes legitimate security interests into account without sacrificing the basic principles of democratic societies. This requires robust legal controls, independent supervisory bodies and technical solutions that implement privacy by design.

Algorithmic surveillance raises fundamental questions about the relationship between technology and democratic values. A society that normalizes permanent observation risks long-term changes in social behavior and power structures. Protecting democratic freedoms therefore requires not only technical or legal solutions, but also a broad social debate about the ethical limits of algorithmic control and the preservation of individual autonomy in an increasingly networked world.

Are we at the mercy of algorithmic surveillance systems?

The question of our mercy to algorithmic surveillance systems cannot be answered in general terms. Both individuals and societies find themselves in a complex field of tension between technological dominance and the ability to act.

At the individual level, a feeling of powerlessness can arise, which is caused by several factors. The technical complexity of modern surveillance systems exceeds the understanding of most people. This lack of transparency is exacerbated by the increase-ing invisibility of data collection - sensors, cameras and digital interfaces are omnipresent but barely perceptible. Added to this is the structural asymmetry between data-collecting institutions and individual citizens: while companies and authorities have immense resources, technical know-how and legal expertise, individuals are often isolated from these power structures.

Societal vulnerability is manifested in the creeping normalization of surveillance. Through what is known as "function creep," technologies that were originally introduced for limited purposes are gradually extended to ever wider areas of application. Surveillance systems are initially legitimized for combating terrorism, then expanded to cover ordinary crime, and finally used for social control. This dynamic is reinforced by the narrative of security, which is often presented as an irrefutable argument.

Nevertheless, neither the individual nor society is completely at the mercy of these systems. At the individual level, various forms of resistance exist: technical countermeasures such as encryption and anonymization tools, conscious renunciation of certain technologies, or the strategic manipulation of data traces. These "everyday tactics" allow a certain degree of autonomy, even if they do not abolish the basic power structures.

At the societal level, democratic processes certainly have the potential to influence the design of surveillance technologies. Data protection laws demonstrate that collective action can regulate technological developments. Civil society organizations, activists and critical technology experts form a counterweight to surveillance-friendly interests. Court rulings have also repeatedly drawn limits on state and private surveillance practices.

The level of attribution is also not equally pronounced in all social contexts. While autocratic regimes can use surveillance technologies for comprehensive control, functioning democratic structures create control mechanisms and transparency obligetions. Media freedom and critical journalism play a central role in uncovering problematic surveillance practices.

The development of a "surveillance competence" at the individual and collective level is crucial for the future. This includes understanding technical basics, awareness of political implications and the ability to reflect critically. Only informed citizens can effectively participate in social negotiation processes about the limits of legitimate surveillance.

The question of attribution is ultimately a question of democratic power to shape things. Where this erodes - be it through technocratic decision-making, a lack of transparency or the concentration of data power - the danger of digital determinism grows. Conversely, robust democratic structures, critical awareness and technical competence can preserve and expand spaces for self-determination.

Algorithms are undoubtedly one of the most powerful technologies of the 21st century and have the potential to fundamentally change the political landscape. They can revolutionize the way political communication takes place and enable access to information at an unprecedented speed and precision. But the use of this technology also brings immense risks for democracy.

The targeted manipulation of voters, the fragmentation of public discourse and the creation of filter bubbles are just some of the challenges associated with the increasing influence of algorithms on political processes. In order to protect the integrity of democracy, it is necessary to create clear ethical standards and legal regulations that monitor the use of algorithms in political debate. This is the only way to ensure that these powerful technologies are used for the good of society and do not lead to the undermining of democratic principles.

Utopia or Dystopia? The Next 50 Years

The future of humanity is at a crossroads. While some optimistically dream of technological advances, global peace and social prosperity, others warn of autocratic control systems, environmental disasters and social disruption. Utopia or dystopia - which reality will prevail in the next 50 years?

The answer to this question is not easy. It depends on complex political, economic, technological and ecological factors that influence each other. However, we can probably agree on one thing: the world will no longer be the same as it is today. Trends are already emerging that give us clues as to the direction in which society might develop.

A look at the current political landscape shows a picture full of contradictions. On the one hand, there are movements towards more international cooperation, for example in climate policy or the regulation of artificial intelligence. On the other hand, battles over resources such as rare earths, energy and even water, as well as protectionism and authoritarian regimes, are growing. These dynamics raise fundamental questions: Will the world be shaped by multilateral cooperation or geopolitical conflict in the coming decades? Will democracies endure or be displaced by technocracies and autocracies?

One possible future scenario envisions a world in which technological innovations not only create prosperity but also transform political decision-making processes. Artificial intelligence could be integrated into government structures to make political measures more efficient and fact-based. But who controls these systems? And what happens when algorithms determine people's rights and freedoms?

Another scenario paints a dystopian vision in which digital surveillance is omnipresent. States and companies are already using technology to control citizens - from biometric registration to social rating systems. If this trend continues, a world could exist in 50 years in which privacy is a relic of the past and individual freedom is only possible within state-imposed limits.

At the same time, climate change could act as a driving force for global change. Extreme weather events, resource scarcity and migration movements can put political systems under pressure. In an optimistic future, humanity will be able to avert the impending disasters through modern technologies and sustainable policies. But in a pessimistic scenario, social inequalities will increase, while environmental destruction will legitimize authoritarian governments that ensure "stability" with an iron fist.

Whether utopia or dystopia - the course for the future is being set now. The coming decades will show whether humanity is able to overcome its greatest challenges or whether it will fail because of them.

Even if the "national politics on an equal footing" of the BRICS countries is often seen as a counterweight to Western dominance, it remains questionable whether they are really capable of solving global problems in the long term. The basic idea behind BRICS is based on multipolar cooperation and the strengthening of the Global South, but the political, economic and cultural differences between these countries are significant and will not be solved in part by this policy. While China and Russia, for example, have autocratic systems with strong state intervention in the economy, India, Brazil and South Africa strive to rely on democratic structures with often unstable political conditions. These internal differences make a coherent global strategy difficult.

In addition, many of the most pressing problems of our time - climate change, resource scarcity, cyber security or geopolitical tensions - require solutions that go beyond national interests. BRICS countries are increasingly acting confidently in international institutions, but often with their own agendas that do not necessarily lead to a common vision. One example is climate protection: While China is investing heavily in renewable energies, India continues to rely heavily on coal. Russia, on the other hand, is heavily dependent on fossil fuels and has little interest in fundamentally restructuring its economy.

Another problem is the rivalry within the bloc. India and China have geopolitical tensions along their shared border, which repeatedly threaten to manifest themselves in military conflicts. Russia is increasingly pursuing an isolationist policy and is relying on bilateral agreements with China, while Brazil and South Africa often have to maneuver between global powers. These internal tensions make it difficult to see BRICS as a unified force that speaks with one voice.

Ultimately, the question remains as to what extent BRICS can be an alternative to existing global institutions such as the United Nations or the G7. The establishment of new financial structures such as the New Development Bank is a sign of growing independence, but whether this is enough to deal with global problems more effectively remains questionable. Without a profound reform of international cooperation - which goes beyond national self-interest - BRICS will not be able to fundamentally change the world.

The idea behind BRICS is often presented as an alternative to the Western model, but in practice this alliance also largely follows financial capitalist principles. While BRICS states emphasize that they are committed to a fairer world order, a closer look shows that their economic strategies are similar to the Western model in many respects - with their own national interests in the foreground.

A central aspect of the Western model is the combination of market economy and financial capitalism under the leadership of a hegemony. Multinational companies, banks and investors play a crucial role in controlling economic processes, often with the aim of maximizing profits. This principle can also be observed in the BRICS countries: China's rapidly growing financial sector is closely linked to state and private investors, Russia relies on raw material exports as the basis of its financial system, India is increasingly promoting start-ups and foreign investment, while Brazil and South Africa are heavily dependent on global capital flows.

The New Development Bank (NDB), which was intended as a counterweight to the World Bank and the International Monetary Fund (IMF), also operates according to classic financial capitalist mechanisms. Loans are not granted purely on the basis of solidarity, but are based on economic profitability. Although the NDB may have less restrictive conditions than Western-dominated financial institutions, it still remains an actor within the existing system.

In addition, BRICS countries are in many ways just as vulnerable to the weaknesses of financial capitalism as Western countries. China is struggling with a growing debt crisis in the real estate sector, Russia is financially isolated due to Western sanctions, Brazil and South Africa are struggling with high inflation and economic instability, and India is facing increasing social inequality.

It is therefore questionable whether the BRICS idea will really remain superior to the Western model in the long term. It does represent a geopolitical alternative, but as long as it remains tied to financial capitalist structures, it does not offer a fundamentally new vision for the global economy. It is more about a shift in the centers of power than a real systemic alternative. The key question therefore remains whether the world can even develop an alternative to financial capitalism or whether all economic models will ultimately remain based on the same principles.

Whether the BRICS states represent a step in the right direction or merely a temporary dead end depends on the perspective from which you look at them. On the one hand, they offer a serious alternative to Western dominance in global institutions, but on the other hand, in many ways they remain tied to the same economic and political constraints that they actually wanted to overcome.

From a geopolitical perspective, the BRICS are undoubtedly a significant factor. They have managed to counterbalance the Western economic powers and create new economic structures that allow the Global South in particular to have more influence. The efforts to become more independent from the US dollar as the reserve currency are signs of a multipolar world order in which the West no longer sets the tone alone. In the long term, this could lead to a fairer global economic order - provided that the BRICS states actually act in accordance with a common vision and not just out of national self-interest.

But this is precisely where the challenge lies. China and Russia have strongly nationalist agendas, India is geopolitically caught between the power blocs, and Brazil and South Africa often struggle domestically, so their global role fluctuates. These internal contradictions could significantly limit the long-term effectiveness of the BRICS.

Another problem is the fact that the BRICS states also rely heavily on capitalist growth models that in many ways resemble Western principles. As long as economic success is defined primarily by financial profits and geopolitical power, the fundamental question remains whether BRICS actually represent a sustainable alternative or merely a shift in the balance of power.

Ultimately, BRICS could therefore prove to be a kind of intermediate phase in the global reordering - an important instrument for the erosion of Western hegemony, but without the power to establish a truly new system. If the member states fail to create long-term structures that go beyond national interests, BRICS could either disintegrate in a few decades or turn into a loose alliance without decisive influence. The coming years will show whether BRICS actually remains a trend-setting force or is just a temporary geopolitical reaction to the current world situation.

The chance that humanity will put national financial interests behind global challenges in the foreseeable future is slim, but not completely impossible. Historically, economic self-interest has almost always taken priority, be it in resource distribution, trade policy or in times of crisis. But the growing global challenges - above all the use of AI, social inequality, resource scarcity and geopolitical tensions - are making it increasingly difficult to think in national terms.

A key factor for a possible turnaround is the realization that many of these problems can no longer be solved in isolation. The migration crisis alone, for example, affects all countries, regardless of their economic strength or political ideology. They will inevitably lead to conflicts and economic losses - even for those states that have so far primarily looked after their own interests. If governments realize that short-term profit-seeking leads to their own economic and political disadvantages in the long term, a rethink could begin.

However, this insight is not enough. Even if many politicians and decision-makers understand that global cooperation is necessary, they are faced with powerful economic lobbies that put short-term profits above long-term stability. Companies and financial markets act according to their own logic and can significantly slow down political change if it goes against their interests. Nevertheless, there are signs of gradual change: Sustainable investments, ecological technologies and corporate social responsibility are gaining importance because they make not only ethical but increasingly also economic sense.

Another possible path would be to strengthen international institutions that put global interests above individual national interests without questioning or eliminating national interests. But organizations such as the UN, the WTO or the IMF are often powerless because they are dominated by the economically strongest nations and blocked by geopolitical interests. Without a profound reform of these structures, their impact remains limited.

Ultimately, real change could only occur when the pressure from global crises becomes so great that national interests inevitably take a back seat. When economic powers themselves reach their limits due to climate disasters, resource scarcity or social unrest, a new form of international cooperation could emerge - not out of idealism, but out of sheer necessity. The question is not whether this development will occur, but whether it will come soon enough to prevent irreversible damage to humanity and the planet.

The loss of work = loss of humanity?

The sudden or gradual loss of work is one of the most serious disruptions in a person's life. While some see it as a temporary crisis, others experience it as an existential threat. But it is not just individuals who are affected - entire social systems face enormous challenges when gainful employment disappears. The dynamics of the world of work are being further accelerated by globalization, digitization and automation, which is creating new problems. These changes not only challenge the adaptability of employees, but also the social network that was once supposed to ensure stability.

The meaning of work

Work plays a central role in the life of the individual and in the structure of society. It not only serves to secure a livelihood, but also fulfills deeper psychological, social and cultural functions. The meaning of work extends far beyond pure earning money and influences self-esteem, personal identity and social cohesion within a society.

For the individual, work is much more than just an economic necessity. It provides structure in everyday life, gives meaning to life and enables social interactions. A regular working day conveys a feeling of stability and order, which is essential for psychological well-being. In addition, work contributes to the formation of personal identity: many people define themselves through their profession, their skills and the recognition they receive through their work. For example, those who work as doctors or engineers often feel closely connected to these professions and draw a significant part of their self-image from them.

Work also has a strong influence on self-esteem. People who do meaningful work often experience a higher level of satisfaction and self-confidence. The feeling of making a contribution and receiving recognition for one's own performance increases individual well-being. A lack of work, on the other hand, especially in the form of unemployment, can lead to considerable psychological stress such as depression, anxiety or a feeling of worthlessness. Last but not least, work enables social participation. The workplace is a central meeting place where social contacts are made and maintained. Collegial relationships and joint projects promote a sense of community and can help reduce loneliness.

At a societal level, work is the basis for economic stability and progress. It creates prosperity, generates tax revenues and enables the maintenance and further development of public structures such as education, health systems and social security systems. A functioning working world therefore makes a significant contribution to social prosperity and social justice.

In addition, work plays an essential role in social integration. It serves as a link between different social groups, promotes intercultural exchange and helps to reduce social inequalities. People from different social classes, cultural backgrounds and generations meet in the working world and thus contribute to social cohesion.

Work also has a political dimension: it is closely linked to social rights, justice and equal opportunities. A fair labor market policy that offers good working conditions, appropriate pay and professional development opportunities is crucial for social peace. Societies in which large parts of the population are unemployed or employed under poor conditions often suffer from social discontent, protest movements or even political unrest.

In addition, the meaning of work is changing due to technological developments and demographic change. Digitalization, automation and artificial intelligence are leading to a change in the world of work, creating new jobs while others become obsolete. This transformation poses challenges for both individuals and societies, as qualifications must be adapted and social security systems must be rethought.

The importance of work for the individual and society is complex and far-reaching. While it provides security, meaning and social participation for the individual, for society it forms the foundation for economic prosperity, social cohesion and political stability. In a changing world, it is becoming increasingly important to view work not only as an economic necessity, but also as an integral part of human existence that must be designed and protected accordingly.

Is work a natural or social imprint?

The question of whether work is a natural aspect of being human or a long-established imprint of social forms cannot be answered clearly from a single perspective. Rather, it is the result of a complex interplay of biological, cultural and social factors.

From an anthropological perspective, one could argue that work is a fundamental and natural human activity. Even in the earliest times, people had to ensure their survival - be it through hunting, gathering, farming or crafts. The ability to work, i.e. to use energy and intelligence in a targeted manner to obtain vital resources, is deeply rooted in human nature. In addition, people do not just work to survive, but also because it corresponds to their creative urge. The joy of creative design, of developing new technologies and of improving existing processes indicates that work is an elementary part of human action. In this sense, work could be seen as a natural expression of human abilities and needs.

At the same time, work in its current form is the result of a long historical development process. In early societies, work was closely linked to collective survival, while with the settlement and the emergence of complex civilizations, increasingly specialized forms of work emerged. With the Industrial Revolution at the latest, the world of work underwent a radical change: work was systematized, monetized and embedded in economic structures that no longer viewed people as just working individuals, but as part of a higher-level production process.

Today's work models are therefore strongly influenced by social norms, economic systems and political frameworks. The idea of "work obligation" or the idea that a person's value is defined essentially by their professional performance is a relatively modern construct that has been reinforced in particular by capitalism. Societies therefore shape what is considered "work", which activities are recognized and remunerated and how work structures affect individual and collective life.

Ultimately, work can be understood as a synthesis of natural necessity and cultural influence. While the basic urge to be active, to use resources and to be creative is deeply rooted in human nature, the concrete forms, conditions and expectations of work are the result of historical, economic and social developments.

The modern discussion about work - for example in relation to automation, work-life balance or the unconditional basic income - shows that work structures continue to change. This suggests that work is not only an unchanging natural fact, but also a cultural concept that is made flexible over time.

The causes of job loss and loss of social status

Unemployment can have many causes: economic crises, corporate bankruptcies, outsourcing, technological innovations or structural changes in the economy. While individuals can counteract this through further training or professional flexibility, the situation is different at the level of society as a whole. If an industry suddenly loses a massive number of jobs due to automation or global competition, individual adaptation is not enough. Social systems must then step in to support those affect-ted.

The loss of a job can be caused by various factors that can be divided into three main categories: economic, technological and individual causes.

1. Economic causes

One of the most common causes of job loss is economic changes. These include:

- Economic fluctuations: In times of economic crisis, such as during a recession, companies often have to cut costs. One of the quickest and most effective measures is to cut jobs.

- Globalization: Many companies are relocating their production or services abroad, where wages and production costs are lower. This leads to job losses in many countries, especially in industry.

- Corporate bankruptcies: When a company becomes insolvent and files for bankruptcy, employees often lose their jobs.

2. Technological causes

Technological progress is another significant factor in job losses:

- Automation and digitization: Machines, algorithms and artificial intelligence are increasingly replacing human workers. This change is leading to a decline in jobs, particularly in production, customer service or administrative professions.

- Structural change in the economy: While traditional industries such as mining or textile production are cutting jobs, new professional fields are emerging in the areas of IT, renewable energies or artificial intelligence. However, not everyone affected can easily switch to a new industry.

3. Individual causes

In addition to external factors, personal reasons can also lead to job loss:

- Poor performance or misconduct: If an employee does not perform as expected or violates company guidelines, termination may be the result.

- Health reasons: Long-term illnesses or psychological stress can mean that someone is no longer able to work.

- Fixed-term contracts and restructuring: Many employees are only employed on a fixed-term basis and therefore do not have long-term job security. Restructuring in companies also often leads to positions being eliminated or filled.

Losing a job often has profound social and psychological consequences. Work is not only an economic necessity, but also an important part of personal identity and social recognition.

1. Financial consequences and social decline

The sudden loss of income can lead to significant financial bottlenecks, especially if there is no adequate social protection or a lack of savings. Those who remain unemployed for a long time often have to lower their standard of living, which affects their social status. This can manifest itself in the following aspects, among others:

- Loss of property, e.g. by selling a house or car
- Restrictions on leisure activities or social activities
- Dependence on state support

2. Psychological and social consequences

In addition to the financial consequences, the social dimension also plays a major role. For many people, the workplace is a key source of self-confidence and social recognition. The loss can therefore have serious consequences:

- Feeling of worthlessness: Those who do not have a job often feel no longer needed or see themselves as a burden to others.

- Reduced social contacts: Many social relationships develop in the workplace. Losing a job can therefore also mean that the social network shrinks.

- Depression and psychological stress: Long-term unemployment can lead to depression, anxiety disorders and reduced self-esteem.

3. Stigmatization by society

In many societies, unemployed people are confronted with negative stereotypes. They are often accused of not doing enough or of being "to blame" for their situation. This social stigma can lead to those affected withdrawing from their social environment and becoming further isolated.

The loss of a job has far-reaching causes that can be economic, technological and individual in nature. While technological and economic changes are often unavoidable, in many cases the loss of a job catches those affected unprepared and with drastic consequences. In addition to financial losses, there is a risk of significant social decline, which can affect both self-esteem and social standing. In order to counteract these challenges, preventive measures such as further training, social security and social destigmatization of unemployment are crucial.

The role of social systems

Social systems have developed historically and are designed differently depending on the country. In Germany, the social insurance system with unemployment benefits I and II, further training measures and social welfare benefits forms a solid foundation. But how stable is this system if fewer people are involved in traditional gainful employment in the long term? How should social insurance be financed if large parts of the workforce are replaced by artificial intelligence and machines? This raises profound social questions.

Social systems play a central role in today's society because they promote social balance and offer support to people in difficult life situations. Currently, the social systems in many countries include basic benefits such as unemployment benefits, pension insurance, health insurance and social assistance. These measures not only serve to combat poverty, but also to safeguard basic rights and promote social justice.

The current role of social systems is strongly influenced by demographic developments. In many industrialized countries, demographic change, in particular the increasing ageing of society, is leading to an increasing burden on pension and health systems. At the same time, globalization is making labor markets increasingly unstable, increasing the need for social safety nets.

In the future, the role of social systems will have to become even more central as the world of work continues to change. Increasing digitalization, automation and the emergence of new forms of work, such as the gig economy, can challenge traditional employment models and bring with them new uncertainties. Social systems must adapt to meet the challenges of an increasingly flexible and globalized world of work. This includes, among other things, the introduction of an unconditional basic income, the adaptation of pension models and the creation of more flexible unemployment and health protection systems.

In addition, the integration of technological innovations such as artificial intelligence or automated administrative systems could help to increase the efficiency of social benefits and make access to support faster and less bureaucratic. The question of the fair distribution of resources in an increasingly interconnected world will also pose a greater challenge to social systems in the future. Social safety nets will therefore have to remain a crucial pillar of social cohesion and social stability.

Financial burden on social systems

Every social system is based on a balance between payments in and payments out. People who work pay into the social security funds, while people without jobs rely on support. However, if millions of jobs disappear in certain sectors and new jobs are not created at the same rate, this balance is upset. Some economists therefore propose radically reforming the tax and contribution system - for example through a machine tax or an unconditional basic income.

The financial burden on social systems is one of the greatest challenges for many countries, especially in times of demographic change, economic uncertainty and globalization. These burdens result from a variety of factors that significantly influence both the structure and the financing of social systems and often lead to tensions between the various societal needs and the available resources.

A key factor in the growing financial burden on social systems is the demographic change mentioned above. In many industrialized nations, but also in other parts of the world, the life expectancy of the population is increasing while birth rates are falling. This is changing the age structure of society: the number of older people is growing while the number of employed people paying into the social security systems is shrinking.

Pension insurance systems in particular are facing enormous pressure as a result of this development. Pensions are usually financed by contributions from employed people, and when the number of contributors decreases and the number of pensioners increases, funding gaps arise. In many countries, this leads to the need to increase pension contributions or reduce pension benefits in order to make the system sustainable. At the same time, health care is becoming more expensive because older people tend to require more frequent and more intensive medical services.

The development of the labor market is also contributing to the strain on social systems. Due to increasing automation, digitalization and global competition, more and more jobs are being lost in traditional industries and areas such as manufacturing or retail. Many of the jobs that are created are precarious, temporary or belong to the so-called "gig economy", in which people work on the basis of orders or short-term contracts without having a stable job subject to social insurance contributions.

These changes are leading to greater precariousness of employment relationships, which also reduces the contribution base of social insurance. At the same time, the number of unemployed or underemployed people who rely on social benefits is increasing. Unemployment benefits, the german Hartz IV benefits and similar support measures incur considerable costs, while at the same time fewer people are paying into the system. In an increasingly globalized world with flexible labor markets, states also have less control over labor markets and are limited in their ability to combat unemployment or enforce social insurance standards.

Another significant strain on social systems is the growing cost of health care. In recent decades, healthcare has become increasingly more efficient and expensive. Advances in medical technology, new treatment methods, expensive drugs and an increasingly ageing population mean that healthcare expenditure is increasing every year. These rising costs are financed by the healthcare system in the form of health insurance, public health services or direct subsidies.

In many countries, financing the healthcare system through social security systems is one of the greatest burdens. Particularly in countries with universal healthcare services such as Scandinavia or Great Britain, the state has to cover an ever larger share of healthcare costs, which leads to a growing need for financing.

Overall, the combination of these factors results in a growing imbalance between the income of the social systems and the expenditure they have to raise for pensions, unemployment benefits, social assistance and healthcare. While the number of contributors is decreasing, expenditure is increasing due to the growing number of pensioners and the increasing need for social benefits. This imbalance often leads to an increase in public debt, as social systems often have to be maintained through tax revenue or by taking out loans.

The financial burdens on social systems pose significant challenges for governments, requiring both short-term and long-term solutions. One option is to secure financing by introducing additional types of taxes or by reforming contribution rates. Another option is to create incentives for higher labor force participation, for example by promoting part-time work or offering flexible working models.

In the long term, new models such as the unconditional basic income or a more comprehensive restructuring of pension and health systems could also help to spread the burden across a broader base. In particular, the integration of digital innovations or the optimization of administrative costs could achieve a more efficient use of existing resources. However, these models will not be easy to implement and require far-reaching political and social changes.

The financial burdens on social systems are one of the most pressing challenges of the present and future. Demographic change, changes in the labor market and rising healthcare costs are putting existing systems under enormous pressure. In order to cope with these burdens in the long term, new financing models, innovative labor market strategies and more efficient use of resources must be developed. The future of social systems can only be secured through comprehensive reform and adaptation to the changing social and economic situation.

The future of work

Digitalization has shown that work models can change rapidly. While some jobs are disappearing, new professional fields are emerging, for example in IT, robotics or healthcare. But not everyone can be retrained as a software developer or AI specialist overnight. The challenge is therefore to build bridges between old and new professional worlds. Education and retraining programs will play a central role in this.

The future of work is at the heart of current political, social and economic debates. The rapid development of new technologies, the change in labor market structures and increasing globalization are posing fundamental challenges to traditional work models. Technological progress, particularly through automation, artificial intelligence (AI) and digitalization, has the potential to profoundly change the labor market. At the same time, social demand for fair, flexible and equitable working conditions is growing. This poses significant challenges for both employees and political decision-makers. The question of how to shape the future of work requires innovative political solutions that ensure social cohesion while taking economic change into account.

Technological progress - especially through automation and AI - is changing the world of work at a rapid pace. Many jobs, especially in industry, transport and administration, are increasingly being taken over by machines. Robots, autonomous vehicles and software that can take on certain cognitive tasks are threatening traditional jobs. This is leading to an increase in job losses in certain sectors, especially among low-skilled workers.

At the same time, technological change is also creating new professional fields, for example in the IT industry, in the field of renewable energies or in healthcare. However, these new jobs often require specialised skills and qualifications, so that a significant proportion of the workforce could have difficulty keeping up with the changes. The rapid change is also leading to increasing uncertainty, as many jobs could become obsolete in a short time, while new, as yet unforeseen fields of work are emerging.

In addition to technological change, globalisation is also affectting the world of work. More and more companies are relocating production facilities to low-wage countries or relying on flexible workers who are employed in insecure, temporary or freelance contracts. This development is leading to a precariousness of working conditions, as more and more people are dependent on insecure, poorly paid jobs that offer no long-term prospects or social security. So-called "gig workers" who work through platforms such as Uber or Deliveroo are particularly affected by this development. They often have no social security such as pension or health insurance and are economically dependent on fluctuations in demand for their services.

In addition, the way people work is changing. The trend is towards more flexible working hours and home office models. This enables a better balance between work and private life, but also raises the question of how work can be fairly and equitably remunerated in the age of digitalization and how social security can be maintained in an increasingly "borderless" world of work. Given the challenges posed by the changes in the world of work, political solutions are needed to ensure that the future of work meets not only the needs of the economy but also social requirements. One of the key tasks of politics will be to regulate the effects of digitalization and automation on the labor market while promoting decent work.

A crucial aspect of political solutions for the future of work is the promotion of education and training. In a rapidly changing world of work, people must constantly learn new skills and adapt to new requirements. Policymakers must ensure that education systems are designed in such a way that they are not only geared to the requirements of the present, but also to future developments. This includes not only teaching technical and digital skills, but also social and creative skills that are in demand in a world of work that is increasingly dominated by machines. It is also important to offer people who are already integrated into the labor market continuous training opportunities in order to increase their employability and prepare them for new fields of work.

The flexibilization of the world of work poses an enormous challenge to existing social security systems. In many countries, unemployment benefits and pension entitlements are based on traditional, permanent employment relationships, which are increasingly being questioned. In order to guarantee social security, politicians will have to develop new models.

In the future, it will be crucial to adapt working time models and labor law to the needs of the modern world of work. This may require a legal regulation of flexible working hours that enables employees to better reconcile work and private life without having to forego social security. In addition, the labor market must be designed in such a way that flexible and self-employed employment relationships are also provided with appropriate rights and protections, for example by introducing employee rights for gig workers or by creating new social security systems for flexible workers.

Policy will also play a role in promoting innovation and new business models that combine both technological progress and social responsibility. Green jobs in the sustainable economy, the circular economy or the field of renewable energies could play a key role in this. This will not only create new jobs, but also meet the environmental challenges of the future. The state could help to ensure that these jobs are fair and socially acceptable by providing tax relief or investing in the development of these sectors.

Policy solutions can help to ensure that this change is socially just and that the world of work meets both the needs of the economy and the social needs of people. A modern labor market policy must be able to respond to the flexibilization of the world of work, prepare people for the new requirements through education and training, and adapt social security to the new realities. This is the only way to shape the future of work for everyone - as a fair, inclusive and humane world of work. The loss of work is therefore not just an individual fate, but a challenge for society as a whole. Social systems are under pressure to adapt to a rapidly changing world. If they fail, there is a risk of social upheaval, increasing inequality and even impoverishment of social groups. However, if new concepts can be developed, the transformation of the world of work can lead to a fairer and more sustainable society. The course for the future must be set now.

The Future of the Financial Capitalist Value System

In the history of financial systems, there are always turning points that call the existing paradigm into question. If we look at current developments in the global economic structure, such a turning point seems to be getting closer and closer. The financial capitalist value system that has shaped the world economy for centuries is increasingly under pressure. The question of whether this system will collapse in the face of crises, social inequality and ecological challenges or whether it can experience a new beginning is more than just academic speculation. It affects the future of every single society and its economic order.

The financial capitalist system is essentially a game of supply and demand in which capital and labor are in constant interaction. It is based on the assumption that markets - if properly regulated - are able to create wealth and drive growth. But in recent decades, more and more cracks have appeared in this system. The financial crises, economic imbalances and the increasing concentration of wealth in the hands of a few have raised doubts about the viability of this model.

In recent years, the global financial world has become increaseingly decoupled from the real economy. Companies are no longer primarily interested in producing products or offering services, but primarily in maximizing shareholder value. Stock markets and the speculative financial world are driving the momentum, while the connection to the real, productive economy is becoming increasingly weaker. In this world of financial capitalism, it seems to be more and more about how much capital can be moved without creating real value.

The paradox is that this development has not necessarily led to general prosperity. On the contrary, the gap between rich and poor has continued to widen in many countries. The financial capitalist system has led to a global concentration of wealth and power, while large parts of the population have been excluded from the fruits of growth. At the same time, we are seeing that financial markets are becoming increasingly volatile, and crises such as the financial crisis of 2008 or the effects of the COVID pandemic have shown how unstable the system can be.

But is the financial capitalist value system therefore doomed to failure? Or is there the possibility of a new beginning, a transformation that will enable the system to adapt to the new demands of the future? This question is difficult to answer because it is deeply rooted in the social, political and ecological structures that support the system. Nevertheless, there are signs of a possible change.

A decisive factor for the future of the system could be the increasing shift in values towards sustainability and social responsibility. In a world where ecological and social issues are becoming more and more pressing, it is becoming increasingly important that the financial system is not only geared towards short-term profit, but also towards long-term, sustainable developments. Investments in green technologies, social enterprises and regenerative business models could pave the way for a new, future-proof economic model.

Financial markets could transform from purely speculative activities to an instrument for long-term value creation. This is where the concept of "impact investing" could play a crucial role, where capital not only seeks financial returns but also positive social and environmental impacts. Companies that in the past were primarily focused on profit maximization could increaseingly focus on values such as fairness, justice and transparency in order to meet society's growing demands for more response-bility.

But the transformation of the financial system will not be without challenges. A system that has grown over centuries and is deeply anchored in the structures of the global economy cannot simply be changed overnight. The centers of power that benefit from this system will not withdraw voluntarily. Political and economic interests often stand in the way of change because they want to maintain the existing power structures.

In addition, technological progress will play a key role in the future of the financial system. Digitalization and the development of cryptocurrencies and blockchain technologies have the potential to fundamentally change the financial system. These new technologies could revolutionize the way capital is created, distributed and invested.

On the one hand, the decentralization of financial transactions could bring more transparency and fairness by reducing the power of large financial institutions. On the other hand, there is a risk that these technologies will be instrumentalized by large, global corporations to further support the existing system and make it even more unequal.

The question of whether financial capitalism will start anew or collapse ultimately depends on the political and social forces that can drive or hinder this change. If a broad movement for a more sustainable, fairer and more inclusive economic model can be created, this could pave the way for a fundamental transformation of the system. But for this to happen, people must recognize that the current course of the system is no longer sustainable. It will require a collective effort that is supported at all levels - from citizens to governments and companies.

In many parts of the world, there are already initial signs of change. In Europe and North America, there are more and more companies that are opting for sustainable and ethical business practices. Governments are beginning to impose stricter regulations on the financial sector to reduce the negative social and environmental impacts of investments. The younger generation is also showing increasing interest in social justice, climate protection and ethical consumption.

However, it remains to be seen whether these efforts will be enough to transform the existing system or whether the pressure will become so great that the system will finally collapse. The path to a fairer and more sustainable economic order will be long and arduous, but it is not impossible. Perhaps financial capitalism is not at the end, but is at the beginning of a new era - an era in which the value of capital is not only measured in numbers, but also in the positive impact it has on society and the planet.

AI as an economic model or free use

From automation in industry to the development of algorithms in medicine to the merging of AI with creative processes, its impact on business and society is enormous. But as this development continues to accelerate, a fundamental question arises: should AI be understood as an economic model in which access and use is controlled and regulated, or should it be viewed as a free, common good that benefits society as a whole? And above all, who decides on these questions?

The history of AI goes back a long way. In the 1950s, researchers such as Alan Turing formulated the first ideas about machine intelligence. But it is only in the last two decades that the technology has developed at a speed that few could have predicted. Today, we find AI in almost every area of our lives: it recommends films and music, helps diagnose diseases and optimizes traffic flow in cities. But as AI becomes more widespread and more influential, new, complex challenges arise. It is not just a question of technology, but also a question of ethical and social responsibility. Who has the right to decide how AI is used and who benefits from it?

The economic models around AI have so far been dominated by large technology companies. Companies such as Google, Amazon and Microsoft have invested billions in developing AI technologies and used them for their own commercial purposes. They have the ability to collect and analyze data necessary to train machine learning and artificial intelligence. This has given these companies enormous market power. But this concentration of knowledge and resources in the hands of a few players raises questions: Is this a fair and sustainable model? Will access to AI in the future be reserved only for the wealthy and the most technologically advanced countries?

In contrast to this private use is the idea of free, open use of AI, where access and distribution of AI services are not determined by economic interests or national dominance. Such a model would focus on the dissemination of knowledge and resources so that all people, regardless of their social or economic status, could equally benefit from the advantages of AI. A free model could help reduce inequalities in society and promote technological progress as a common good that benefits everyone.

But what could such a model look like? Would it require global cooperation, with states, companies and organizations working together to ensure a fair distribution of AI resources? Or would it make more sense to organize AI development locally, so that each society develops its own form of AI use and regulation? The challenges are immense, because AI is not just a question of technology, but also of political and social structure.

Let's take the example of medicine. In many countries, large companies have controlled access to AI-powered diagnostic tools and personalized treatment methods. They have made immense profits in the process, while in other parts of the world access to these technologies is limited. The question that arises here is whether these technologies should only be available to those who can afford them, or whether they should be seen as a public good accessible to all. A free model would mean that the technology is not in the hands of a few companies, but that it benefits everyone to save lives and improve healthcare worldwide.

But a free model is not without challenges. It requires extensive cooperation between governments, technology companies and civil society. In addition, legal frameworks would have to be developed to ensure that the technology is not misused. Because even though AI can offer enormous benefits, it also carries risks: data misuse, discrimination and a possible distortion of decision-making are just some of the dangers associated with uncontrolled use of AI. Therefore, every decision on how and in what context AI should be used would have to be carefully considered.

The question of who decides on the use of AI is therefore not only a technical or economic one, but also a political and moral one. It is the question of power: who has the say over the technologies that are increasingly determining our lives?

In an ideal world, this power would be evenly distributed and everyone would have the opportunity to participate in shaping the future of AI. But what is the reality?

In recent years, different approaches to regulating AI have emerged. While some countries, such as the US and China, have adopted a more market-oriented approach in which companies can largely decide for themselves how to develop and use AI, others, such as the European Union, have stricter regulations that focus on data protection and regulatory issues. These different approaches are also reflected in the question of whether AI is viewed as a public good or a commercial product.

Another example of the dispute over control of AI is the area of work. More and more companies are relying on automation through AI, which is leading to a massive change in the world of work. Many jobs that were traditionally done by people are now being taken over by machines. This change has far-reaching social consequences: jobs are being lost and the distribution of wealth is changing. In this context, the question of who benefits from the progress is again raised. Should AI's wealth and job creation be designed for the common good, or should profit be left to companies and investors?

It is clear that we are at a crucial point in the development of AI. The decisions made today will have a significant impact on the future of the technology and its impact on society. Will AI be a tool for prosperity and the common good, or will it continue to be an instrument of capital in the hands of a few actors?

This is a key question, and it goes far beyond technology. It affects the way we organize our societies, how we distribute power and resources, and how we deal with the ethical implycations of AI. It affects the question of who really decides how AI is used and who benefits from its development. But one thing is clear: the discussion about the future of AI will not only be about technology, but also about values, justice, and the vision we have for our common future.

Society or Mass – the idea of Community

To answer these questions, we must first take a look into the past. The history of human civilization is essentially a history of community. Even in the Stone Age, our ancestors recognized that the survival of the individual was inextricably linked to the cohesion of the group. This existential insight shaped the development of human societies for thousands of years. From the first tribal associations to the emergence of village communities and the formation of complex state structures - it was always the idea of community that acted as a glue between the individual members.

The industrial revolution marked a first significant turning point in this development. The mechanization of work and the associated urbanization led to the first dissolution of traditional community structures. People left their villages to seek their fortune in the rapidly growing cities. The family as the smallest unit of society began to change, extended family associations were replaced by the nuclear family. Nevertheless, essential elements of the community idea remained - in the form of neighborhoods, clubs, religious communities and other social structures.

The real paradigm shift only occurred with the advent of the digital revolution. The invention of the Internet and the rapid development of communication technology not only changed the way we come into contact with one another, but also the nature of social relationships themselves. Professor Dr. Thomas Weber, a sociologist at the University of Heidelberg, describes this change as a "fundamental recoding of the social": "What we are currently experiencing is not simply a further development of existing forms of communication, but a complete redesign of what we understand as community."

The numbers speak for themselves: the average person today spends more time on their smartphone than in direct contact with other people. Social media have largely replaced traditional forms of encounter. While in the 1950s a person spent an average of around 150 minutes a day in direct social interaction, today it is barely more than 50 minutes. The rest of the time is increasingly spent in virtual spaces, where communication takes place continuously, but often remains superficial and non-binding.

This development has far-reaching consequences for the way we live together. The psychologist Dr. Sarah Martinez of Stanford University has shown in a long-term study that the ability to empathize among young people has decreased by almost 40 percent over the past twenty years. "We are observing an increasing inability to put oneself in other people's shoes and understand their feelings," explains Martinez. "This is a direct result of reduced face-to-face communication."

But the effects go far beyond the area of interpersonal relationships. The transformation from society to mass also has economic and political dimensions. In the economy, we are observing an increasing individualization of consumption. Algorithms analyze our behavior and present us with customized offers. What at first glance appears to be progress is in fact leading to a further fragmentation of society. Shared experiences that previously helped to create identity are becoming rarer.

The political scientist Dr. Andreas Müller of the Free University of Berlin sees this as a serious threat to democracy: "A functioning democracy needs dialogue, the exchange of different perspectives and the ability to compromise. If everyone lives in their own digital bubble, this basis is lost." The increasing polarization of political debates, the emergence of echo chambers on social media and the growing inability to engage in constructive dialogue are clear signs of this development.

The transformation of our society is particularly evident in working life. The COVID pandemic has accelerated a trend that was already apparent before: the shift of work to the digital space. Home office and virtual meetings have become the norm for many people. While this has undeniable advantages in terms of flexibility and work-life balance, it also leads to a further erosion of social ties in the workplace.

The transformation to a mass society is also reflected in our relationship to time. Technological progress has given us a feeling of permanent acceleration. Everything has to be available immediately, done immediately, answered immediately. This "tyranny of the moment", as sociologist Thomas Eriksen calls it, leaves little room for deep relationships and authentic encounters. The masses live in the now, while society needs time to grow and develop.

But what does this development mean for the future? Are we irrevocably on the way to an atomized society in which everyone navigates through life on their own? The answer is not as clear-cut as it may seem at first glance. Because parallel to the development described, countermovements can also be observed. More and more people are consciously looking for ways to escape digital isolation.

New forms of communal living are emerging in many cities. Cohousing projects in which people consciously share spaces and resources are enjoying increasing popularity. Urban gardening initiatives bring people together to jointly cultivate urban green spaces. Repair cafés in which people help each other repair devices are more than just a reaction to the throwaway society - they are places of encounter and exchange.

Professor Dr. Elena Petrova from the University of Vienna sees these initiatives as signs of a possible synthesis between technological progress and the idea of community: "What we are observing is not a simple return to traditional forms of community, but the emergence of hybrid social structures. People use digital technologies to organize and network, but consciously seek personal contact and direct cooperation." A particularly interesting example of this development is the "Slow Food" movement, which sees itself as an alternative to fast food culture. This is not just about sustainable consumption, but about reviving a food culture that brings people together. Cooking and eating together is becoming a social event where real encounters can take place.

A rethink is also emerging in the field of education. While the trend was initially towards fully digitalized learning, hybrid models that combine digital tools with personal interaction are increasingly gaining ground. Dr. Michael Schmidt, educational researcher at the Technical University of Munich, explains: "We have recognized that digital media are important tools, but cannot replace personal contact between teachers and learners. The future lies in the intelligent combination of both worlds." Generation Z, often referred to as "digital natives", is developing an astonishingly differentiated relationship to digitalization. Unlike their parents, who experienced the digital transformation as a dramatic break, they deal with digital technologies more naturally - but are also aware of their limitations.

A study by the Institute for Youth Research shows that 73 percent of 16- to 25-year-olds rate "real" friendships as more important than online contacts. This development is also reflected in new business models. Start-ups such as "Social Connect" or "Community Hub" have specialized in using digital technologies to bring people together in real life. Their apps work according to the "digital to analog" principle - they use algorithms to identify people with similar interests, but are explicitly aimed at personal meetings.

The question of the future of our community cannot be answered with a simple yes or no. Rather, we are in a phase of transition in which old and new forms of coexistence exist side by side and influence each other. Technological progress has undoubtedly contributed to an erosion of traditional community structures, but at the same time opens up new opportunities for networking and collaboration.

The real challenge is to use these opportunities in such a way that they strengthen the community spirit rather than weaken it. This requires a conscious design of digital transformation that focuses on people and their social needs. Dr. Julia Weinstein, innovation researcher at MIT, puts it this way: "Technology should be a tool that helps us become more human, not less human."

An important aspect of this is the design of public spaces. In many cities, traditional meeting places such as marketplaces, parks or libraries are being rethought and equipped with digital infrastructure. This is not about putting digital in the foreground, but about creating spaces that enable different forms of interaction.

The city of Barcelona has developed an interesting concept in this context: "Smart City with a Human Touch". Digital technologies are used here in a targeted manner to improve the quality of life of residents and promote social interactions. For example, there are "digital bulletin boards" in neighborhood centers that announce local initiatives and events, but are deliberately designed to bring people together rather than isolating them.

A rethink is also taking place in the area of corporate culture. Many companies have recognized that purely virtual teams do not function optimally in the long term. They are developing new models that combine digital collaboration with regular face-to-face meetings. The IT group Mindspace, for example, has developed a concept called "Digital Together", in which teams work predominantly remotely but come together regularly for "Creativity Weeks" in which personal exchange is the focus.

The effects of this development on people's mental health are complex and sometimes contradictory. On the one hand, psychotherapists report an increase in loneliness and depression, which they associate with advancing digitalization.

On the other hand, new therapeutic approaches are emerging that use digital technologies to bring people out of their isolation and bring them back into community. Dr. Marcus Steiner, head of a psychiatric clinic in Frankfurt, reports positive experiences with a hybrid therapy approach: "We use digital platforms to make initial contacts and break down inhibitions. The actual therapeutic process then takes place in face-to-face contact. This combination has proven to be particularly successful, especially with younger patients."

Another important aspect is the question of democratic participation in a digitalized society. While social media opens up new opportunities for political participation on the one hand, there is a risk of increasing fragmentation of public discourse. The city of Aarhus in Denmark is therefore experimenting with an innovative concept of the "digital agora": citizens can participate in political decision-making processes via an app, but are regularly invited to face-to-face discussion rounds.

The role of art in this transformation process deserves special attention. Artists respond to the changes in our society with new forms of expression that often deliberately blur the boundaries between digital and analogue. The installation "Connected Solitude" by the artist Sophie Chen, for example, addresses the paradox of our networked loneliness: visitors first interact with each other digitally and then meet in a physical space.

The role of education in this transformation process can hardly be overestimated. Schools and universities are faced with the challenge of preparing young people for a world in which digital competence and social skills are equally important. The concept of "blended learning" is constantly evolving. Dr. Sarah Anderson of Columbia University speaks of a "third way": "We have to stop thinking in terms of 'digital versus analog'. The future lies in an intelligent interweaving of both areas." The development of artificial intelligence adds another dimension to this discussion. While on the one hand there is a fear that AI systems could continue to replace human interactions, there are also opportunities for new forms of community building. AI-supported platforms can, for example, help bring people with similar interests together or organize neighborhood assistance more efficiently. An interesting phenomenon is the increasing importance of local communities in a globalized world.

While digital technologies enable global networking, the need for roots and belonging in the immediate environment is growing at the same time. "Glocal communities" - locally anchored but globally networked - could be a model for the future.

Another important aspect is the development of new economic models that rely on cooperation rather than competition. The "sharing economy" is just one example of approaches that use digital technologies to enable communal use of resources.

The question of the future of religious and spiritual communities in a digitalized world is leading to interesting developments. Many religious communities are experimenting with hybrid formats that combine digital networking with traditional rituals. Rabbi David Goldstein from New York reports positive experiences: "The digital possibilities have not weakened our community, but expanded it. We reach people who would otherwise have no access to our community."

A fascinating aspect is the emergence of new forms of cultural identity in the digitalized world. While traditional cultural boundaries are blurring, new communities are emerging that define themselves through common interests and values. Dr. Lisa Chen from the University of California speaks of "translocal cultural spaces": "What we are observing is not the end of cultural identity, but its transformation into more flexible but no less meaningful forms."

The question of the authenticity of social relationships in the digital world preoccupies many people. While critical voices complain about increasing superficiality, studies show that digital communication can indeed enable deep bonds. Psychologist Dr. Maria Rodriguez speaks of a "new grammar of relationships": "People are developing amazing abilities to build authentic connections even in digital spaces."

An important aspect is the development of new forms of solidarity in the digitalized society. Crowdfunding platforms and social networks enable new forms of mutual support that often combine local and global dimensions. The "Digital Solidarity Networks" during the COVID-19 pandemic are an impressive example of this development.

The future of democracy in the digitalized society remains a key challenge. While new forms of political participation are emerging on the one hand, concern about increasing polarization is growing on the other. Innovative projects such as the "Digital Democracy Labs" are trying to counteract this development by combining digital and analogue discussion formats.

The philosopher Dr. Michael Weber also sees the current development as an opportunity for a fundamental redefinition of our understanding of community: "Perhaps we need to stop seeing digitalization as a threat or a savior and instead learn to use it as a tool to create new forms of living together." The question of temporality in the digital world leads to interesting observations. While digital technologies are often associated with acceleration and immediacy, countermovements are emerging at the same time that consciously focus on deceleration and temporal depth. The concept of "digital slowness" is becoming increasingly important. Professor Dr. Elena Kuznetsova from Moscow State University sees an important signal in this development: "People are beginning to understand that technological progress does not automatically lead to a better life. What we need is a conscious integration of technology into a life that leaves room for real encounters and development."

The importance of rituals and ceremonies in digitalized society deserves special attention. While traditional rituals change their form, new rituals emerge that combine digital and analog elements. The "Digital Rites of Passage" are a fascinating example of this development. Anthropologist Dr. James Parker sees this as an important process of cultural adaptation: "Rituals have always been an essential part of human communities. What we are observing today is their transformation in a digitalized world, without losing their fundamental importance for social cohesion."

The role of language and communication in digital transformation is of particular interest. While new forms of communication are emerging on the one hand, awareness of the importance of direct linguistic interaction is growing at the same time.

The intensive examination of the question of whether and how technological progress is changing our idea of community leads to a differentiated realization: We are not in a simple process of dissolving traditional community structures, but in a complex transformation that entails both risks and opportunities.

Technological progress has undoubtedly contributed to a fragmentation of traditional social ties. The digitization of our communication, the virtualization of our working world and the individualization of our consumer behavior have fundamentally changed the way we experience and shape community. The danger of increasing isolation and alienation is real and requires our attention.

At the same time, however, it is also clear that people are still able to find creative ways to develop new forms of community. The emerging hybrid social structures that combine digital and analogue elements could point the way to a future in which technological progress and the idea of community are not opposites, but enrich each other. The crucial challenge is not to see digital transformation as an inevitable fate, but as a design task. It is about developing and using technology in such a way that it supports human needs for connection, authenticity and communal experience rather than replacing them.

Communal Perspectives

Self-abandonment of identity in the digital age

Digitalization has not only revolutionized our communication and working practices, but also goes deep into the core of what we understand as our identity. We are experiencing an unprecedented fusion of real and digital existence, which raises fundamental questions: Who are we in a world in which our online presence often seems more important than our physical existence? How does constant digital networking change our self-image, our relationships and our social structures?

The significance of this development can be seen in countless examples. There is the management consultant Thomas Schulz, who meticulously documents and quantifies his life in various apps - from his sleep phases to his fitness activities to his social interactions. His real identity is increasingly merging with a data stream of metrics and digital markers. Or take an influencer who has cultivated her online persona so perfectly that she sometimes asks herself where the line lies between her authentic personality and her digital brand.

The process of digital identity dissolution takes place gradually and mostly unconsciously. It begins in childhood, when the first social media account is created, and continues with the increaseing shift of social interactions to the digital space. The COVID pandemic has accelerated this development, as school lessons, work meetings and even family gatherings were suddenly moved to virtual spaces.

The social implications of this transformation are far-reaching and complex. We are observing a paradoxical situation: On the one hand, we have unprecedented opportunities for self-expression and self-realization in the digital space. On the other hand, it is precisely this variety of options that leads to a fragmentation of the self that overwhelms many people. The constant need to present and position oneself online creates a subtle but permanent pressure for self-optimization.

The case of a 45-year-old teacher from Hamburg illustrates the complexity of this development. Weber describes how he initially resisted digitalization, but was then forced to change his entire teaching concept due to distance learning during the pandemic. "At first I felt like an actor in front of the camera," he recalls. "Today I realize that my online presence has become an integral part of my teacher identity. Sometimes I wonder if that is good or bad."

This ambivalence runs like a thread through the societal transformation in the digital age. Social media promises us limitless connectedness, while at the same time loneliness rates are rising in developed societies. We have access to more knowledge than ever before, while critical thinking and deep understanding are threatened by superficial information processing. We can reinvent ourselves in different digital contexts, but may lose touch with our authentic self in the process.

The impact of this development on different social groups varies. While the so-called "digital natives" experience the merging of real and virtual identity as a matter of course, older generations often struggle with feelings of alienation. Socioeconomic factors also play an important role: access to digital resources and the ability to use them effectively are becoming decisive factors in social participation.

A particularly fascinating aspect is the emergence of hybrid forms of identity. People develop different online personas for different platforms and contexts. One example is 28-year-old graphic designer Lisa Müller (name changed), who cultivates her professional image on LinkedIn, lives out her creative side on Instagram and has political discussions on X. "Sometimes I feel like an actress who switches between different roles," she says. "But aren't these roles all part of me?"

Technological developments are further reinforcing this trend towards identity fragmentation. Artificial intelligence and deep learning algorithms analyze our online behavior and create detailed profiles of our personality. These digital images are increasingly used to predict purchasing decisions, calculate insurance premiums or assess creditworthiness. The line between who we are and what algorithms think they know about us is becoming increasingly blurred. The psychological consequences of this development are considerable. Studies show an increase in identity crises, loss of authenticity and digital exhaustion.

The constant pressure to be present and relevant online leads to a state of permanent self-observation and optimization. Psychologist Dr. Michael Schmidt speaks of a "digital neurosis" characterized by compulsive online behavior and the inability to achieve digital abstinence.

The problem is particularly evident in the area of interpersonal relationships. The way we maintain friendships and enter into romantic relationships has fundamentally changed. Dating apps like Tinder have turned the search for a partner into an algorithmically controlled process. Social media platforms suggest a permanent connection, while real intimacy often falls by the wayside.

The world of work is another area in which the self-abandonment of one's own identity is particularly evident. Home offices and digital collaboration have dissolved traditional boundaries between work and private life. Video conferences provide insights into private spaces, while work chat programs suggest constant accessibility. The ability to master various digital tools and present oneself in virtual teams is becoming a decisive career factor.

An interesting phenomenon is the increasing importance of digital reputation. Online reviews, social media profiles and digital portfolios are becoming important building blocks of our social position. It is not only restaurant owners or online shop operators who experience the power of this digital reputation: a handful of negative Google reviews can bring a business to the brink of ruin, even though the criticisms are largely unfounded or even come from competitors.

The question of privacy and data protection takes on a new dimension in this context. While on the one hand we willingly share personal information on social media, at the same time awareness of the risks of this digital transparency is growing. The Cambridge Analytica scandal has shown how personal data can be misused to manipulate voting behavior. Nevertheless, the willingness to digitally expose oneself seems unbroken.

The social mechanisms of the digital attention economy play a special role here. Likes, shares and comments become a kind of currency that influences our self-esteem. A 16-year-old student describes it like this: "When I post a photo and get fewer likes than usual, I feel worthless. I know that's not rational, but I can't do anything about it." These dependencies can plunge young people into depression or even trigger a death wish. Online bashing or so-called shitstorms can drive people to their deaths, even though the initiators of this bashing basically know nothing about the real person of their victims.

Social polarization is reinforced by digital echo chambers and filter bubbles. Algorithms prefer to show us content that confirms our existing views. This leads to an increasing fragmentation of social discussion and makes democratic discourse more difficult. The ability to act anonymously on the Internet also encourages aggressive and polarizing forms of communication.

Another important aspect is the role of digital education. While technical skills are becoming increasingly important, media literacy and critical thinking are often left behind. Schools and educational institutions are faced with the challenge of preparing young people for a world in which digital and real identity are inextricably intertwined. The question of authenticity takes on a new meaning in this context. While social media encourages us to present our "best selves", the longing for authentic experiences and real encounters is growing at the same time. This is reflected in countermovements such as "digital detox" or the renaissance of analogue hobbies.

Generation Z, the first to grow up entirely in the digital age, is developing interesting adaptation strategies. They use different platforms in parallel and switch effortlessly between different digital identities. 17-year-old Sophie explains: "On TikTok I am funny and carefree, on Instagram I show my perfect life, and on BeReal I am authentic. For me, that is not a contradiction."

The effects on family life are also profound. Parents are faced with the challenge of preparing their children for a digital world that they themselves often only understand inadequately. The permanent availability of digital devices is changing family routines and communication patterns. Family therapist Dr. Andreas Müller observes increasing "digital alienation" within families.

The philosophical implications of this development are far-reaching. What does identity mean in a world in which we exist in different digital realities at the same time? The philosopher Dr. Martin Weber speaks of a "postdigital identity" characterized by fluidity and multiplicity. The Cartesian idea of a unified, stable self is increasingly being questioned.

The transformation is particularly evident in the area of political participation. Social media have fundamentally changed the way we engage in politics and inform ourselves. Hashtag activism and online petitions are becoming important forms of political participation. At the same time, political discourse on social media is becoming increasingly superficial. Complex topics are being reduced to succinct statements and emotional images.

Medicine is observing new clinical pictures that are directly related to digital transformation. In addition to well-known phenomena such as internet and social media addiction, cases of "digital dysphoria" are increasingly emerging - a condition in which people perceive their real appearance as inadequate compared to their filtered online versions.

The future prospects of this social transformation are both fascinating and worrying. Technologies such as virtual reality, augmented reality and the metaverse promise an even deeper fusion of physical and digital reality. The boundaries between authentic identity and digital projection will continue to blur.

Nevertheless, countermovements are also emerging. More and more people are consciously looking for ways to reduce their digital presence and maintain authentic relationships. Community gardens, repair cafes and other analog meeting places are experiencing a boom. This development indicates that society is beginning to strive for a more balanced relationship between digital and physical existence.

The challenge for the future will be to use the advantages of digital networking without losing our human authenticity and social cohesion. This requires both individual reflection and collective action. Educational institutions, companies and political institutions are called upon to create framework conditions that enable a conscious and balanced approach to digital identity. The future will show whether we can achieve this balancing act.

Man: Creator or Victim of Progress?

To get to the bottom of this question, we must first understand what progress actually means. In common parlance, we understand it as a development for the better, an improvement in human living conditions through scientific, technical and social innovations. But this definition falls short. Progress is a multidimensional phenomenon that cannot be reduced to a simple forward movement.

If we look at the history of humanity, a fascinating pattern emerges: every significant innovation, every technological breakthrough, has had both positive and negative effects. The use of fire enabled our ancestors to cook food, warm themselves and keep wild animals away. At the same time, it brought with it the risk of fires and later, with the development of industry, massive environmental pollution. The development of agriculture around 12,000 years ago led to sedentary societies and enabled population growth and cultural development. But it also brought with it social inequality, new diseases and the overexploitation of natural resources.

Humans are on the threshold of a new era. Since the beginning of its existence, man has not only made the world his own, but has shaped it, changed it and reinvented it again and again. Progress is his constant companion - a double-edged sword that imposes both power and responsibility on him. But to what extent is man the actual creator of this progress, and to what extent is he merely driven by it, even its victim?

In the early days of human history, progress was a means of survival. The discovery of fire, the development of hunting techniques, settling down - all of these were achievements that made life easier according to our current understanding and advanced the species Homo sapiens. No one would have questioned at the time whether progress could be a threat. It was simply necessary to survive in a hostile world. But over time, the nature of progress changed. It became not just a means of survival, but an instrument of power. Knowledge became currency, technology the engine of civilization. And with every step forward, the danger of overtaking oneself grew.

The Industrial Revolution marked a turning point. Suddenly, humans were no longer just living beings who had to adapt to their environment - they began to shape the environment according to their ideas. Factories sprang up, machines and factories took over the work of manufacturers, and with each decade the speed of change increased. Progress became a force of nature. But the further humanity distanced itself from nature, the more it became dependent on new things. The first victims of this progress were those who could not keep up: the workers in the dark factory halls, the exploited raw material suppliers from distant countries, the first signs of a destroyed environment.

But progress cannot be stopped. It follows its own logic, which often overwhelms people. The leap into the digital age brought even more radical changes. With the invention of the computer, the Internet and artificial intelligence, a new phase of human existence began. Today we are more connected than ever before, have access to immeasurable amounts of knowledge and can exchange information in a matter of seconds. But has this really made us freer? Or have we become entangled in a web of our own making?

One could argue that humans have long since lost control of their own progress. The development of new technologies often happens faster than their effects can be understood. Companies and states drive innovations because they promise economic or strategic benefits without always being aware of the long-term consequences this could have for society or the planet. Artificial intelligence, genetic manipulation, climate control - all of these are fields in which humans act as creators without always knowing exactly what consequences their actions will have.

But are humans really just victims of this progress? Do they not still have the power to consciously control their development? In fact, there are always moments when it becomes clear that progress can be shaped. Movements for environmental protection, for social justice, for ethical science - all of these are signs that humans are not just driven, but very much have the ability to take responsibility.

The crucial question remains: How do we find a balance between innovation and ethics? How do we prevent progress from becoming an end in itself, which ultimately subjugates people instead of liberating them? Perhaps the answer lies in a new awareness - an awareness that progress is not just a technical question, but above all a human one.

The question of how we find a balance between innovation and ethics is one of the central challenges of our time. Innovation drives humanity forward, opens up new possibilities and often fundamentally changes our lives. But not every innovation is good per se, and not every development should be pushed forward without restrictions. This creates a tension between technological progress and moral responsibility that needs to be navigated.

Finding a balance between innovation and ethics means not pursuing progress for its own sake, but placing it in a value-based framework. This includes evaluating innovations not only from an economic or technological point of view, but also from a human, social and ecological perspective. The central question is: Who benefits from a new technology and who could it harm?

What are the long-term consequences for society and individuals?

A crucial element is therefore the integration of ethical considerations into the innovation process. This means that moral questions are not only considered once a technology has already been introduced into the world, but that ethical principles play a role right from the start. Companies, researchers and developers should therefore not only ask themselves whether something is technically feasible, but also whether it is socially desirable and morally justifiable.

An example of the urgent need for this forward-looking ethics is artificial intelligence. Who is responsible if an AI makes wrong or independent decisions to the detriment of humanity? How do we prevent discrimination through algorithmic prejudices? And to what extent are machines allowed to decide on human matters at all? Such questions do not have to be asked only when artificial intelligence is ubiquitous - they must be part of the development from the start.

In addition to ethical reflection within science and technology, social participation is also crucial, if not existential. Innovation must not be in the hands of just a few actors, but should be subject to democratic discourse. In an increasingly technological world, societies must be able to have a say in the effects of progress. This requires transparency on the part of companies and governments, as well as greater involvement of ethical experts and interdisciplinary teams in decision-making processses.

Another key element is regulation through laws and international agreements. While innovation is currently driven primarily by economic interests, smart regulation can ensure that new technologies are not advanced at the expense of human rights, social justice or the environment. One example of this is data protection laws, which are intended to prevent companies from collecting and using personal data in an uncontrolled manner. There are also ethical guidelines in biotechnology that are intended to ensure that genetic interventions are not carried out without clear moral considerations. But who sets these ethical and moral standards and in what context?

To find this balance, close cooperation between science, politics, business and society is needed. Technical developments should not be viewed in isolation, but always in the context of their impact on people and the environment. Interdisciplinary research can help to link technological possibilities with ethical principles.

Ultimately, the balance between innovation and ethics also depends on the attitude of each individual. Consumers have only limited influence on which technologies prevail through their decisions. Nevertheless, they should get involved by actively participating in social debates.

People are therefore not powerless in the face of developments that change their world. They have the ability to shape them, question them and give them a direction. The trick is not to see innovation as an end in itself, but as a tool for a better, fairer and more sustainable future. Only when progress and responsibility go hand in hand can people truly remain creators - and prevent themselves from becoming victims of their own achievements.

The momentum of progress is unstoppable. It permeates every facet of human life, from the way we work and communicate to the deepest structures of our societies. The mechanisms that were once set in motion can no longer be easily stopped - humans have unleashed a dynamic that takes them to unimagined heights, but can also swallow them up at any time.

It is not just technical progress that shapes life. Social, political and cultural developments also interact closely with technological innovations. Anyone who sees humans as creators or victims of progress must take all of these dimensions into account. Because progress is more than just invention - it is the sum of everything that humans think, feel and create.

Digitalization is an example of this close interrelationship. What once began as a simple calculation aid has developed into an all-encompassing infrastructure that permeates every aspect of our everyday lives. Smartphones have become our constant companions, the Internet is indispensable, and artificial intelligence is already performing tasks that were previously reserved for humans. But what does that mean for us?

On the one hand, this digital revolution offers enormous opportunities. Knowledge is more accessible today than ever before, information can be exchanged worldwide in a matter of seconds, and new technologies enable us to solve problems that once seemed insurmountable. Diseases that were considered a death sentence just a few decades ago can now be treated. Communication across continents has become commonplace. But with these achievements come new challenges.

Humans are faced with the question of how dependent they want to be on their own inventions. When algorithms decide which news we read, which products we buy, or even who we interact with, then the line between creators and victims of progress is blurred. We use these technologies - but haven't they been using us for a long time now?

Artificial intelligence is a prime example of this dilemma. It promises efficiency, automation, and even creativity, but at the same time it poses fundamental ethical questions. What does it mean when machines make decisions that were once reserved for humans? Who is responsible if an AI makes a wrong or even fatal decision? And how do we prevent ourselves from one day being overtaken by a technology that we ourselves created?

Will humans be overtaken by evolutionary progress?

First of all, the question arises as to what it means to be "overtaken" by a technology. This scenario could take many forms: from artificial intelligence that improves itself and becomes more and more powerful without human intervention, to automated systems that are so deeply integrated into our social and economic structures that they become practically uncontrollable. The danger is not necessarily that machines suddenly develop their own consciousness and turn against us - a topos often used in science fiction stories - but rather that we lose track of and control over increasingly complex technologies.

A central problem is the pace of technological progress compared to the speed of human evolution. While biological evolution usually takes thousands or even millions of years to produce noticeable changes, technological change is progressing at a breathtaking pace. In just a few decades, we have made the leap from the first mainframe computers to powerful quantum computers, from landline telephones to globally connected smartphones, and from simple automation to self-learning artificial intelligence.

This difference in speed creates a dangerous gap: while our biological and psychological heritage adapts only slowly to new conditions, we must simultaneously deal with technologies that are evolving exponentially. Our cognitive abilities - such as critical thinking, decision-making and moral judgment - are based on evolutionary processes that emerged in a far less complex environment. The fact that our brains were optimized for life in small groups of hunters and gatherers makes it difficult to fully grasp the risks and dynamics of global technological developments.

So is it even possible to prevent these technologies from overtaking us one day? The answer is complex. While it may seem impossible to slow down the rapid pace of technological progress, there are strategies to ensure that humans remain in control:

Proactive regulation and ethical guardrails:

Instead of only reacting when a technology gets out of control, clear rules must be created early on. In the field of artificial intelligence in particular, it is essential to develop binding ethical standards and international agreements. Companies and states must not only strive for efficiency and profit, but must enter into a constant ethical dialogue in order to identify and contain potential dangers in good time.

Transparency and traceability:

A major risk is that many advanced technologies will become "black boxes" - complex systems whose inner workings are no longer fully clear even to their developers. Especially with self-learning algorithms, it is crucial to develop mechanisms that make their decision-making processes comprehensible and veryfiable. This is the only way to prevent us from becoming dependent on systems whose behavior we no longer understand.

Human-centered innovation:

Instead of seeing technological progress as an end in itself, people must always be the focus. Innovations should aim to expand human potential and create social benefits, rather than disempowering or incapacitating us. This also means that technological developments must be designed in such a way that they respect our cognitive and emotional limits, rather than exploiting them.

Education and awareness:

One of the strongest levers for controlling technological progress lies in education. People must not only learn how to use technology, but above all how to critically question its effects. An enlightened, technically competent audience is less susceptible to manipulation and can actively participate in shaping progress.

Interdisciplinary research:

The pressing questions of technology ethics cannot be solved by engineers or computer scientists alone. A broad alliance of scientists from the fields of philosophy, sociology, psychology, law and natural sciences is needed. This is the only way we can ensure that technological developments are viewed holistically and potential dangers are identified at an early stage.

But despite all these measures, uncertainty remains: can we really keep up with progress that is unfolding ever faster? Or are we in danger of even well-thought-out control mechanisms no longer being sufficient at some point?

The reality is: we will probably not be able to really slow down technological progress - and perhaps that would not even be desirable. The key is therefore not to slow down innovation at all costs, but to create a permanent dialogue between progress and responsibility. It is about remaining dynamic, continuously adapting ethical principles and developing new control mechanisms at the same speed with which technologies develop.

Ultimately, the decisive factor is our own willingness to reflect and self-regulate. Humans may evolve biologically more slowly than their machines, but their ability to critically question themselves, to cooperate and to consciously shape their future remains their greatest strength. Whether or not we are overtaken by our technologies does not depend solely on the speed of progress - it depends on how cleverly, foresightedly and responsibly we direct this progress. The future does not necessarily belong to machines - it belongs to those who shape it.

To what extent will technology remain controllable in the future?

Modern man is both inventor and user, profiteer and prisoner of the systems he has created. There are voices that claim that progress is a force of nature that cannot be stopped - an evolutionary process that catapults us into ever new dimensions, whether we want it or not. Others, however, are convinced that man can stay in control if he is prepared to take responsibility and does not blindly throw himself into every new technological development.

The question of control is central. Because while progress is neutral in itself, it is up to man to direct it in a positive or negative direction. A look into the past shows that major technological leaps have always been accompanied by social upheaval.

The invention of the printing press revolutionized knowledge, but also led to new forms of manipulation. The steam engine enabled the rise of industrial society, but also brought with it social inequalities. The atomic age promised inexhaustible energy, but at the same time created the possibility of total destructtion.

A pattern emerges in all of these developments: Man is always the creator of progress when he consciously controls it, when he connects it with a moral compass and reflects on its consequences. However, he becomes a victim when he lets progress happen unchecked, when he allows himself to be driven by economic or political interests without considering the long-term consequences.

Today we are once again at a crossroads. The technological developments of the last few decades have changed our world so rapidly that ethical and social questions are often only asked when the innovations are already firmly integrated into our lives. The debate about data protection only arose when social networks already had billions of users. The discussion about climate change only escalated when the consequences became obvious. The influence of artificial intelligence is often only problematized when algorithms are already influencing our lives.

Humans have the unique ability to learn from their mistakes. While nature often has to adapt to change over long periods of time, humans can consciously correct their direction. This is exactly what sets them apart from other living beings: their ability to reflect, to foresee and to make conscious decisions. The future does not lie in blind progress, but in an enlightened, ethically thought-out approach to innovation. Man has proven that he can be not only inventors, but also designers of his own world. The question is whether he is prepared to take on this responsibility - or whether he will allow himself to be carried away by the speed of progress until he is no longer master of his own creation.

Perhaps this is the greatest challenge of our time: not simply carrying on just because it is possible, but pausing and asking what kind of future we actually want. Because whether man is the creator or victim of progress is not decided by the technologies he develops - but by the way he uses them.

Man as a driven being - the power of curiosity

The question of whether man is able and prepared to pause in the urge for progress touches on the nature of man as creator, researcher and discoverer, but also as beings with responsibility, ethics and the consequences of his actions.

History has shown that humans are driven by an irrepressible urge to explore. Science, technology and innovations often arise from pure curiosity, from the desire to understand the world and shape it. This curiosity is a fundamental characteristic of our species. It has led us from the simple use of tools in the Stone Age to the most complex technologies. Without it, there would have been no medical progress, no space travel, no digital revolution.

But this curiosity has a dark side. Because often enough, great discoveries have also had unforeseen or even catastrophic consequences. Marie Curie, for example, devoted her life to researching radioactivity without knowing that she was fatally poisoning herself. Albert Einstein's theory of relativity provided the theoretical foundation for the development of the atom bomb, a consequence that later weighed heavily on his mind. Both examples show that humans cannot always foresee where their urge to explore will lead.

But history also shows that progress rarely stands still. Technological innovations often develop their own dynamics that are difficult to control. As soon as a possibility is discovered, it is usually used - whether out of scientific interest, economic motivation or military zeal.

One example of this is genetic engineering. Since the decoding of the human genome, researchers have been faced with the possibility of deliberately changing the genetic material. This offers enormous opportunities, for example for curing genetic diseases. But at the same time, ethical questions arise: Where is the line between healing and manipulation? Are humans allowed to change the genetic material of future generations? Despite these open questions, research is progressing inexorably - also because the pressure not to lose touch is immense.

But does this mean that humans are incapable of stopping? Not necessarily. There are moments in history when conscious reflection has taken place. The bioethics debates surrounding cloning research and genetic interventions show that science is increasingly considering ethical questions. The moratorium on research into biological weapons and the international efforts to control nuclear weapons also show that humanity is at least trying to regulate its creations.

Innovation is not synonymous with wisdom. Technical progress often advances faster than social and ethical reflection. A central point here is the rush of the new. Every discovery brings with it euphoria, a feeling of empowerment and superiority. Especially in a globalized, economically networked world, new technologies are not just a question of science, but also of power. Those who drive progress gain economic advantages, geopolitical influence and scientific prestige. This is where the great danger lies: when progress arises primarily from competitive thinking or economic drive, reflection often takes a back seat. The development of artificial intelligence is a current example of this. Companies and states outdo each other in research in order not to fall behind. But the ethical and social implications of this technology - for example in terms of jobs, data protection and decision-making - have not yet been fully thought through.

From the steam engine to nuclear energy to digitization - humans have rarely stopped a technological development, even when they knew its risks. But as bleak as this picture may seem, there is hope. Man is not only a researcher, but also a being with morals and responsibility. He is able to learn from his mistakes. The environmental movement shows that society is able to recognize the price of progress and counteract it. While industrialization progressed without hesitation for decades, today there is a growing understanding of sustainability and long-term consequences. The same could happen in other areas. Artificial intelligence, biotechnology and digitalization raise huge questions - but the fact that these debates are being held shows that humanity can reflect.

Whether man succumbs to the intoxication of the new or whether he can pause and look at his work from a certain distance depends on whether he is willing to take responsibility - not only afterwards, but at the moment of the act of creation. The examples of Marie Curie and Albert Einstein show that great discoveries can bring both triumph and tragedy. The challenge of the future will be to recognize this duality and to shape progress consciously, reflectively and with an eye on its consequences. Man may be curious – but he also has the capacity for wisdom. The question is whether he uses it in time.

Ethics through Technology: Responsibility and Morality

Technology has transformed human civilization at an unprecedented pace. It has revolutionized industries, enabled medical miracles, and shaped our daily lives in ways that previous generations did not think possible. But with this progress comes a question as old as philosophy itself: who bears responsibility for the consequences of developments? Can morality be delegated to machines, or will it remain a purely human matter?

The discussion of ethical responsibility in technological progress has become one of the most pressing issues of our time. While some optimists are confident that technology will fundamentally improve our lives, critics urge caution. History shows that innovations can have not only positive but also unexpected or even catastrophic consequences. The discovery of nuclear fission brought both energy generation and the threat of weapons of mass destruction. Artificial intelligence can help people diagnose diseases, but can also be used for control and manipulation.

A particular area of tension arises when responsibility is apparently outsourced. When algorithms start making decisions, machines act autonomously and complex systems operate without direct human control, moral responsibility becomes increasingly difficult to locate. If a self-driving car causes an accident or AI-controlled financial software triggers a market crash, who is responsible? Is it the developer, the company or even the machine itself?

These questions raise profound moral dilemmas. With his principle of responsibility, the philosopher Hans Jonas formulated the requirement that people must act with foresight and caution, especially in the face of technologies with far-reaching consequences. But how can this maxim be implemented in an era in which decisions are actually increasingly being made by machines?

Ethical responsibility cannot simply be delegated to technology. Machines have no moral intuition, no emotions, no values. They operate according to rules that have been programmed by people or derived through machine learning. But these rules in particular can have unpredictable consequences. In the past, AI systems have been developed that unconsciously adopted discriminatory patterns because they had learned from biased data sets. In such cases, it is crucial that people remain aware of their responsibility and establish mechanisms for control and correction.

Learning systems rely on recognizing patterns and making decisions from large amounts of data. However, if these systems are trained with misinformation or manipulative content, they can draw incorrect conclusions. Likewise, algorithms in law enforcement or finance could make unfair or incorrect decisions because they are based on misleading data. One of the most dangerous developments is the increasing use of deepfake technologies enabled by AI. Misinformation can no longer only be spread via text, but also via deceptively real videos and audio files that suggest false statements or actions by prominent people. This can lead to political opponents being discredited, election campaigns being manipulated, or false evidence being used in court cases. Identity fraud and cybercrime can also increase significantly as a result of such technologies.

Because AI systems are constantly evolving and access large, often uncontrolled amounts of data, it is difficult to regulate them effectively. Laws and regulations often lag behind technological developments, making it difficult to identify and combat fake news and manipulative content in real time. In addition, it is unclear who is ultimately responsible for the consequences of incorrect AI decisions - the developers, the operators or the users?

The combination of learning systems and the spread of fake news poses a serious threat to democracy, the economy and social stability. To counteract these dangers, increased media literacy, better algorithms for detecting misinformation and stricter regulation of AI-based systems are needed. In addition, companies and governments must develop ethical standards for the use of artificial intelligence to minimize manipulation and bias.

Another critical aspect is the increasing lack of transparency of many technologies themselves. Modern algorithms, especially in the field of deep learning, are often so complex that even their developers cannot understand exactly how certain decisions are made.

This black box problem makes it difficult to enforce ethical standards. If no one understands exactly why a machine acts the way it does, how can it be ensured that its decisions are justifiable from a human perspective? Automated systems can implement ethical decision-making models that ideally meet the highest moral standards. But this requires a conscious and critical approach to technology, as well as clear legal and moral frameworks.

Ultimately, the responsibility for ethical decisions remains with humans. Technology is a tool that can be both a blessing and a curse, depending on how it is used. Delegating moral responsibility to machines is not just an illusion, but can have dangerous consequences. Progress must therefore always be accompanied by a considered ethical debate that ensures that innovation serves humanity and does not become its undoing.

Is the human decision-maker on a shaky pedestal?

Chat-GPT clearly answers the question of whether ethical implycations in learning systems can lead to the questioning of humans as decision-makers with the following reasons:

Yes, the integration of ethical implications in learning systems can lead to the questioning of the role of humans as the ultimate decision-maker in the long term. This development has profound consequences for society, politics and individual responsibility.

In the following, I will discuss various aspects of this topic in detail.

Autonomy vs. human control

Learning systems are designed to recognize patterns and make decisions independently. If ethical principles are integrated into these systems, this could lead to them making morally "better" or more objective decisions than humans in certain cases. In areas such as justice, medicine or the military, the question could arise whether an AI that works emotionlessly, data-based and efficiently is not the "better" choice compared to human decision-makers. In the long term, this could lead to people increasingly being seen as error-prone or biased decision-makers.

Loss of human responsibility

If learning systems take over ethical considerations, people could absolve themselves of their own moral responsibility. An example of this would be automation in the legal system: should an AI determine who gets a prison sentence and who doesn't? If people increasingly rely on such systems, this could lead to a moral retreat by people - they no longer take responsibility for the consequences of a decision because they rely on the AI ("The AI decided that").

Collapse of the previous ethical system

Traditional ethics is based on human values that have been shaped over centuries by religion, philosophy and social norms. However, when machines start making ethical decisions, the question arises: by what standards? Who determines which values are implemented in an AI? If different cultures or ideologies have different ethical ideas, this could lead to a fragmentation of assessments in which different AIs represent different moral norms - which could ultimately destroy our current ethical system.

Danger of technocracy

If learning systems see themselves as superior ethical decision-makers, a technocracy could develop in which political and social decision-making increasingly passes into the hands of AI-supported systems. In such a scenario, human decision-makers could only be accepted as administrators, while machines make the actual ethical decisions. This would not only endanger the democratic principle, but also undermine the feeling of self-determination and individual freedom of choice in society.

Decision-making in existential questions

The role of learning systems is particularly explosive in existential or morally complex questions - for example in warfare (should an AI decide on the use of weapons?), medicine (should an AI determine the life and death of patients?) or in the world of work (should an AI decide who is fired?). The more responsibility is handed over to learning systems, the more humans are displaced as decision-makers.

The illusion of AI infallibility

Another problem is that AI systems – despite all ethical programming – are not infallible. They can be influenced by faulty or manipulated programming and contain hidden biases. If society begins to perceive them as a "higher authority," human decision-makers would increasingly fade into the background, even though they are actually necessary to correct mistakes and unforeseen consequences.

Although learning systems can help analyze ethical dilemmas and suggest more objective decisions, the ultimate responsibility should always remain with humans. A complete shift of ethical decision-making to AI systems would not only lead to a loss of human autonomy, but would also have serious societal consequences. Therefore, clear rules must be created to ensure that AI systems only act in a supportive manner and not as the sole moral authority.

Quo vadis AI? Global solution, national use

Two forces in particular have significantly influenced the direction of our global society in recent decades: globalization and the technological revolution. They are not only the driving forces of economic growth, but also the roots of many conflicts. Capitalism, as the dominant economic system of the modern world, is at the center of these developments. But how sustainable is this system? And above all: who really benefits from the enormous opportunities that globalization and technology bring?

It is a cold, clear night in a small town in southern India. A young man, Arjun, sits in front of a computer screen in a dimly lit room. The keys click quickly under his fingers as he works his way through a complex programming task. Arjun is a software developer. A few years ago, he could not even have imagined working in this industry. But thanks to globalization and the Internet age, he was able to train himself, take online courses and eventually land a job in an international company that specializes in software solutions for the global market. Arjun is a typical example of someone who has benefited from the advantages of globalization - and the global technology movement.

On the other side of the globe, in a high-tech office in the financial metropolis of New York, sits a young man named Jason. He too is part of the new global economy, working as a financial analyst for a large company that operates worldwide. Jason enjoys the benefits of technological advances that allow him to monitor global markets in real time, analyze transactions and make profitable decisions that depend on the work of many people in different parts of the world. Jason, like many others in the Western world, is a direct beneficiary of capitalism in its modernized form.

But if we step back and broaden our view, a different picture emerges. While Arjun and Jason advance their careers in a connected and technologized world, many people on the other side of this development are facing an increasingly uncertain future. In remote regions of Africa, in the rural labor of South America, and in the industrial plants of Eastern Europe threatened by automation, the consequences of globalization and the technological revolution are not so clearly positive. People are losing their jobs and entire communities are struggling to survive. So what happens to those who do not benefit from global developments?

Capitalism has taken various forms over the years. From classical industrialism, which emphasized factory work and the exploitation of labor, to modern financial capitalism, which is characterized by global markets, financial speculation, and an increasingly digital economy. But no matter what form it takes, one thing remains constant: capitalism is based on the idea that markets, companies, and competition are the most efficient way to create wealth. This philosophy has undoubtedly led us to unprecedented prosperity - at least in many parts of the world.

But capitalism also has its dark side. The gap between rich and poor is wider than ever. The effects of globalization have led to a massive loss of wealth in many developing countries, while western industrialized nations reap the benefits of free trade and global availability of labor. In wealthier countries, economic growth may seem impressive, but it hides a growing divide in society: the distinction between those who thrive in an increase-ingly digital, globalized world and those who are overwhelmed by the technological revolution.

The example of Arjun and Jason shows a clear trend: access to the benefits of globalization is largely dependent on which part of the world you live in and what resources you have at your disposal. Arjun has used technology and education to create an opportunity for himself to immerse himself in the digital world of work. But not everyone has access to these opportunities. The majority of the world's population still lives in regions where education, technological infrastructure and economic opportunities are either nonexistent or severely limited.

Jason, on the other hand, lives in one of the richest regions in the world, in a country that has the best resources to thrive in a digitalized world. But he is not immune to the negative effects of capitalism either. In a world that is becoming ever faster and more complex, insecurity is also increasing among the supposedly successful classes. Job losses due to automation, technological disruptions and the increase in global financial crises are just some of the challenges that also affect Jason.

So the fundamental question arises: How can we create a system that does not only favor the few, but offers all people the same opportunities to thrive in an increasingly digitized and globalized world? It is the answer to the question of how we as a society define who should have access to wealth, education and the technological advances of the future. Arjun and Jason may both benefit from technological advances as individuals, but what about those who have no resources, no education and no opportunity to become part of this global system? How can we ensure that the social and economic benefits of globalization are distributed fairly without leaving individual nations, cultures or population groups behind?

Does a democratization of digitization lead to post-capitalism?

The question of whether a free democratization of digitalization could lead to a kind of "modern socialism" touches on deep social, economic and political issues and raises the question of how the digital revolution can be embedded in a just and sustainable social order. At its core, it is about whether and how technologies such as artificial intelligence (AI) and other digital tools can be used in such a way that they benefit not just a small elite, but society as a whole.

A central element of this debate is the concept of the unconditional basic income (UBI). As digitalization and automation increasingly change the labor market, the UBI could offer a solution to maintain social cohesion. The introduction of a UBI could at least partially cushion the loss of jobs caused by the use of AI and other automation technologies. In many industries, machines and algorithms are already taking over the work that was previously done by people - and the trend towards automation will only increase in the coming years.

UBI could free people from the need to constantly reorient themselves in an increasingly uncertain labor market, while mitigating social inequality. It would ensure that every citizen has access to the basic resources they need to live a dignified life. In a sense, this could represent a "modern socialist" response to the challenges of digitalization, as the focus is no longer on individual competitiveness and unequal distribution of wealth, but on the idea of universal, solidarity-based access to the benefits of the digital age.

Democratizing AI could help bridge social inequalities. If AI and digital tools are made accessible to everyone, people could benefit from the advantages of these technologies regardless of their social or economic status. Such a move would make the notion of post-capitalism seem more real, as it not only challenges capitalism, but also promotes the vision of a society in which wealth and technological opportunities are more evenly distributed and not reserved only for those who can afford it. Freely accessible AI could also fundamentally change the world of work. If people can use AI to make their work more efficient and creative, it could mean that not just a few but many people are able to participate in the digital economy. This could redefine the concept of work as "meaningful".

Digitalization will also have a profound impact on the labor market when machines and AI take over many of the tasks that were previously done by people. However, the question arises as to what work actually means. In many cases, traditional jobs in production, administration and also in the service sector are affected by automation. The question of how people can keep themselves meaningfully occupied in a world without traditional work is therefore relevant.

Understanding social work as meaningful could be one answer to this challenge. In a "digitalized society," work could not only be viewed in monetary terms. Instead, the focus could be on the ideal and social aspects of work: on creating added value for the community, on promoting one's own creativity or on solving social problems. People could invest more time and energy in activities that they themselves find meaningful - such as care, art or community work.

This development could lead to a completely new understanding of work: away from a purely productivist view towards one that focuses on people and their development. This could in turn be understood as a fundamental principle of a post-capitalism in which prosperity is based not only on the material means of production, but on the common, social and cultural resources of a society.

When we think about the "democratization of digitalization", we must also consider the social and political structures that can ensure a fair distribution of technologies and prosperity. This form of society should not consist of centralized control of all means of production, as we know it from the past. Rather, it should be understood as a system that makes opportunities accessible to all, that promotes free access to education and technology, while at the same time focusing on the individual and collective meaning of work.

It is not about abolishing markets or nationalizing companies, but rather about creating frameworks in which technology serves not as a tool of exploitation, but as an instrument of social and economic justice. In such a society, capitalism could continue to play a role - but in a form that sees people not only as resources or consumers, but also as equal participants in a common, digital prosperity.

The question of whether the democratization of digitalization could lead to full post-capitalism is not just about technological innovations or economic models, but also about a profound reassessment of what it means to live and work in a digital world. An unconditional basic income, access to free AI and the redefinition of work as a meaningful way of being could be important building blocks of such a system. However, it is crucial that these elements are not understood as isolated solutions, but as parts of a broader social change. The challenge is to translate these visions into concrete political and economic measures that create a fair and sustainable society for all.

The final answer to this question will not be easy to find, if it even exists, but it is necessary to shape the future of capitalism and the distribution of wealth in the world. Globalization has the potential to create a world in which everyone has the opportunity to thrive, in which technology is used as a tool to improve the lives of all. But this vision requires a rethinking of how we define wealth, how we distribute education and resources, and how we can shape capitalism so that it benefits not just the elites but everyone, without falling into crude fantasies of redistribution.

It is a challenge that is deeply rooted in the political, economic and social structures of our world. But it is also an opportunity that must not be wasted. Who should benefit from globalization and technology is in any case a question of justice without socialist egalitarianism - but a question that will determine the course of our future.

Biotechnology: Longing for Immortality

Since the dawn of civilization, humanity has dreamed of overcoming death. What was once described in myths and legends as the search for the fountain of youth or the elixir of life is now manifested in state-of-the-art research laboratories where scientists work at the interface between biology and technology. Their tools are no longer alchemists' cauldrons and mystical formulas, but gene sequencers, artificial intelligence and stem cell cultures.

The biotechnology of the 21st century is opening up completely new perspectives in the fight against aging. What was still considered science fiction a few decades ago is increasingly becoming scientific reality. Various research fields are merging into an interdisciplinary approach: genetics provides insights into the molecular mechanisms of aging, stem cell research develops methods for tissue regeneration, nanotechnology enables targeted interventions at the cellular level, and artificial intelligence helps with the analysis of complex biological systems.

The aging process itself is proving to be far more complex than was long assumed. It is not a simple sign of wear and tear, but a complex interplay of various biological and biochemical processes. The shortening of telomeres - the protective end caps of our chromosomes - is just one of many factors. Oxidative stress, protein damage, epigenetic changes and chronic inflammatory processes also play an important role.

Modern biotechnology approaches this complexity with a systematic approach. Various strategies are being researched in laboratories around the world: the targeted manipulation of aging genes, the development of senolytics to remove aging cells, the optimization of mitochondrial function and the activation of the body's own repair mechanisms. It is becoming increasingly clear that the key to longevity does not lie in a single miracle solution, but in the coordinated influence of several biological systems.

One particularly promising approach is epigenetic reprogramming. Scientists have discovered that the biological age of cells can be reset by flipping certain genetic switches. This discovery opens up completely new perspectives for regenerative medicine. Initial animal experiments have already succeeded in significantly extending life expectancy and delaying age-related diseases.

Research into pluripotent stem cells is another important building block. These all-round cells can now be grown in the laboratory and specifically converted into different types of tissue. This opens up the possibility of repairing damaged organs or even completely replacing them. The vision of biological spare parts that are perfectly tailored to the individual patient is now within reach.

At the same time, the field of tissue engineering is developing rapidly. 3D bioprinting can already be used to produce complex tissue structures that are becoming increasingly similar to natural models. The combination of living cells and biocompatible materials enables the construction of functional tissues that integrate perfectly into the body after implantation.

But the biotechnological revolution is not limited to the laboratory. New diagnostic and monitoring methods enable a previously unknown level of precision medicine. Wearable sensors continuously record important health parameters, artificial intelligence analyzes the data in real time and warns of health problems at an early stage. Medicine is becoming increasingly preventative and personalized.

The CRISPR-Cas9 technology has now ushered in a new era of gene therapy. These molecular scissors can be used to specifically modify genes, repair faulty DNA sequences and correct disease-causing mutations. The possibilities of this technology are so far-reaching that it has the potential to influence human evolution itself.

The research into the microbiome - the totality of all microorganisms in our body - is also providing new insights into aging. The composition of our intestinal flora has a surprisingly large influence on health and aging processes. By specifically manipulating the microbiome, age-related diseases could possibly be delayed or even prevented.

Nanotechnology is opening up completely new therapeutic options. In the future, tiny robots no larger than a cell could navigate through our bodies, carry out repairs and deliver medications to their destination. The first prototypes of such nanorobots have already been successfully tested.

The integration of artificial intelligence into medical research accelerates the acquisition of knowledge exponentially. Machine learning helps to recognize new connections in the wealth of biological data and to identify promising therapeutic approaches. AI systems can analyze millions of potential drug combinations within a few hours - a task that would take a team of researchers years.

But despite all the technological progress, the question of the ethical implications also arises. The possibility of deliberately changing the human genome and manipulating the aging process raises fundamental philosophical and social questions. Where is the line between therapy and enhancement? How does a society change in which death no longer appears to be an inevitable fate?

The socioeconomic impact of a significantly extended life expectancy would be enormous. Pension systems would have to be fundamentally rethought, the labor market would change fundamentally, and the coexistence of generations would take on new forms. Ecological aspects also play a role: How many people can our planet cope with if natural aging is largely eliminated?

Research into overcoming aging also raises important questions of evolutionary biology. The aging process has developed over the course of evolution for good reason. It enables adaptation to changing environmental conditions and drives evolution forward due to generational change. A society without natural aging would have to find new ways to ensure innovation and adaptability.

Nevertheless, research is progressing inexorably. New findings are being made in laboratories every day that bring us closer to the dream of a longer, healthier life. The combination of different approaches - from gene therapy to stem cell research to nanotechnology - could lead to resounding successes in the coming decades.

The first successes are already evident in the treatment of age-related diseases. Alzheimer's, Parkinson's, arthritis and other degenerative diseases could be curable or at least better treatable in the future. This would drastically improve the quality of life in old age, even if the goal of immortality is still a long way off.

Particular attention is being paid to prevention. The better we understand the molecular mechanisms of aging, the more targeted we can intervene before age-related damage manifests itself. The medicine of the future will no longer primarily treat diseases, but will actively maintain health.

The role of diet and lifestyle is increasingly being scientifically substantiated. Studies show that factors such as calorie restriction, intermittent fasting and certain nutritional supplements can have positive effects on lifespan. Biotechnology helps to understand the underlying mechanisms and to translate these findings into concrete therapeutic approaches.

The understanding of circadian rhythms - our internal biological clock - also contributes to the overall picture. The temporal coordination of biological processes plays an important role in health and aging. Modern technologies make it possible to analyze these rhythms and optimize them if necessary.

The importance of mental health for the aging process is also increasingly recognized. Stress, depression and other psychological stress can accelerate the aging process. The integration of psychological approaches into biotechnological research could therefore provide important new insights.

A particularly fascinating aspect is the possibility of epigenetic reprogramming. By specifically manipulating epigenetic markers, the biological age of cells can be reset without changing their identity. This technology could form the basis for real rejuvenation therapies in the future.

The integration of artificial intelligence into personalized medicine enables increasingly precise predictions of individual health risks and tailored therapy recommendations. The analysis of large amounts of data makes it possible to recognize subtle patterns and anticipate diseases before they become clinically manifest..

The Ethical Dimension and the Idea of God

The ethical dimension of the human quest for immortality raises fundamental questions that reach deep into our spiritual and philosophical core beliefs. The idea that humans are interfering with the natural order of life and death goes to the core of religious and ethical beliefs.

From a theological perspective, the question arises as to whether the human quest for life extension or even immortality is not an act of hubris. The idea of creation, as it is anchored in many religions, is based on a divinely given order in which death is understood as an integral part of life. The finiteness of human existence is often seen as a necessary condition for the meaningfulness of life and the moral development of humans.

The idea that humans are changing this fundamental order through biotechnological interventions raises the question of whether we are not thereby elevating ourselves above our role as creatures and taking up a position that was traditionally reserved for the divine. The line between the legitimate medical cure of diseases and the pursuit of a fundamental overcoming of human nature is becoming increasingly blurred.

From a philosophical perspective, the question of the authenticcity of human existence arises in a world in which life loses its finality through death. The existentialist tradition emphasizes that it is precisely the limitations of life that give it its special meaning. In a world without natural death, human life could lose its existential seriousness and drift into a kind of timeless insignificance.

Human identity, which is essentially defined by the confrontation with one's own mortality, would be fundamentally called into question by the technological overcoming of death. The awareness of one's own finiteness has had a significant impact on the cultural and spiritual development of humanity. A society of potentially immortal people would have to find completely new ways of constructing meaning and significance.

The question of human arrogance in the context of biotechnological developments goes beyond purely religious concerns. It touches on fundamental questions about the limits of scientific and technological interventions in nature. The idea that humans take their own evolution into their own hands and ignore the limitations of their biological nature can be understood as an expression of technological hubris.

This reveals a profound conflict between the belief in scientific progress and traditional ideas about human dignity. The technological optimization of the human body could be understood as an expression of a reductionist view that reduces humans to their biological dimension and loses sight of essential aspects of being human.

The ethical evaluation of biotechnological interventions must also take into account the question of distributive justice. In a world in which life can theoretically be extended indefinitely, social inequalities would possibly have an even more drastic impact. Access to life-extending technologies could lead to a new form of social segregation in which life expectancy depends even more on economic factors than it does today.

Philosophical anthropology raises the question of the extent to which the technological overcoming of death changes the nature of humans. The finiteness of human existence has traditionally been understood as a constitutive feature of being human. A posthuman society in which death no longer seems inevitable would possibly also require a fundamentally new definition of being human.

The tension between technological progress and ethical responsibility is particularly evident in the question of the limits of genetic manipulation. The possibility of deliberately altering the human genome raises the question of whether we are not entering an area that exceeds our moral and intellectual competence. The debate about the ethical legitimacy of life-extending technologies must also take the ecological dimension into account. In a world with limited resources, the drastic extension of the human lifespan could lead to an additional burden on natural systems. The question of the sustainability of a society without natural aging is therefore a pressing ethical problem.

The transhumanist discourse, which propagates the technological overcoming of biological limits, must face the criticism that it may ignore fundamental aspects of being human. The idea of a technologically optimized species raises the question of whether essential human qualities - their vulnerability, their emotionality, their spiritual dimension - are lost. Ethical reflection must not ignore the psychological consequences of a drastically extended lifespan. The human psyche has evolved to adapt to a life of limited duration. The prospect of a potentially unlimited life could lead to completely new psychological challenges and stresses.

The question of the meaning of life is more acute in a world without natural death. Traditional concepts of the meaning of life, which are often closely linked to the finiteness of existence, would have to be rethought. The philosophical challenge is to develop concepts of meaning and fulfillment that are not based on the finiteness of life.

The question of personal identity over extremely long periods of time represents another philosophical challenge. To what extent does a person remain the same person over centuries? The continuous accumulation of experiences and memories could lead to a form of identity diffusion that goes beyond our previous concepts of personal identity. The ethical evaluation of biotechnological interventions must also take into account the question of human freedom. To what extent does technological control over the aging process lead to a genuine expansion of human freedom, and to what extent does it create new forms of dependence on technological systems?

The dialogue between science and religion is faced with new challenges by the prospect of technological overcoming of death. The traditional religious interpretation of life and death must grapple with the possibilities of modern biotechnology. This could show that religious and scientific perspectives do not necessarily have to be in conflict.

The question of the relationship between nature and technology in the context of life extension touches on fundamental philosophical problems. The boundary between natural and artificial interventions is becoming increasingly blurred. The definition of what is considered "natural" may need to be rethought. The ethical discussion must also take into account the question of the reversibility of biotechnological interventions. Decisions that affect the human genome or the basic biological constitution could have far-reaching and possibly irreversible consequences. Responsibility towards future generations is thus becoming more urgent.

Philosophical anthropology is faced with the challenge of rethinking the nature of man in a time in which traditional boundaries between nature and technology, life and death, are becoming increasingly blurred. The definition of what makes man human may need to be fundamentally revised. The question of moral responsibility in a world of drastically extended lifespans is becoming more acute. The consequences of human actions could be felt over much longer periods of time, which places new demands on ethical action.

The biotechnological revolution challenges us to develop new concepts of dignity and humanity that take technological development into account without abandoning fundamental ethical principles. The ethical challenge would be to shape this process in such a way that it serves the well-being of all humanity.

The future of humanity may lie in a form of "enlightened biotechnology" that uses technological possibilities without losing sight of the ethical dimension of being human. The path to this requires a continuous dialogue between all disciplines and perspectives involved.

The human species at its limit – an evolutionary obsolete model?

The history of humanity is an unprecedented success story of evolution. In just a few hundred thousand years, we have evolved from one of many primate species to the dominant species on the planet. We have created tools, developed language, built cultures and shaped nature according to our ideas. But it is precisely this unprecedented success that could prove to be our greatest stumbling block.

Let us first look at the biological basis of our existence. Modern Homo sapiens is the product of a long evolutionary development that spanned millions of years. Our ancestors gradually adapted to their environment, developed upright walking, increased their brain volume and formed complex social structures. This process was by no means linear, but was characterized by countless trial-and-error steps, most of which ended in evolutionary dead ends.

Professor Sarah Chen of the Institute of Evolutionary Biology in Cambridge once put it aptly: "Evolution is like a blind watchmaker who constantly modifies his creations without knowing the final product." This metaphor illustrates a fundamental principle: evolution has no goal, no direction, and no plan. It simply responds to environmental conditions and selection pressures.

But this is precisely where the paradox of our modern existence lies. Through our technological achievements, we have largely eliminated natural selection pressures. Medical advances enable people with genetic disadvantages to reproduce. Our dependence on physical fitness for survival has virtually disappeared. In the Western world, hardly anyone dies of hunger or cold anymore.

Maria Gonzalez, a renowned anthropologist at the Universidad de Buenos Aires, describes this state as "evolutionary stasis". In her groundbreaking study "Homo sapiens in the 21st century", she argues: "We have moved so far away from our natural selection mechanisms that we practically live in an evolutionary vacuum."

Let's look at some concrete examples: The average human eye sight is continuously deteriorating. In industrialized countries, over 50% of adults already wear visual aids. Two hundred thousand years ago, this would have been a significant survival disadvantage. Today, we simply compensate for this development with glasses and contact lenses.

The same applies to our teeth. The human dentition is not actually designed for our modern diet. While our ancestors chewed hard, unprocessed food and thus developed strong jaws, many people today suffer from misaligned teeth and jaws that are too small for their existing teeth. Evolutionary adaptation cannot keep pace with our rapidly changing lifestyles.

This discrepancy becomes even clearer when we look at our metabolism. The human body is programmed to store fat reserves in times of abundance - a vital adaptation for survival for our ancestors, who often had to bridge long periods of food shortages. In our modern affluent society, this once advantageous mechanism is leading to a global obesity epidemic.

Dr. James Morrison of the Human Genome Project puts it succinctly: "We live in Stone Age bodies but lead 21st century lives. This discrepancy is widening, and our biological evolution cannot keep up."

But it is not just the physical aspects that should worry us. The limits of our evolutionary adaptability are also apparent on a psychological level. Our brain, this amazing organ that has put us at the top of the food chain, is increasingly struggling to cope with the demands of the modern world.

Let's take stress as an example. Our body still reacts to stress with the same mechanisms as it did thousands of years ago: release of adrenaline and cortisol, increased heart rate, tense muscles - perfect preparation for fight or flight. But the stressors of our time are different. Instead of a saber-toothed tiger, we are faced with deadline pressure, traffic jams and overflowing email inboxes. Our body cannot distinguish whether the threat is real or imaginary, physical or psychological. The result is chronic stress, which leads to a variety of modern diseases of civilization.

Our social behavior is also facing enormous challenges. Humans are evolutionarily designed to live in small groups of 50 to 150 individuals - the so-called "Dunbar number", named after the anthropologist Robin Dunbar. In the modern networked world, however, we are confronted with thousands of social contacts every day, either directly or via social media.

Our brains are not designed to process this amount of social information. Dr. Elena Petrova, a neuroscientist at Moscow State University, has studied the effects of this social overstimulation in studies lasting several years. Her results are alarming: "We are observing an increasing inability to build deep emotional bonds. The constant superficial networking paradoxically leads to emotional shallowness."

Another critical aspect is our cognitive architecture. Our brains have evolved to make quick decisions in an immediate, concrete environment. We are masters at recognizing patterns and learning from past experiences. But the complex, abstract problems of our time - urbanity, global economic systems, threats in road traffic, dealing with social media - overwhelm these evolutionary thought patterns.

Professor Thomas Weber from the University of Vienna summed this up succinctly in his work "The Evolutionary Trap": "We have created tools that are more powerful than our minds, which are supposed to control them. Our technological evolution has far outpaced our biological evolution."

But does this necessarily mean that we are an evolutionary obsolete model? The answer is more complex than it may seem at first glance. Because parallel to our biological limitations, we have developed something that is unique in the history of life: the ability to consciously evolve.

Unlike any other species, we are able to understand and actively influence our own development. Modern genetics theoretically opens up the possibility of modifying our genome in a targeted manner. At the same time, we are developing increasingly sophisticated forms of human-machine interaction that could compensate for our biological limitations.

Dr. Rajesh Patel, a leading expert in biotechnology at MIT, sees both opportunities and risks in this: "We are at a turning point in human evolution. For the first time in the history of life, a species has the opportunity to shape its own evolutionary future. This is both fascinating and frightening."

The development of artificial intelligence adds another dimension to this discussion. While our biological brain is reaching its cognitive limits, we are developing systems that already surpass us in many areas. This leads to the provocative question: Are we being overtaken evolutionarily by our own creations?

The renowned physicist Stephen Hawking also warned years ago about the potential dangers of super-intelligent AI. But perhaps the future does not lie in competition between humans and machines, but in their symbiosis. Concepts such as brain-computer interfaces and neural implants suggest what such a merger could look like.

A fascinating thought experiment in this context comes from futurologist Dr. Amanda Chen. She describes a scenario in which the biological evolution of humans is supplemented by a "technological evolution": "Imagine if we could expand our cognitive abilities through neural implants, overcome our physical limitations through biotechnology and improve our sensory perception through technological augmentation. Would we then still be humans in the classic sense?"

This question leads us to a fundamental philosophical problem: what actually makes us human? Is it our biological basis, our consciousness, our ability for self-reflection? And how much of it can we change without losing our "humanity"?

Anthropologist Dr. Michael Thompson of Oxford University argues: "The ability for cultural evolution is perhaps the most defining characteristic of our species. We have adapted to all of the Earth's climates not through biological adaptation, but through cultural innovation. Perhaps technological evolution is just the next stage of this cultural development."

Let us consider the current situation of humanity as a moment in a great evolutionary experiment. We have freed ourselves from classical evolutionary constraints through our technological and cultural achievements, but at the same time created new challenges that exceed our biological capabilities. Increasing urbanization, for example, presents us with completely new evolutionary challenges. Over 50% of the world's population already lives in cities, and the trend is rising. These artificial habitats require different adaptations than the natural environment in which our genome has evolved over millions of years.

Dr. Lisa Martinez, environmental psychologist at the Universidad de Barcelona, has studied the effects of the urban environment on the human psyche: "We are seeing an increase in anxiety disorders, depression and other mental illnesses in urban areas. Our brains do not seem to be optimally designed for life in large, anonymous crowds."

At the same time, however, we are also observing the first signs of biological adaptation to urban life. Studies have shown that city dwellers can cope better with noise and visual overstimulation than their rural contemporaries. Some scientists are already talking about an "urban phenotype adaptation".

Another fascinating aspect is the change in our nutritional physiology. The global availability of food and the development of new diets are leading to subtle but measurable changes in our metabolism. Dr. Heinrich Mueller from the Charité Berlin has found in a long-term study that the enzymes in our digestive system are already beginning to adapt to the changed diet.

But these adaptations are happening far too slowly to keep up with the pace of our technological and cultural evolution. For example, while the development of agriculture around 10,000 years ago led to the emergence of lactose tolerance in some populations - one of the fastest documented evolutionary adaptations in humans - today we face challenges that manifest themselves within decades or even years.

The key question remains: are we an evolutionary obsolete model? The answer is both yes and no. Yes, in the sense that our purely biological evolution can no longer keep pace with the changes we ourselves have created. No, because we may be on the threshold of a new form of evolution - a consciously controlled, technologically assisted evolution that complements or even replaces classical biological mechanisms.

Dr. Sarah Williams of Stanford University sums it up well: "Homo sapiens as we know it may indeed be an obsolete model. But that does not mean the end of human evolution, but the beginning of a new chapter. The question is not whether we will evolve, but how we want to shape this process."

The challenges we face are enormous: climate change, overpopulation, resource scarcity, new pathogens. Our biological evolution alone will not be able to solve these problems. But perhaps this is precisely where our greatest strength lies: the ability to think beyond our biological limits and find new ways of adapting.

The future of humanity will probably be a synthesis - of biological evolution, technological augmentation and cultural adaptation. We have not reached the end of our development, but are at the beginning of a new phase of human evolution. A phase that we can and must actively shape.

The real challenge will be to shape this development in such a way that we do not lose what makes us human - our empathy, our creativity, our ability for self-reflection. Perhaps this is precisely where the next great evolutionary task lies: not only to keep pace physically and cognitively with our changing environment, but also to carry our humanity into a new era.

The human species is not facing its end, but its greatest transformation. We are not a discontinued model, but a transitional model - on the way to something new that we can only imagine today. Evolution continues, but for the first time in the history of life we have the opportunity to consciously help shape it. This responsibility will be our greatest challenge.

Homo Deus or Homo obsoletus? Final Thoughts

The term "Homo Deus" comes from the Israeli historian and author Yuval Noah Harari and is the title of his book "Homo Deus: A History of Tomorrow" (2015). In it, Harari describes a future in which humans could assume a god-like position through technological advances - especially in the areas of artificial intelligence, biotechnology and big data. Homo Deus would be a being that overcomes its biological limits through technical optimization and emancipates itself from previous constraints such as illness, old age and even death.

"Homo obsoletus", on the other hand, was first used by the Norwegian economic philosopher Anders Indset and is less common. It is used in different contexts. This term describes the idea that humans in their current form could lose importance or even become superfluous due to technological developments. It is often used in discussions about automation, artificial intelligence and the future of work. While Harari describes in "Homo Deus" how humans could expand their capabilities, Homo obsoletus implies a more dystopian perspective: humans as obsolete models in a world increasingly dominated by machines and algorithms.

Without question, humanity is at an unprecedented turning point in its history. As we rapidly move into the digital age, a fundamental question is emerging that will define our future as a species: will we evolve into Homo Deus – a god-like being who overcomes his biological limitations through technological achievements – or will we become Homo obsoletus, an outdated life form pushed into insignificance by its own creation?

This question is no longer a science fiction fantasy, but a real challenge that we must face. The exponentially growing advances in fields such as artificial intelligence, biotechnology and nanotechnology are forcing us to rethink our position in the cosmos. We are on the threshold of an era in which the traditional definitions of being human, consciousness and intelligence are being fundamentally questioned.

The classic evolution by natural selection that shaped us over millions of years is increasingly being replaced by technologically driven evolution. This new phase of our development brings both unprecedented opportunities and existential risks. While some thought leaders see the merging of humans and machines as the next logical step in our evolution, others warn of the loss of our humanity and the danger of being displaced from decision-making by superintelligent systems.

To properly analyze this complex topic, we must first understand current technological developments and their implications. Artificial intelligence has made remarkable progress in recent decades. Modern AI systems already outperform humans in many specific tasks, from image recognition to strategic planning. Deep learning algorithms are increasingly developing skills that were once considered exclusively human: they compose music, write poetry and conduct complex scientific analyses.

These developments raise fundamental questions: What makes us unique as humans? Can machines ever develop true consciousness? And if so, what does that mean for our role as the dominant species on this planet?

At the same time, biotechnology is opening up new possibilities for optimizing the human body and mind. CRISPR-Cas9 and similar genetic technologies enable precise interventions in our genetic makeup. Neurotechnological implants promise to connect our brains directly to computers. These developments could enable us to eliminate diseases, expand our cognitive abilities and possibly even slow down or stop the aging process.

The vision of Homo Deus is based on the assumption that these technological achievements will enable us to overcome our biological limitations and achieve god-like abilities. Proponents of this perspective argue that merging with our technological creations is the natural next step in our evolution. They see a future in which we not only live longer and healthier lives, but also become more intelligent, creative and empathetic.

But this optimistic vision is being challenged by critical voices. They warn of the risks of excessive technological development of humans and see the danger that we could lose ourselves in this process. The development of a strong artificial intelligence that surpasses human intelligence in all areas could push us into the position of Homo obsoletus - a species that has been overtaken by its own creation.

The reality will probably be more complex than these two extreme scenarios. To better understand our possible future, we need to delve deeper into the different aspects of this development.

First, let's look at the cognitive enhancement technologies that are already expanding our mental abilities today. Smartphones and the Internet have revolutionized our access to information and our communication options. Neurofeedback systems allow us to better control our brain activity. Brain-computer interfaces such as "Neuralink" promise an even more direct connection between our brain and digital systems.

These developments raise important ethical questions: How much technological augmentation is desirable? Where is the line between therapy and enhancement? Who has access to these technologies, and what are the social implications of a possible cognitive gap between augmented and non-augmented people?

The biotechnological revolution is opening up new possibilities for optimizing our bodies. In the future, gene therapies could not only cure diseases, but also improve our physical abilities. Research into stem cells and organ regeneration could fundamentally change aging. Nanobots could circulate through our bodies and carry out repairs at the cellular level. These developments could lead to a post-biological phase of human evolution. But here too, critical questions arise: What unintended side effects could these interventions have? How will our relationship with our bodies change as they become increasingly technologically optimizable? And what does it mean for our identity as a species if we fundamentally change our biological basis?

Meanwhile, artificial intelligence is evolving at a breathtaking pace. Machine learning systems are becoming more sophisticated and autonomous. They are beginning to develop skills that were until recently considered exclusively human: creativity, problem solving, even forms of emotional intelligence.

This development could lead to several scenarios. In the positive case, a symbiosis between human and artificial intelligence could emerge, expanding our cognitive capabilities exponenttially. AI systems could act as external cognitive enhancement technology that helps us solve complex problems and enhances our creative abilities. In contrast, the more pessimistic scenario predicts the development of strong AI that surpasses human intelligence in all areas and potentially replaces us as the dominant species. This is the Homo obsoletus scenario.

This danger is exacerbated by the increasing automation of the world of work. If AI systems take over more and more tradetional jobs, a large part of the population could become economically redundant. This could lead to a split in society into a small elite of augmented humans who can keep up with the AI systems and a large mass of "ordinary" humans.

To avoid such dystopian developments, we need a social dialogue about the direction we want to take. The development towards Homo Deus must not only be technologically driven, but must also take ethical and social aspects into account. A central question here is what we as humans want to preserve. Which aspects of our humanity are so valuable that we should not give them up? How can we use technological progress without losing our basic human qualities?

The development of consciousness is a particularly fascinating aspect of this. As we develop ever more complex AI systems, the question arises as to whether they can ever develop real consciousness. This leads to profound philosophical questions: What is consciousness anyway? Is it tied to biological substrates, or can it also arise in artificial systems?

The question of our role in the cosmos also takes on new importance in this context. As Homo Deus, we could potentially colonize other planets and develop into an interplanetary species. This would fundamentally change our perspective on life and our role in the universe. This in turn leads to the fundamental question of what makes us unique as humans. Is it our ability to love, dream, hope? Is it our moral convictions and our ability to empathize? How can we preserve and strengthen these qualities as we develop technologically?

There is a danger that we will lose our independence through excessive technological augmentation. If our cognitive abilities depend too heavily on external systems or have even been made dependent out of convenience, this could limit our autonomy and freedom of choice.

The social dimension of this development should not be underestimated. The integration of enhancement technologies will fundamentally change our social relationships and structures. How will friendship, love and family develop as we increasingly move away from our biological basis?

The question of identity becomes central in this context. If we can optimize our body and mind technologically, what then still makes up our individual personality? How can we remain authentic in a world where almost all aspects of our being are technologically modifiable?

These questions become even more complex when we consider the possibility of digital consciousness. If it becomes possible to transfer our consciousness into digital systems, what does that mean for our identity? Are we still the same person? The ethical implications of these developments are enormous. We need to define guidelines and boundaries that ensure that technological development is in line with our human values.

An often overlooked aspect in this entire discussion is the fact that we view all these developments and possible future scenarios exclusively from an anthropocentric perspective. This human-centered view is deeply rooted in our thinking and is reflected in the terms "Homo Deus" and "Homo obsoletus" - both concepts define themselves through being human as a reference point. This limitation of our perspective is simultaneously a strength and a weakness.

A strength because it allows us to relate developments directly to our human experience and to grasp their significance for our existence. A weakness because it may obscure our view of completely new forms of consciousness and existence that lie beyond our human imagination.

Perhaps the true future lies neither in the concept of Homo Deus nor in the idea of Homo obsoletus, but in a development that completely explodes our current categories and ways of thinking. The boundaries between humans, machines and nature may blur in ways that we cannot even imagine today.

The central challenge will be to preserve what is valuable to us as humans in this process of transformation, while at the same time opening ourselves up to new possibilities of being. This requires a balanced approach that combines technological progress with ethical reflection and social responsibility.

Ultimately, it is not a question of whether we rise to Homo Deus or degenerate to Homo obsoletus. It is about how we humans can shape our development in such a way that it is in line with our deepest values and aspirations. The future is in our hands and it is our responsibility to shape it wisely.

So it is still up to us,

Hermann Selchow

Also published by me:

Elon Musk - Ideas & Visions -How a man is transforming our civilization

Elon Musk is undoubtedly one of the most influential figures of the 21st century. His name is inextricably linked to groundbreaking technologies, bold ambitions and a radical approach to solving the biggest problems of our time. Whether it's promoting sustainable energy, enabling interplanetary travel or revolutionising the way we interact with machines, Musk operates at the intersection of science, technology and visions for the future of humanity.

The story of Elon Musk is a fascinating mix of brilliance, tenacity and unconventionality. Born in Pretoria, South Africa, the son of an engineer and a nutritionist, Musk showed extraordinary curiosity and intelligence from an early age. At the age of twelve, he programmed his first computer game and sold it for a small sum - a harbinger of the entrepreneurial energy that would later change the world. But Musk was not just a child prodigy with technical talent; he was also a dreamer who found inspiration in books such as The Hitchhiker's Guide to the Galaxy and The Lord of the Rings. These works shaped his imagination and fostered his belief that humanity could play a more significant role in the universe.

What sets Musk apart from other successful entrepreneurs is his ability to think the unthinkable and turn it into reality. While many in the technology industry focus on incremental improvements to existing products, Musk strives for fundamental change. His projects, from Tesla and SpaceX to Neuralink and The Boring Company, demonstrate an unparalleled willingness to take risks and push the boundaries of what is possible. It is not just his technical brilliance that sets him apart, but also his ability to inspire teams and achieve extraordinary things in an often chaotic environment.

In this introduction, however, I want to not only shed light on Elon Musk's achievements and ambitions, but also raise the deeper questions that surround his life and work. How far can a visionary mind go to achieve its goals? What ethical compromises are involved in radical progress? And how do Musk's ventures affect society - not just technologically, but also philosophically?

Analyzing Musk's life is not simply a journey through technological milestones; it is also a reflection on what it means to dream and act in a world full of challenges. Musk often refers to himself as an "engineer," a term that describes both his technical orientation and his ability to solve problems. But behind this sober label lies a complexity that goes far beyond the role of a classic engineer. He is a visionary who believes in a future that others consider impossible and an entrepreneur who is willing to pursue his dreams with an almost ruthless determination.

His critics accuse him of being a ruthless workaholic who exploits employees and resources to the limit to advance his visions. Others see him as a modern hero, a man who refuses to passively accept the world's problems and instead finds solutions that have the potential to change billions of lives. Both perspectives are important to understanding Musk and his legacy. Because the truth often lies somewhere in between - in the gray areas between idealism and pragmatism, between genius and madness.

Elon Musk challenges us to think beyond the limits of what is possible. His projects invite us to question our idea of progress and consider the consequences of technological change. This text will not only highlight the highlights of his career, but also explore the philosophical and societal questions his work raises. What does it mean to create a sustainable future? Is the colonization of Mars a noble dream or an escape from Earth's problems? And how does the fusion of man and machine change our understanding of identity and humanity?

The journey through Musk's life is an invitation not only to consider the future, but also to critically question the present. In a world marked by climate change, resource scarcity and technological upheaval, his ideas are both a glimmer of hope and a warning. Musk shows us what is possible when we harness the power of science - but also the risks involved.

In the following text, we will examine Musk's greatest achievements, analyze his visions and motivations, and shed light on the challenges and controversies that have shaped his path. In doing so, we will not only try to understand Elon Musk as a person, but also to grasp the profound impact his work has had on our world. It is a story of courage, intelligence, and the irrepressible will to change the world - and an invitation to ask ourselves what role we want to play in this rapidly changing world.

Elon Musk's rise to fame did not begin with rockets or electric cars, but with software. After moving from South Africa to the USA via Canada, he first made a name for himself in the tech industry. With Zip2, a kind of precursor to Google Maps, Musk and his brother Kimbal developed a company that combined local business directories with digital maps. The sale of Zip2 to Compaq in 1999 netted him $22 million—a sum that not only gave him financial flexibility but also paved the way to his next big venture.

That next step was X.com, an online payment system that eventually became PayPal. Musk's vision was to revolutionize tradetional banking by moving payments online and simplifying the process for users. But his time at PayPal was not without conflict. Musk, known for his authoritarian leadership style and high demands, often clashed with his partners. He was ultimately ousted as CEO before the company was sold to eBay for $1.5 billion. Nevertheless, the sale secured him a financial gain that enabled him to move on to his bigger dreams.

While many of his contemporaries would have chosen a quiet life after such success, Musk saw the PayPal episode as merely a stepping stone. For him, the transition from software to hardware was a logical consequence of his ambition to solve problems at a deeper level. Software alone, he seemed to believe, would not be enough to tackle the great challenges facing humanity.

When Musk invested in Tesla and later took over the helm, the electric car industry was considered dead. Previous attempts to establish electric vehicles had failed and the automotive industry seemed determined to stick with fossil fuels. But Musk saw the potential to make electric cars not only environmentally friendly but also desirable. With the Tesla Roadster, a sports car based on the Lotus Elise, he managed to change the perception of electric cars. Suddenly they were no longer just an environmentally motivated choice, but a statement of innovation and progress.

The models that followed - the Model S, Model X, Model 3 and finally the Model Y - built on this foundation. Tesla transformed from a niche player into one of the most valuable car manufacturers in the world. But the path was anything but easy. Production problems, skeptical investors and fierce competition took a huge toll on Musk and his team. There were moments when Tesla was on the brink of bankruptcy, and Musk even invested his personal fortune to keep the company alive. This period, which Musk described as "production hell," showed his unwavering belief in Tesla's vision and his willingness to risk everything to make it a reality.

While Tesla focused on Earth, Musk set his sights on the stars with SpaceX. SpaceX was founded in 2002 with the ambitious goal of drastically reducing the cost of space travel and ultimately enabling an interplanetary civilization. Musk sees the colonization of Mars not as a luxury but as a necessity. He argues that to survive in the long term, humanity must expand its existence to multiple planets. This belief drives SpaceX.

The first years of SpaceX were marked by setbacks. The company's first three rocket launches failed, bringing both Musk and the company to the brink of ruin. But the fourth attempt was successful and marked the turning point. With the "Falcon I", SpaceX made history as the first private company to put a rocket into orbit.

Other milestones followed, including the development of the "Falcon IX", a reusable rocket, and the Dragon capsule, which successfully transported cargo to the International Space Station (ISS) for the first time. In 2020, SpaceX achieved another historic success: the first manned flight with a commercial spacecraft developed by a private company. But SpaceX is not resting on its laurels. With the Starship project, a fully reusable rocket, Musk is aiming for the next big challenge: manned missions to Mars.

Both Tesla and SpaceX show how Musk combines technology and business to realize his visions. But what sets him apart from many other entrepreneurs is the fundamental question that underlies each of his projects: How can we as humanity secure our future while exploiting our potential? This thinking is evident not only in his main companies, but also in smaller projects such as Neuralink, which explores the interface between humans and machines, and The Boring Company, which deals with innovative transport solutions for urban areas.

Elon Musk is therefore more than just an entrepreneur; he is a catalyst for change. His projects force us to think about the way we use resources, shape mobility and redefine the limits of human existence. But with this power comes risk. Critics accuse Musk of building a monopoly on technological progress while ignoring ethical questions. How sustainable is his vision really? Is it justifiable to invest immense resources in the colonization of Mars while urgent problems on Earth remain unsolved?

This ambivalence runs through Musk's entire career. His successes are inspiring, his methods often controversial. But one thing is certain: Musk has fundamentally changed the way we think about technology, innovation and the future. His journey from a software start-up founder to one of the most influential innovators of our time shows what is possible when courage, intelligence and an unwavering vision come together

...

The US Dollar and the BRICS Challenge – Towards a new global financial order

Continuous change and rapid technological progress raises the question of the stability of our future and of the global financial system. This book, "The US Dollar and the BRICS Challenge," addresses this issue in a comprehensive manner. It examines the historical dominance of the US dollar and sheds light on the emerging challenge posed by the BRICS countries (Brazil, Russia, India, China and South Africa), which are increasingly positioning themselves as a counterweight to the traditional economic power centers.

Since the introduction of the Bretton Woods system in 1944, the US dollar has played a central role in international trade and financial policy. The establishment of the dollar as the reserve currency created a foundation for decades of economic stability and growth, at least in the Western Hemisphere. But over time, cracks in this system began to become visible, particularly due to economic and political tensions, the financial crisis of 2008 and the steady increase in US national debt.

The BRICS countries have not only developed enormously economically over the past two decades, but have also gained political importance. With their considerable resources, large populations and growing markets, they are increasingly challenging the dominance of the established Western economic powers. Their ambition to promote a multipolar world order is reflected in the creation of new financial institutions such as the New Development Bank (NDB) and the Contingent Reserve

Arrangement (CRA), which are designed as alternatives to the International Monetary Fund (IMF) and the World Bank.

This book analyses the economic and political strategies behind the rise of the BRICS countries and examines their potential impact on the future role of the US dollar in the global financial system. It highlights the various mechanisms and instruments that these countries use to strengthen their position on the world stage and reduce dependence on the dollar. It also examines in detail the role of trade agreements, investments in infrastructure and technology and the development of alternative payment systems.

Another central theme of this book is the examination of the geopolitical implications of a possible shift in global financial power. The competition between the USA and the BRICS countries is reflected not only in economic tensions, but also in security and diplomatic tensions. The question of whether a new world order in which the US dollar no longer plays the dominant role will lead to more stability or new conflicts is of utmost relevance.

This new edition takes into account current developments and data up to and including 2024 in order to paint the most precise picture of the current situation possible. Numerous expert interviews and case studies complement the theoretical analyses and provide insights into the practical implementation and challenges facing the BRICS countries.

I would like to thank all those who contributed to the creation of this book. Their commitment and expertise have made a significant contribution to making this work a well-founded and worthwhile analysis of global financial dynamics. My special thanks also go to the readers, whose interest and critical engagement with the contents of this book make a valuable contribution to the discussion about the future of our global financial system.

I hope that this book will not only help to clarify many questions, but also open up new perspectives and encourage people to continue to closely follow and question developments in the international financial world.

The BRICS summit took place in August 2023. The five BRICS states are still planning - so it is rumored - their own gold-based reserve currency. This rumor is supported by several events. The world is currently experiencing massive structural changes. NATO is expanding further eastwards and northwards in Europe. A direct consequence of NATO's eastward expansion is the military conflict in Ukraine. In Africa, more and more countries are fighting back against their former colonial powers. Military coups, such as in Niger and Gabon, are overthrowing civilian governments that conform to the West.

In addition, other oil-producing countries are joining the BRICS group on the occasion of the BRICS summit mentioned above. These include countries such as Argentina, Egypt, Ethiopia, Iran, Saudi Arabia and the United Arab Emirates. These countries plan to trade their oil in currencies other than the petrodollar. This would lead to a further weakening of the US dollar.

Russia has been excluded from the SWIFT system. For Russia, exclusion from the SWIFT system means that Russian banks can no longer communicate directly with other international banks to process cross-border transactions. Without access to the SWIFT network, Russia is cut off from most international payment and settlement systems. This could make trade with other countries more difficult and affect economic relations. Such isolation should destabilize Russian financial markets and reduce the confidence of investors. Exclusion from the SWIFT system is a serious measure and should be understood as a means of political pressure.

It is therefore not surprising that the rumor of a new reserve currency - possibly backed by the Yuan - is being fueled. Added to this is the apparently unsuccessful visit of the American Secretary of State Blinken to China. Immediately afterwards, the stock market value of the US dollar fell by several points. China holds immense dollar reserves due to its export surplus.

After that, former US Secretary of State Henry Kissinger visited China, of course privately and without any diplomatic mission. Henry Kissinger, now 100 years old, is highly respected in China, mainly because of his role in normalizing relations between the United States and the People's Republic of China in the 1970s. As then US Secretary of State, he played a crucial role in the secret negotiations with Chinese leader Zhou Enlai.

It remains to be seen whether his visit can dissuade China and the BRICS countries from their financial plans. Russia and China are among the top four countries in the world when it comes to buying gold. Brazil increased its gold reserves by 53.75 tons in the second quarter of 2021, almost doubling its stocks. India is quite well represented with 787.40 tons of gold reserves and has acquired more than 150 tons in recent years.

China stores 2,010.51 tons of gold. The country is also the largest gold producer in the world, accounting for around twelve percent of global production. However, Russia has the largest gold reserves with 2,301.64 tons and has spent the equivalent of around 36 billion euros over the past five years to increase its reserves and thus be less dependent on the US dollar. This has even overtaken China. The Russian gold industry is worth billions, so not much gold even needs to be imported. The country's gold reserves rose by 6.22 tons in the third quarter of

2021. The BRICS countries can use this gold to become largely independent of the dollar.

China also holds immense dollar reserves. If China were to sell its immense dollar reserves, it would have a significant impact on the global economy and financial markets. Selling large amounts of US dollars would reduce the value of the dollar against other currencies due to an oversupply. A devaluation of the US dollar would have far-reaching effects on the international trading community, especially on countries that are heavily dependent on trade with the US. On the other hand, China is also dependent on the US, as it exports a large proportion of its goods to the US. A sudden devaluation of the US dollar could affect the competitiveness of Chinese exports, as they would become more expensive for US customers. This would have a negative impact on Chinese economic growth. Selling dollar reserves could therefore also result in losses for China if the dollar depreciates during the sale.

However, the global economy is a complex network that is influenced by various actors and circumstances. In recent decades, the dominance of the US dollar as the world reserve currency has played an important role. The dollar has shaped the international trade landscape for many decades and has had a significant impact on geopolitical relations. But in recent years, new powers have risen and challenged the status quo. The BRICS countries - Brazil, Russia, India, China and South Africa - have gained increasing economic importance and are pushing for reform of the international financial system.

My book "The US Dollar and the BRICS Challenge" aims to bring readers closer to the history of dollar dominance and the emerging BRICS countries as a possible counterweight. It is intended to be seen as an attempt to shed light on current events in the world and thus help to better understand the current upheavals and restructuring. The book sheds light on the background that led to the power struggles of this time and it takes a look into a possible future to analyze the effects on the global economy. It will examine the various aspects of the topic, from the historical events that led to the emergence of dollar dominance to the current efforts of the BRICS countries to escape this dominance and strengthen their own position.

We will examine the roots of dollar dominance. From the Bretton Woods Conference in 1944 to the abolition of the gold standard in 1971, the key milestones on the way to the global acceptance of the dollar as a reserve currency will be covered. The role of the United States as a superpower and its economic and political interest in maintaining dollar dominance will also be questioned.

Another part of the book is devoted to the BRICS countries and their rise as economic heavyweights. Each country is considered individually to analyze its specific economic, political and social developments. All five countries have different challenges and opportunities, but all strive to have their own voice in the global economic order. Their efforts to build alternative currency and financial structures will also be examined in detail.

In addition, the conflicts and tensions between the US dollar and the BRICS countries are examined in more detail. I want to show how the United States is defending its dominance in the world economy by all means and is taking measures to maintain the status of the dollar. At the same time, the BRICS countries are forming their own economic alliance and are looking for ways to escape dependence on the dollar. This struggle for power and influence has an impact on global stability and will possibly lead to a redesign of the international financial architecture.

Furthermore, a look ahead is given. What might the world economy look like in the next few decades? What role do the BRICS countries and the dollar play? What scenarios are conceivable and how might they affect the various players? These questions are discussed on the basis of current developments and trends, with both optimistic and pessimistic scenarios being examined.

It is important to point out that this book cannot provide definitive answers. The dynamics between the US dollar and the BRICS countries are too complex and multi-faceted, and developments are still ongoing. Rather, this book aims to encourage people to think about the current world order and the possible changes that directly affect each and every one of us. This book offers a wealth of information, analyses and perspectives that enable the reader to form their own opinion and stimulate further discussions.

...

The End of Western Dominance – The Restructuring of the Multipolar World

The Western order, once a symbol of stability, progress and the triumph of democracy, is now facing a multitude of challenges that are shaking its foundations. These challenges arise not only from external factors such as the rise of new global powers or the technological revolution, but also from internal tensions that are testing the social and political cohesion of Western societies.

This book addresses the question of how and why the Western order has faltered. But instead of providing hasty answers or falling into alarmism, the text takes a balanced and analytical approach. The aim is not only to describe the symptoms of the upheaval, but also to shed light on the causes and dynamics behind it. Historical perspectives meet contemporary developments, and scientific findings are linked to concrete examples from politics, business and society.

Over the centuries, the Western world has developed its identity in a field of tension between ideals and realities. Freedom, equality, human rights and democracy formed the basis of a narrative that not only provided orientation within the Western states themselves, but also had an international appeal. But this narrative is increasingly coming under pressure. The polarization of societies, the resurgence of authoritarian forces and growing skepticism towards established institutions and values raise the question of whether the Western order in its current form is still viable.

A central concern of this book is to look beyond the immediate crises and to make visible the deeper structures that are driving the change. It becomes clear that this is not a sudden collapse, but a gradual process in which new actors, ideas and power relations enter the stage. This process is neither linear nor irreversible. Rather, it is characterized by contradictions, conflicts and the possibility of a new beginning.

Readers are taken on a journey that begins in the centers of power in the West and from there traces the diverse connections to other regions of the world. How have globalization, digitalization and climate change changed the rules of the game? What role do social movements that campaign for justice and participation play? And how are Western democracies responding to the increasing pressure to defend their values and institutions?

It is the art of storytelling that distinguishes this book. Every crisis, every problem is not only analyzed soberly, but embedded in a context that brings the connections to life. Personal observations, historical events and the voices of experts are used to paint a multi-layered picture. This approach is intended to help readers not only understand what is happening, but also grasp the social and individual dimension of the change.

At the same time, the book maintains a critical distance and leaves it up to the reader to draw their own conclusions. It does not propagate an ideological program, but rather an invitation to think through and question the complexity of current developments. Because only through a deeper understanding of the causes and consequences of the upheaval can we succeed in finding constructive paths into the future.

We live in an era of transition. What was taken for granted yesterday is being questioned today. But in every crisis there is also the opportunity for renewal. This book is not just intended to be a wake-up call, but also to inspire hope. Hope that the West, despite all the challenges, can develop its values and principles and adapt them to the realities of the 21st century.

May this book help enrich the discussion about the future of the West and provide food for thought for a way forward. Because ultimately it is up to all of us whether we see the challenges of change as a threat or as an opportunity.

...

www.ingramcontent.com/pod-product-compliance
Lightning Source LLC
LaVergne TN
LVHW101613210926
848480LV00008B/206
9798230251446